Stop Press

With hardly three weeks to go for the Democratic convention, the FBI director's statement on July 5, 2016 about the private email saga of Hillary Clinton sends conflicting signals. While it clarifies that the agency will not recommend pressing of criminal charges, the director clearly indicates that the emails did contain classified information and security protocols were severely compromised, as noted in Chapter 11 of this book. What seems to have saved Hillary is their perception that there was no criminal intent. Does the law see it the same way though? Chapter 11 provides a clear and unambiguous interpretation of the law, both in letter and spirit!

Chapter 11 has indeed foreseen this scenario of "no criminal indictment". That said, while Hillary may have escaped "criminal prosecution", she surely cannot shrug off the fact that the FBI investigation has confirmed serious security breaches and compromise of classified information? What can she tell the American people about her various explanations that have now completely fallen flat? Can she offer yet another weak apology and be done with it?

Similar to what she has done in the past — be it the vote on the Iraq War or the Libya situation or the private server saga itself? Can the nation's security and welfare be entrusted to an individual who has consistently revealed singular lack of judgment or an understanding of the consequences of crucial decisions? And indeed one needs to ask what have her 'lapses' in judgment come to mean for the United States?

Praise for *Madam President: History in the Making?*

"A formidable grand picture ... this is a fascinating compilation of information available in the public domain — no fiction! — on the intricacies and interdependencies of American campaign politics and [lack of] financial sector regulation and supervision. ... I have not seen so clearly that America is really confronting a choice between Scylla and Charybdis."

— Prof. (em.) Dr. Hans Dieter Seibel, Germany

"Simply brilliant, unbiased, timely and thorough investigative journalism on what the world can expect of the Hillary Clinton Presidency. Woodward and Bernstein would be proud of it. This extensively researched, verified and cited work is certain to impact and change the dynamics of the 2016 U.S. Presidential Elections. America has only been allowed to see the "tip of the iceberg". In this beautifully written, organized and riveting book, Ramesh exposes the "rest of the iceberg". A "must read" for every American!!!"

— Ajit Patel, Chief Technology Officer, WWA Advisors LLC, USA

"The breathtaking analysis by Ramesh S Arunachalam can be profitably applied to understand any popular politician pursuing public office with passion and single minded ambition. The author's fidelity to facts is absolute. His ability to connect the dots is astounding. He takes us through hard data with an easy stride. Madam President will never become dated. While serving as a prism to scrutinize and understand Hillary Clinton's future actions, this work is actually a clarion call to rescue American democracy from the fatal embrace of money-power."

— G.R. Swaminathan, Assistant Solicitor General of India

MADAM
PRESIDENT

MADAM
PRESIDENT
History in the Making?

Ramesh S Arunachalam

First published in USA in 2016 by: Shruthikka Media World

Dedication

This book is dedicated to the people of
the United States of America!

"The liberty of a democracy is not safe if the people tolerated the growth of private power to a point where it becomes stronger than the democratic state itself. That in its essence is fascism: ownership of government by an individual, by a group, or any controlling private power."

– Franklin D. Roosevelt, 1938

Contents

Introduction   1

Campaign Financing   9

The Wall Street Speeches   58

Corporate Crime, Tax Evasion, Paid Speeches and
Conflicts of Interest!   83

Panama Papers, Off-Shore Accounts, Tax Evasion
and Contributions to the Hillary Campaign   92

Climate Change and Contributions   112

The Foreign Corrupt Practices Act, Campaign
Contributions and Related Issues   121

Wall Street Regulation, Revolving Door, Conflicts of
Interest, and the Hillary Clinton Campaign   132

The Clinton Foundation, Its Donors/Trustees and the
2016 Hillary Clinton Campaign   148

Hillary Clinton, the Trans-Pacific Partnership and
Free Trade-Agreements (1993–2016)   178

The Hillary Clinton Email Saga   198

Hillary Clinton's Track Record In Foreign Policy   222

Conclusion   235

Chapter 1

Introduction

The 2016 United States presidential primaries have been very controversial, both from the perspective of the Democrats as well as Republicans. Whether it is the Hillary Clinton "email saga" or the Donald Trump "Mexican wall," the process of electing the candidates for the U.S. presidential election has indeed been generating a lot of drama and controversy.

As the primary process winds down, the choices have become clear – Donald Trump for the Republicans versus Hillary Clinton for the Democrats. The interesting fact though, is that both Trump and Clinton have astonishingly high negative ratings[1].

The primaries have been one controversy after another — the chaotic Nevada Democratic Convention,[2] the New York election fiasco, the Arizona primary debacle — all of these events were not only controversial but are undoubtedly blots on the United States democratic process itself! What happened in New York deserves particular mention here:

---

1   See, 'Fox News Poll: Clinton's negatives surpass Trump's' — The article argues that a large percentage of the American voters dislike, both Hillary Clinton and Donald Trump. Specifically, it states that while a record 61 percent had a negative view of Hillary, 56 percent had an unfavorable view of Trump. — http://www.foxnews. com/politics/2016/05/18/fox-news-poll-clintons-negatives-surpass-trumps.html

2   http://www.realclearpolitics.com/video/2016/05/22/mediabuzz_panel_was_ nevada_democratic_convention_chaos_reported_fairly.html

- Over 120,000 individuals were supposedly purged from the voters list in Brooklyn alone;[3]

- People who had registered as Democrats found that they had been unregistered or had to go to faraway places to cast their vote in districts they did not belong to;

- In addition, several other strange happenings at various polling stations including the breakdown/non-functioning of voting machines and other mysterious occurrences.

There is no question that these incidents have shown the United States Democratic Party in a very poor light. Even the Mayor of New York, Bill de Blasio, was quite astonished that over 120,000 voters had apparently been purged off the list in Brooklyn. Where did they go? How could they disappear?

The election drama reached a crescendo on April 19, the day of the New York primary, when an NGO under the name of "Election Justice of USA" filed a lawsuit requesting the opening of the Democratic primary to enable Democrats (who were previously registered[4]) and independents to vote.

It seems sadly ironic that a country, which has actively worked to promote fair electoral practices globally, has itself become the object of democratic and electoral scrutiny. Increasing talk of a "rigged electoral system" in America has come as quite a shock.

Without a doubt, American politics is on the cusp of a watershed moment and the current electoral process and its outcome are sure to have a significant impact on the process of establishing ethical standards for political governance going forward. Given the above, it also naturally follows that the candidature of the nominees of the different political parties will face significant scrutiny on the basis of their public positions, transparency, and accountability vis-à-vis the various critical issues that

---

3   http://edition.cnn.com/2016/04/19/politics/new-york-primary-voter-problem-polls-sanders-de-blasio/

4   These were mostly people whose registrations were changed, apparently without their knowledge, to either independent or Republican.

concern the American public and emerge through this dynamic electoral process.

As a former First Lady, Senator, Secretary of State, and the Democratic Party's presumptive nominee as candidate for President of the United States, Hillary Clinton occupies a unique position when compared to her fellow contenders in this electoral battle. Inarguably, she brings a certain experience to the table that neither of the other candidates[5] still in contention do.

She holds the qualification of having been intimately involved in the running of the White House for eight years by virtue of having been the First Lady. Later, she served as Secretary of State in the Obama administration, where she had been actively involved in shaping strategy in foreign affairs among other issues. Her unique advantages, however, also expose to public scrutiny her actions and positions on topics of national and international relevance. Having already been an occupant of the White House and having held the third most important office[6] in the United States Government, her established track record in terms of her position on critical and contentious issues is baggage in a sense as it makes it impossible for her to start off with an altogether clean slate. This is particularly true of some of the parameters that the current electoral debate has dredged up — campaign finance, for example. In this context, as per the data of the Federal Election Commission (FEC[7]), it needs to be emphasized that Hillary Clinton is the only one, among the three contenders left in the fray, who has received very large corporate donations to finance her electoral campaign.

Thus, given her unique qualifications and advantages and her established public track record on issues of national and international significance, Hillary's candidature offers ample scope for an analyst keenly observing events surrounding the run up to the 2016 presidential polls.

---

5   The other two candidates currently in the fray are Bernie Sanders and Donald Trump, as at June 8, 2016, although Hillary Clinton and Donald Trump are regarded as the presumptive nominees of their respective parties.

6   In notional hierarchy, The Secretary of the State Department is third in line in terms of importance. This may however vary if national security is considered.

7   www.fec.gov — FEC data used is of April 1, 2016, unless specified otherwise.

It is for this reason that I chose to make Hillary's candidature and her campaign the focus of this book to the exclusion of any strengths and weaknesses of her competitors. Indeed, I made a conscious choice to attempt a fact-based evaluation of the Hillary Clinton candidature — which is the most interesting in my opinion — based on information meticulously culled and collated from the public domain and objectively analyzed thereafter. Having been earlier involved in research into and evaluation of strategic and governance related issues in the global financial sector, I have adopted a similar framework and methodology in this endeavor too. The book thus provides a comprehensive factual account of several inter-linked strategic issues in Hillary Clinton's 2016 run for the U.S. presidency.

While writing this book, I have established several ground rules for myself:

(a) The book must be fact based. There is no place for rhetoric and unsubstantiated claims that would make it almost impossible for anyone to challenge the facts, findings, and consequent analysis presented in the book!

(b) The book should be written in an easy-flowing style, ought to have simple language, and should *not* be verbose! Short simple sentences therefore form the bulk of the book and the chapters are crisp and to the point. Footnotes, contextual explanations and additional material are provided (where required) to ensure greater clarity and depth of analysis.

(c) The material must be presented in an easy-to-assimilate manner. Where required, I do use interesting tables in the book.

(d) The book must be up-to-date, as of the time of its publication.

The outline of the chapters is as follows:

(1) **Chapter 1**, the **Introduction** provides an overview of the strategic context — the United States Elections, 2016 — in which the book is rooted. It also offers an overview on how the book is organized.

(2) **Chapter 2** discusses Hillary Clinton's strategy of campaign financing and the consequences of the same for her presidential run. It specifically focuses on conflicts of interest and the commonly brought up money in politics, topics that have been at the forefront of the discussions surrounding the 2016 U.S. presidential campaign. Accordingly, **Chapter 2** looks at who has contributed campaign money for the Hillary Clinton campaign and takes a closer look at their antecedents. Five case studies are presented and analyzed in detail. This is a very important chapter providing an eclectic analysis of the Federal Election Commission (FEC) data and other antecedent material in a manner hitherto unknown.

(3) **Chapter 3** looks at Hillary Clinton's on-going relationship with Wall Street (a metaphor used to refer to the larger financial sector) and its impact on her candidacy. While attempting this, I use the findings from the final report of the Financial Crisis Inquiry Commission (FCIC)[8]. These findings make the linkages and inter-relationships very interesting! The FCIC was the statutory body that looked at the causes and consequences of the 2007/2008 financial crisis in the United States.

(4) **Chapter 4** looks at paid speeches made by Hillary and Bill Clinton[9] to organizations in various industries. Interestingly, several of those institutions were involved in corporate crime and had issues with the Federal Government at the time

---

8   http://fcic-static.law.stanford.edu/cdn_media/fcic-reports/fcic_final_report_full.pdf

9   Bill Clinton's speeches to Wall Street firms are relevant in so far as the fact that several of them were given at a time when Hillary Clinton was Secretary of State and the company concerned was having serious problems with the Federal Government. An example is UBS AG, to whom Bill Clinton delivered several speeches when Hillary was Secretary of State and UBS AG was in the midst of a very serious problem with the Internal Revenue Service (IRS) regarding American tax evader accounts. The IRS in fact had a court order against UBS AG and that apart, there are conflicts of interest issues involved here. Therefore, Bill Clinton's speeches are also looked at while analyzing Hillary's Wall Street speeches.

when Hillary and Bill Clinton spoke. Without a doubt, this raises potential conflicts of interest, just as it does in the case of receiving campaign contributions from people who have violated the law. Two specific cases are discussed with regard to taxation and corporate crime. This highly relevant information makes this an important chapter when placed against the fact that, throughout her campaign, Hillary Clinton has talked of the need to take strong action against tax evaders.

(5) **Chapter 5** looks at an event that has taken the world by storm in early 2016 — the Panama Papers expose. Specifically, it looks at people who have supported the Hillary Clinton campaign (both monetarily as well as otherwise) and examines if their names feature in the list that the Panama Papers have thrown up.

(6) **Chapter 6** focuses on the Hillary Clinton campaign and its relationship to the energy industry, including those involved in fracking[10], fossil fuel production, and others who may have some impact on climate change. What follows is a very interesting and thought-provoking analysis.

(7) **Chapter 7** takes a look at large (non-Wall Street) contributors to the Hillary Clinton campaign, as well as large corporations associated with her, and examines their backgrounds, especially with regard to some of the critical issues that have been raised in the 2016 presidential election.

(8) **Chapter 8** focuses on Wall Street regulation, the revolving door phenomenon, conflicts of interest, and the bundlers and Hillblazers who have worked for the Hillary Clinton campaign

---

10   "Fracking refers to the procedure of creating fractures in rocks and rock formations by injecting fluid into cracks to force them further open. The l arger fi ssures allow more oil and gas to flow out of the formation and into the wellbore, from where it can be extracted." — http://www.investopedia.com/terms/f/fracking. asp? layout=orig

and looks at the inter-relationships and key antecedents therein. An eclectic and insightful analysis follows.

(9) **Chapter 9** discusses the Clinton Foundation donors and trustees (past as well as present) and the various inter-relationships to key issues raised and discussed as part of the presidential election of 2016. It also looks at related aspects that could impact Hillary Clinton's 2016 run for presidency.

(10) **Chapter 10** looks at trade and traces Hillary Clinton's support (or lack of it) to various agreements ranging from NAFTA[11] to the most current TPP[12]. This again promises to be exciting because it builds a very objective and fact-based timeline of Hillary Clinton's spoken positions on trade (with objective evidence) across a period of over two decades. It offers a bird's-eye view of Hillary Clinton's overall trade position and outlines the implications of the same for her presidential run.

(11) **Chapter 11** focuses on the "email saga," i.e., the use of a private email and private server by Hillary Clinton when she was the Secretary of State. It also outlines the consequences for her candidacy arising from that email affair. Specifically, the chapter takes a microscopic look at some of Hillary Clinton's released emails and analyzes the content of these emails in terms of whether they concerned United States national security, foreign policy, national defense, foreign government information and the like. The chapter also objectively discusses whether Hillary's use of a private email (as Secretary of State) constituted a violation of law in the United States in letter or in spirit.

(12) **Chapter 12** discusses Hillary Clinton's foreign policy orientation and experience, both before and after she became Secretary of State. It starts with her vote for the Iraq War (October 2002) and the associated consequences and implications of these for her candidacy. It also looks at Hillary Clinton's positions

---

11   NAFTA is the North American Free Trade Agreement.
12   TPP is the Trans-Pacific Partnership.

vis-à-vis the Iraq war over a 13-year period. It culminates with factual details on her other foreign policy efforts, i.e., Libya, Syria, Iran etc.

(13) **Chapter 13** is the concluding chapter and summarizes the key issues with regard to Hillary Clinton, the presidential candidate. From a transparency and accountability standpoint, it raises a number of issues with regard to Hillary Clinton's quest to become the most powerful person on this planet – the President of the United States.

(14) Information relevant to the various chapters apart from tables, references, and endnotes are provided on the book's website — which also contains a number of exhibits in support of the arguments put forth, the facts cited, and the claims made: http://www.madampresident2016.net/

Chapter 2

Campaign Financing

In March 2016, Bernie Sanders — who was running[1] against Hillary Clinton for the Democratic presidential nomination — made a very strong statement against the campaign finance system.

The *Independent* reported in an article[2] that, Bernie Sanders came down heavily on the $353,400-a-ticket fundraising dinner, organized by the Hillary Clinton campaign, featuring George and Amal Clooney and even called it "corrupt and obscene."[3] According to the *Independent*, Bernie Sanders called out Hillary Clinton for seeking the help of big-money folks to finance her presidential campaign. The article also reports that Bernie recognized this as a problem in American politics when a corrupt finance system with "big money interests" had strong influence on the electoral and political processes.

While obscene may seem a harsh word, I would, however, like to

---

1   In fact, Bernie Sanders was running against Hillary Clinton as of June 8, 2016.

2   'Bernie Sanders says Hillary Clinton's $353,400-a-ticket fundraiser with George and Amal Clooney is "obscene"' — http://www.independent.co.uk/news/world/americas/us-elections/bernie-sanders-hillary-clintons-353400-a-ticket-fundraiser-is-part-of-a-corrupt-obscene-system-a6956341.html

3   In fact George Clooney agreed with the Sanders statement calling such fundraising "obscene," in a subsequent article — http://www.cbsnews.com/news/george-clooney-political-fundraisers-cost-an-obscene-amount-of-money/; 'George Clooney Admits Money He Raised for Hillary Clinton Is "Obscene"' — http://time.com/4297055/george-clooney-obscene-hillary-clinton/

state that the issue of campaign finance is an extremely critical one that needs close consideration because it creates potentially huge possibilities for conflicts of interest. For example, what would be the long-term expectations of someone who is willing to cough up a large sum of money (almost a third of a million dollars) to share a table with Hillary Clinton, George Clooney, and Amal Clooney?[4] The short-term gain would be the pleasure and prestige derived from being seen in their company, of course.

What do we mean by "conflicts of interest here?"

A conflict of interest is a conflict between the private interests and the duty, roles, and responsibilities of any official that could improperly and unfairly influence the performance of his/her official roles and responsibilities. Private interests would include financial, pecuniary and other interests that generate a direct personal benefit to the public official as well as personal affiliations, associations, and family ties, that could or would likely improperly and unfairly influence the official's performance of his/her roles, duties, and responsibilities.

Defined in this way, conflicts of interest include the potential to undermine the proper functioning of institutions (public, private, not-for-profit) and government bodies by:

(a) Weakening adherence by officials to the ideals of impartiality, objectivity, fairness, and legitimacy in decision-making; and

(b) Distorting the rule of law, the development and application of policy, the functioning of organizations and markets, as well as the allocation of resources.

Therefore, it is correct to assume that someone contributing significantly to the campaign funds of a presidential candidate could well expect to be granted special favors in the event of the said candidate assuming office as the President of the United States.

Please note that the operative word here is "could," which indicates a

---

4   I like George Clooney as an actor and respect the kind of work he has done for the UN. I also admire Amal Clooney's track record of wonderful human rights work.

possibility rather than a certainty, of a situation or event occurring that may give rise to a conflict of interest where there is a need to compromise power or position. I quote from the Final Report[5] of the Financial Crisis Inquiry Commission (FCIC), which talks about campaign funding, lobbying, and the 2008 financial crisis. This enlightening report drives home the above conflicts of interest argument in a clear and decisive manner.

Talking about Fannie and Freddie, the FCIC Final Report notes:

> "Fannie and Freddie … reported spending more than $164 million on lobbying, and their employees and political action committees contributed $15 million to federal election campaigns."[6] (FCIC Report[7])

Take a look at the amounts that Fannie and Freddie spent on lobbying and the amounts contributed by their employees and political action committees (PACs) to the federal election process.

That is indeed sad because what Fannie May and Freddie Mac did was akin to cutting a big branch off the tree while sitting on that same branch. They had to fall and there was no other way out. Ironically, their political clout (acquired through lobbying and election support to candidates) meant that they resisted the very legislation that could have saved them. Sadly, the "invisible hand" that was to regulate them remained invisible when something went wrong. Conflicts of interest in this case were indeed very powerful it seems!

---

5   'Final Report Of The National Commission On The Causes Of The Financial And Economic Crisis In The United States', Submitted by The Financial Crisis Inquiry Commission, Pursuant to Public Law 111-21, January 2011 — http://fcic-static. law.stanford.edu/cdn_media/fcic-reports/fcic_final_report_full.pdf

6   FCIC Report (2011), Original Footnote 14: Senate Lobbying Disclosure Act Database   (www.senate.gov/legislative/Public_Disclosure/LDA_reports.htm); figures on employees and PACs compiled by the Center for Responsive Politics from Federal Elections Commission data.

7   http://fcic-static.law.stanford.edu/cdn_media/fcic-reports/fcic_final_report_full. pdf

The FCIC report further argues,

> "In 1999, the financial sector spent $187 million lobbying at the federal level, and individuals and political action committees (PACs) in the sector donated $202 million to federal election campaigns in the 2000 election cycle. From 1999 through 2008, federal lobbying by the financial sector reached $2.7 billion; campaign donations from individuals and PACs topped $1 billion.[8]

> In November 1999, Congress passed and President Clinton signed the Gramm-Leach-Bliley Act (GLBA), which lifted most of the remaining Glass-Steagall-era restrictions. The new law embodied many of the measures Treasury had previously advocated.[9] The *New York Times* reported that Citigroup CEO Sandy Weill hung in his office 'a hunk of wood — at least 4 feet wide — etched with his portrait and the words 'The Shatterer of Glass-Steagall.'"[10] (FCIC Report[11])

Note the fact that the FCIC, which was the statutory commission inquiring into the 2008 financial crisis, strongly highlighted the fact that PACs and lobbying indeed played a huge role in the shattering of Glass-Steagall-era restrictions.

So how did the sorry saga end? This is what the FCIC report has to say:

---

8   FCIC Report (2011), Original Footnote 15: FCIC staff computations based on data from the Center for Responsive Politics. 'Financial sector' here includes insurance companies, commercial banks, securities and investment firms, finance and credit companies, accountants, savings and loan institutions, credit unions, and mortgage bankers and brokers.

9   FCIC Report (2011), Original Footnote 16: U.S. Department of the Treasury, *Modernizing the Financial System* (February 1991); Fed Chairman Alan Greenspan, "H.R. 10, the Financial Services Competitiveness Act of 1997," testimony before the House Committee on Banking and Financial Services, 105th Cong., 1st sess., May 22, 1997.

10   FCIC Report (2011), Original Footnote 17: Katrina Brooker, "Citi's Creator, Alone with His Regrets," *New York Times,* January 2, 2010 — http://www.nytimes.com/2010/01/03/business/economy/03weill.html?_r=0

11   http://fcic-static.law.stanford.edu/cdn_media/fcic-reports/fcic_final_report_full.pdf

"Now, as long as bank holding companies satisfied certain safety and soundness conditions, they could underwrite and sell banking, securities, and insurance products and services. Their securities affiliates were no longer bound by the Fed's 25% limit—their primary regulator, the SEC, set their only boundaries. Supporters of the legislation argued that the new holding companies would be more profitable (due to economies of scale and scope), safer (through a broader diversification of risks), more useful to consumers (thanks to the convenience of one-stop shopping for financial services), and more competitive with large foreign banks, which already offered loans, securities, and insurance products. The legislation's opponents warned that allowing banks to combine with securities firms would promote excessive speculation and could trigger a crisis like the crash of 1929. John Reed, former co-CEO of Citigroup, acknowledged to the FCIC that, in hindsight, 'the compartmentalization that was created by Glass-Steagall would be a positive factor,' making less likely a 'catastrophic failure' of the financial system."[12] (FCIC Report[13])

Nevertheless, that was not to be as we saw in 2008 when the financial crisis exploded!

"The new regime encouraged growth and consolidation within and across banking, securities, and insurance. The bank-centered financial holding companies such as Citigroup, JP Morgan, and Bank of America could compete directly with the 'big five' investment banks — Goldman Sachs, Morgan Stanley, Merrill Lynch, Lehman Brothers, and Bear Stearns — in securitization, stock and bond underwriting, loan syndication, and trading in over-the-counter (OTC) derivatives. The biggest bank holding companies became major players in investment banking. The strategies of the largest commercial banks and their holding companies came to more closely resemble the strategies of investment banks. Each had advantages: commercial

---

12   FCIC Report (2011), Original Footnote 18: John Reed, interview by FCIC, March 24, 2010.

13   http://fcic-static.law.stanford.edu/cdn_media/fcic-reports/fcic_final_report_full. pdf

banks enjoyed greater access to insured deposits, and the investment
banks enjoyed less regulation. Both prospered from the late 1990s
until the outbreak of the financial crisis in 2007. However, Greenspan's
'spare tire' that had helped make the system less vulnerable would be
gone when the financial crisis emerged — all the wheels of the system
would be spinning on the same axle." (FCIC Report[14])

Sadly, we are still suffering from the impact of the 2008 financial crisis
that affected the United States first and thereafter impacted several
other countries globally. Moreover, clearly as the FCIC report strongly
argues, the financial crisis in the United States was (primarily) caused
by lax and laissez-faire regulation coupled with banning of regulation
(through legislation) resulting from regular and continuous lobbying
as well as huge contributions made by the financial sector to PACs
including those of potential presidential candidates!

Read the quote from the FCIC report below:

**"We conclude widespread failures in financial regulation and
supervision proved devastating to the stability of the nation's financial
markets.** The sentries were not at their posts, in no small part due to
the widely accepted faith in the self-correcting nature of the markets
and the ability of financial institutions to effectively police themselves.
More than 30 years of deregulation and reliance on self-regulation by
financial institutions, championed by former Federal Reserve chairman
Alan Greenspan and others, supported by successive administrations and
Congresses, and actively pushed by the powerful financial industry at
every turn, had stripped away key safeguards, which could have helped
avoid catastrophe. This approach had opened up gaps in oversight of
critical areas with trillions of dollars at risk, such as the shadow banking
system and over-the-counter derivatives markets. In addition, the
government permitted financial firms to pick their preferred regulators
in what became a race to the weakest supervisor. ...

---

14   http://fcic-static.law.stanford.edu/cdn_media/fcic-reports/fcic_final_report_full.
      pdf

Changes in the regulatory system occurred in many instances as financial markets evolved. However, as the report will show, the financial industry itself played a key role in weakening regulatory constraints on institutions, markets, and products. It did not surprise the Commission that an industry of such wealth and power would exert pressure on policy makers and regulators. From 1999 to 2008, the financial sector expended $2.7 billion in reported federal lobbying expenses; individuals and political action committees in the sector made more than $1 billion in campaign contributions. *What troubled us was the extent to which the nation was deprived of the necessary strength and independence of the oversight necessary to safeguard financial stability.*" (FCIC Report[15])

This is what happens when there is a campaign financing system ridden with conflicts of interest. As stated before, there is no free lunch. If large business interests and/or people with vested interests contribute to the PACs and/or the campaign, then, they are bound to extract their pound of flesh surely. Naturally, the same argument holds good when a couple pays close to a third of a million dollars to share a table with two celebrities and a potential presidential candidate, as part of the candidate's fund raising process. Without any doubt, conflicts of interest are indeed being created by a campaign financing strategy that is fundamentally flawed and we all saw from the FCIC report[16] what happens when these conflicts of interest are at play.

Keeping all of this in mind, one has to perforce question the soundness of Hillary Clinton's fund raising strategy (in using George and Amal Clooney as mentioned earlier in this chapter). Candidates who desire to be perceived as "transparent candidates" by the American public should avoid using such fund raising strategies as these could eventually give rise to unnecessary conflicts of interest.

If there is one former president whose famous speech effectively

---

15   http://fcic-static.law.stanford.edu/cdn_media/fcic-reports/fcic_final_report_full. pdf

16   As an illustration, I gave an example from the financial sector. Media, fossil fuel companies and other large corporations are no exceptions to the conflict of interest phenomenon.

sums up the present discourse in the 2016 U.S. presidential elections with regard to campaign financing, it is that of Abraham Lincoln, who notably said on November 19, 1863 at Gettysburg:

> "Four score and seven years ago our fathers brought forth on this continent, a new nation, conceived in Liberty, and dedicated to the proposition that all men are created equal. ...

> Now we are engaged in a great civil war, testing whether that nation, or any nation so conceived and so dedicated, can long endure. ...

> In a larger sense, we cannot dedicate — we cannot consecrate — we cannot hallow — this ground. The brave men, living and dead, who struggled here, have consecrated it, far above our poor power to add or detract. The world will little note, nor long remember what we say here, but it can never forget what they did here. ...that we here highly resolve that these dead shall not have died in vain — that this nation, under God, shall have a new birth of freedom — and that government of the people, by the people, for the people, shall not perish from the earth — Abraham Lincoln, November 19, 1863."[17]

Indeed, it is on the one fundamental principle in the above speech that the ethos of modern government and democracy lie — "a government of the people, by the people, for the people" and one that works for the entire population, without any conflict of interest!

It is in the above context that election 2016 is a watershed in American electoral history and I quote Bernie Sanders, who noted (in this regard) that:

> "In the year 2016, with a political campaign finance system that is corrupt and increasingly controlled by billionaires and special interests, I fear very much that, in fact, government of the people, by the people, and for the people is beginning to perish in the United States of America."[18]

---

17   http://www.abrahamlincolnonline.org/lincoln/speeches/gettysburg.htm   —   the Bliss Copy.

18   'Getting Big Money Out of Politics and Restoring Democracy' — https://berniesanders.com/issues/money-in-politics/

Indeed, this statement coupled with various happenings (such as the use of the George and Amal Clooney fund raising strategy by Hillary Clinton) prompted me to look closely at the Federal Election Commission (FEC) and other data to understand whether indeed the political financing system in America is corrupt as has been claimed by many people. In short, I wanted to explore whether the "big wealthy money in politics" and the "corrupt finance system" arguments are true of the American political milieu as of today.

I decided that the best way to do this would be to analyze the data from the FEC and look at the backgrounds of those who were contributing to Hillary Clinton, given that she is the subject of this book.

What follows are the case studies of five, high profile, wealthy, and large money contributors and bundlers (called "Hillblazers"[19]) to the Hillary Clinton campaign from among the financial sector, energy related industries, lobbyists, and several other stakeholders.

The Case of Paul Adler

Before we look at Paul Adler (the first case study) and his links with the 2016 Hillary Clinton presidential campaign, let us go back in time to 2001, and look at an interesting event cited through an article (dated March 2, 2001) published on the Jewish Sightseeing[20] site by Author Donald H. Harrison.

Harrison, writing in his article about the grant of presidential pardon to the fugitive financier Marc Rich, noted that the then U.S. Attorney Mary Jo White of New York was apparently concerned not just with regard to former President Bill Clinton's grant of pardon to Rich — on whose behalf several Jewish leaders in Israel and the United States apparently made pleas — but also the clemency granted to four other persons supposedly convicted of misusing federal funds through fraud.

Harrison wrote on his website that the four persons — Kalmen Stern,

19   https://www.hillaryclinton.com/about/hillblazers/

20   'Pardons for New Square Chasidim under investigation by White' — http://www.jewishsightseeing.com/usa/wash_dc/white_house/clinton_bill/sd3-2chasidim_pardons.htm

David Goldstein, Benjamin Berger, and Jacob Elbaum — all of whom were residents of the Hasidic village of New Square, were convicted in 1999 on charges of fraudulently obtaining federal funds to the tune of $40 million (in student grants, small-business loans, and housing subsidies). The article noted that the four were convicted and sentenced to prison terms that ranged from between 30 to 78 months. Harrison further wrote that after Clinton's pardon, Berger's sentence was reduced from 30 months to 24 months, "while Stern, Goldstein, and Elbaum received reductions to 30 months."[21]

The official clemency decisions with regard to these four people — Kalmen Stern, David Goldstein, Benjamin Berger, and Jacob Elbaum — can be viewed at The United States Department of Justice Website.[22] A summary of the offenses, sentence, and terms of the grant of clemency with regard to these four convicts is provided in **Table 2.1**.

Table 2.1: Commutations, Remissions, and Reprieves Granted by President William J. Clinton (1993–2001)	
January 20, 2001	
	Benjamin Berger
Offense:	Conspiracy to defraud the United States, 18 U.S.C. § 371; wire fraud, 18 U.S.C. § 1343; false statement, 18 U.S.C. § 1001; money laundering, 18 U.S.C. §1956(a)(1)(B)(1); filing a false tax return, 26 U.S.C. § 7206(1)
District/Date:	Southern New York; October 18, 1999
Sentence:	30 months' imprisonment; two years' supervised release; $522,977 restitution

---

21   'Pardons for New Square Chasidim under investigation by White' — http://www.jewishsightseeing.com/usa/wash_dc/white_house/clinton_bill/sd3-2chasidim_pardons.htm

22   Commutations, Remissions, and Reprieves Granted by President William J. Clinton (1993–2001) — https://www.justice.gov/pardon/clinton-commutations#janone

Table 2.1: Commutations, Remissions, and Reprieves Granted by President William J. Clinton (1993–2001)	
January 20, 2001	
Terms of Grant:	Sentence of imprisonment commuted to 24 months' imprisonment
	Jacob Elbaum
Offense:	Conspiracy to defraud the United States, 18 U.S.C. § 371; embezzlement from a federally funded program, 18 U.S.C. § 666; wire fraud, 18 U.S.C. § 1343; mail fraud, 18 U.S.C. § 1341; making a false statement, 18 U.S.C. § 1001; filing a false tax return, 26 U.S.C. § 7206; failure to file a tax return, 26 U.S.C. § 7203
District/Date:	Southern New York; October 18, 1999
Sentence:	57 months' imprisonment; two years' supervised release; $11,089,721 restitution
Terms of Grant:	Sentence of imprisonment commuted to 30 months' imprisonment
	David Goldstein
Offense:	Conspiracy to defraud the United States, 18 U.S.C. § 371; wire fraud, 18 U.S.C. § 1343; embezzlement from a federally funded program, 18 U.S.C. § 666; mail fraud, 18 U.S.C. § 1341
District/Date:	Southern New York; October 18, 1999
Sentence:	70 months' imprisonment; three years' supervised release; $10,118,182 restitution
Terms of Grant:	Sentence of imprisonment commuted to 30 months' imprisonment

Table 2.1: Commutations, Remissions, and Reprieves Granted by President William J. Clinton (1993–2001)	
January 20, 2001	
	Kalmen Stern
Offense:	Conspiracy to defraud the United States, 18 U.S.C. § 371; embezzlement from a federally funded program, 18 U.S.C. § 666; wire fraud, 18 U.S.C. §1343; mail fraud, 18 U.S.C. § 1341; filing a false tax return, 26 U.S.C. § 7206(1)
District/Date:	Southern New York; October 18, 1999
Sentence:	78 months' imprisonment; three years' supervised release; $11,179,513 restitution
Terms of Grant:	Sentence of imprisonment commuted to 30 months
Source: Compiled from https://www.justice.gov/pardon/clinton-commutations#janone	

Author Donald H. Harrison citing a *New York Post* report, indicated that Paul Adler, then a Rockland County Democratic Party official, was perhaps a behind-the-scenes player in the clemency of the four people — Kalmen Stern, David Goldstein, Benjamin Berger, and Jacob Elbaum.[23]

Now, let us return to the present. A look at the Federal Election Commission (FEC) website[24] data clarifies beyond doubt that Paul Adler has contributed to the 2016 Hillary Clinton presidential campaign. Specifically, he has individually given $2,700[25]. Another interesting piece of information is that Paul Adler's name appears in the "Hillblazers" list provided on Hillary Clinton's website.[26]

---

23   'Pardons for New Square Chasidim under investigation by White' — http://www.jewishsightseeing.com/usa/wash_dc/white_house/clinton_bill/sd3-2chasidim_pardons.htm

24   http://www.fec.gov/pindex.shtml

25   Ibid.

26   https://www.hillaryclinton.com/about/hillblazers/

So who exactly is Paul Adler? He is the former chairman of the Rockland County Democratic Party, who is reported to have close ties with the Clintons. In fact, a *New York Times*[27] report suggests that Paul Adler had indeed developed a close alliance with Hillary Clinton during her election to the Senate, way back in the early 2000s.

Apart from his reported behind-the-scenes role[28] in the clemency granted to "Kalmen Stern, David Goldstein, Benjamin Berger, and Jacob Elbaum — residents of the Hasidic village of New Square"[29] who "had been convicted in 1999 on charges of swindling the federal government of $40 million in student grants, small-business loans, and housing subsidies"[30], there is some more interesting information on Paul Adler as revealed below.

The *New York Times*[31] dated September 12, 2000, reported that Paul Adler, who was the chairman of the Democratic Party in Rockland County, had been charged with corruption. The same report further added that prosecutors had mentioned the fact that Paul Adler had enriched himself "to the tune of $375,000" by participating in several real estate transactions that were tainted by "fraud, bribery, and extortion."

In fact, Paul Adler in his own admission informed the court[32] as follows:

---

27   'Rockland Democratic Leader Arrested on Corruption Charges' — http://www. nytimes.com/2000/09/12/nyregion/rockland-democratic-leader-arrested-on-corruption-charges.html

28   'Pardons for New Square Chasidim under investigation by White' — http://www. jewishsightseeing.com/usa/wash_dc/white_house/clinton_bill/sd3-2chasidim_pardons.htm

29   'Pardons for New Square Chasidim under investigation by White' — http://www. jewishsightseeing.com/usa/wash_dc/white_house/clinton_bill/sd3-2chasidim_pardons.htm

30   'Pardons for New Square Chasidim under investigation by White' — http://www. jewishsightseeing.com/usa/wash_dc/white_house/clinton_bill/sd3-2chasidim_pardons.htm

31   'Rockland Democratic Leader Arrested on Corruption Charges' — http://www. nytimes.com/2000/09/12/nyregion/rockland-democratic-leader-arrested-on-corruption-charges.html

32   http://www.leagle.com/decision/2003857274FSupp2d583_1817/U.S.%20v.%20 ADLER#

"From 1996 until my arrest in this case, I was Chairman of the Rockland County Democratic Committee. ...On more than one occasion, I accepted payments from the Herskowitzes as partial payment for my work. ... I often used my political contacts to obtain a government job for Caine. I conveyed to Caine that I wanted his help with the Smith Farm approvals in exchange for a job."

Adler further noted to the court[33] as follows,

"I intentionally did not report approximately $52,000 in income ... in 1996 and 1997. ...In 1996, I did not report $150,000 in business income. ...I falsely told the accounting firm that was preparing my tax returns that the $150,000 was income to my neighbor's company in the form of a fee."

As the court document[34] further notes, Paul Adler

"also mentioned other improper deductions taken by the business and conceded that he had specific criminal intent at the time he acted to defraud the Internal Revenue Service."

This makes it very clear that Paul Adler, as per his own admissions to the court, had:

(a)   taken bribes;

(b)   engaged in public corruption;

(c)   displayed specific criminal intent to defraud the Internal Revenue Service; and

(d)   In simple terms, Paul Adler had indeed been a felon in the eyes of the law in the United States and he had served a sentence for the crimes committed!

In fact, when Adler was spotted with de Blasio and Hillary Clinton

---

33   Ibid.
34   Ibid.

at a fund raising event held on October 23, 2013, the *New York Post*[35] carried a report — commenting on his appearance at the event — titled "Ex-felon Clinton ally helps fund de Blasio's campaign". The newspaper observed that the former Rockland County Democratic Chairman and Hillary Clinton ally, Paul Adler — "who served time for felony fraud and federal corruption"[36] — was among the people leading the campaign to put Bill de Blasio into City Hall.

The report[37] further said that Adler, who was also named in Bill Clinton's clemency-for-votes probe case in New Square, had been sentenced to a prison term of 19 months in 2002 after admitting guilt in a federal corruption and bribery case as well as tax evasion and fraud.

In the light of all this, I wonder how Hillary Clinton is using the services of Paul Adler, who has himself confessed to and been convicted on charges of felony, fraud and federal corruption — as a "Hillblazer"[38] (Bundler)[39] to solicit campaign contributions for her 2016 presidential run!

Somehow, her action does not match with the plan put forth by her for campaign finance reform[40] and it makes one wonder whether her campaign finance reform plan will indeed be implemented in real time, if she becomes the President of the United States.

Several questions are relevant here and require an answer from

---

35   'Ex-felon Clinton ally helps fund de Blasio's campaign' — http://nypost. com/2013/10/23/ex-felon-clinton-ally-helps-fund-de-blasios-campaign/
36   Ibid.
37   Ibid.
38   https://www.hillaryclinton.com/about/hillblazers/
39   "A 'bundler' is a person who gathers contributions from many different individuals and presents the sum (or 'bundle') to a campaign in one lump sum. 'Bundlers' are invaluable to campaigns — because of this, campaigns will usually bestow honorary titles upon the bundlers" — http://www.davemanuel.com/investor-dictionary/ bundlers/
40   'Hillary Clinton Announces Campaign Finance Overhaul Plan' — http://www. nytimes.com/2015/09/09/us/politics/hillary-clinton-announces-campaign-finance-reform-plan.html

Hillary Clinton and her campaign in this regard. These questions are listed below:

(a) How has she and her campaign justified accepting contributions from a convict, who himself admitted before the law that he was guilty of fraud, criminal intent, and bribery?

(b) Is this not tantamount to supporting corrupt people, who use fraud and bribery to further their causes?

(c) Does this action by the Hillary Clinton campaign not send the wrong signals to the electorate at large?

(d) Is the Hillary Clinton campaign grateful (as mentioned in the Hillblazers webpage[41]) to a convict, a corrupt person, and fraudster like Paul Adler, who cheated the people of his constituency, just because he helped bundle $100,000 (or more) for Hillary's presidential run?

(e) Is campaign money welcome at any cost and especially, at the cost of integrity?

(f) What implication does this have for the "money in politics" argument that is at the center of the U.S. presidential elections 2016?

(g) What implication does this have for the candidature of Hillary Clinton for the President of the United States?

These and other questions will have to be answered by Hillary Clinton and her campaign, even as they prepare to woo the general electorate in the run up to the U.S. presidential elections!

The Case of Beth Dozoretz

January 20, 2001 would go down as one of the black days in office for Bill Clinton. It was on this day, his very last in office as president, that Bill Clinton issued what was described by the *New York Times*[42]

41　　https://www.hillaryclinton.com/about/hillblazers/

42　　'An Indefensible Pardon' — http://www.nytimes.com/2001/01/24/opinion/an-indefensible-pardon.html#h

as 'An Indefensible Pardon' for the international fugitive Marc Rich, who was on the FBI's most wanted list. The editorial unequivocally condemned Bill Clinton's last-minute pardon of Marc Rich, the shadowy international fugitive who fled in 1983 to Switzerland to avoid American justice, as a serious, shocking, and ultimate abuse of presidential power.

Beth Dozoretz, a longtime Democratic Party donor and a close friend of Denise Rich (wife of Marc Rich[43]), reportedly played a "key role" in helping secure the Marc Rich pardon.[44] Commenting on her role, the Second Report, by The Committee On Government Reform, Volume 1 of 3, United States House Of Representatives, 107th CONGRESS, Washington, 2002 notes and I quote:

> **"The role of Beth Dozoretz.** Beth Dozoretz, another close friend of President Clinton, played a key role in obtaining the Rich pardon. Like Denise Rich, Beth Dozoretz had a relationship with President Clinton built on personal ties and political fundraising. Dozoretz has raised and contributed millions of dollars for the Democratic party and has pledged to raise an additional million dollars for the Clinton library. Beth Dozoretz also has close relationships with Denise Rich and Jack Quinn. Dozoretz used her close relationship with President Clinton to lobby for the Rich pardon."[45]

It is in the above context that we need to understand who Beth Dozoretz is and what her connection with the Clintons is.

Subsequent to the Marc Rich pardon, over the years, Dozoretz seems to have worked closely with the Clintons. She was the finance co-

---

43   'Rich has been listed in the Panama Papers expose' — http://www.mcclatchydc.
      com/news/politics-government/election/article72215012.html

44   'Bill Clinton's pardon of fugitive Marc Rich continues to pay big' — http://nypost.
      com/2016/01/17/after-pardoning-criminal-marc-rich-clintons-made-millions-
      off-friends/

45   Justice Undone: Clemency Decisions In The Clinton White House, Second Report,
      By The Committee On Government Reform, Volume 1 Of 3, United States House
      Of Representatives,107TH CONGRESS, Washington, 2002

chair of Hillary's 2008 presidential run[46] and later, she became a senior State Department official during Hillary's tenure as Secretary of State. Specifically, Beth Dozoretz served[47] as Director of Art in Embassies at the State Department.

In that role she oversaw the placement of art in all of the embassies around the world, as well as enhancing the cultural exchange aspects of the program. It was the soft power opportunities that were her main area of interest.

She has contributed[48] to the PAC "Ready for Hillary"[49] and also to Hillary Clinton's 2016 presidential run. She has given $2,700, as has her husband[50]. Her husband, Ronald, likewise, has supported Hillary's 2016 presidential run individually in addition to having donated substantial amounts[51] to the Clinton Foundation and their other efforts.[52]

It would be fair to conclude from all of the above that Beth and Ronald Dozoretz have close ties to the Clintons and are their staunch supporters.

Getting back to the Marc Rich pardon case, which perhaps made Beth Dozoretz a household name in the United States, it is interesting

---

46   http://cpl.hks.harvard.edu/people/beth-e-dozoretz. "Beth has been actively involved in Democratic politics for several years. ... In the 2004 Presidential Race, she served as Finance Co-chair for the John Kerry Campaign and in 2008 for Hillary Clinton's campaign."

47   http://www.bethdozoretz.com/

48   'Bill Clinton's pardon of fugitive Marc Rich continues to pay big' — http://nypost.com/2016/01/17/after-pardoning-criminal-marc-rich-clintons-made-millions-off-friends/

49   Now called Ready PAC. Please see https://rfh.ngpvanhost.com/ — This website lists Beth Dozoretz as a National Council Member!

50   www.fec.gov

51   There are two entries in the names of Dozoretz: a) Ronald I. Dozoretz Foundation has given a sum of between $100,001 to $250,000; and b) Dozoretz Family Foundation which has donated a sum between $250,001 to $500,000

52   'Bill, Hillary and Chelsea draw Democratic VIPs to closed-door foundation fundraiser' — https://www.washingtonpost.com/blogs/reliable-source/wp/2013/09/10/bill-hillary-and-chelsea-draw-democratic-vips-to-closed-door-foundation-fundraiser

to note what the Congressional hearings had to say and I quote relevant paragraphs from the same:

"The pardons of Marc Rich and Pincus Green were the most controversial and most outrageous pardons issued by President Clinton, and likely, by any President. Rich and Green were fugitives from justice, and were two of the largest tax cheats in U.S. history. In addition, they had a long and disgraceful record of trading with America's enemies, helping prop up the Ayatollah Khomeini, Saddam Hussein, Muammar Qaddafi, and the Russian mafia, among others. This track record has led even Marc Rich's lawyers to call him a 'traitor' and observe that he has 'spit on the American flag.'

It is beyond any dispute that Marc Rich and Pincus Green did not deserve pardons. Therefore, the inevitable question is why the President granted them.

There are a number of reasons to believe that the pardons were not just the product of a sloppy process. After all, even though they did not fully understand the scope of Rich and Green's crimes, the President and White House staff grasped the essentials of the Rich case: Rich and Green were massive tax cheats, fugitives from justice, and had traded with the enemy. Yet, they received the pardons despite these damning facts. ...

Denise Rich and Beth Dozoretz were both close friends of President Clinton and major contributors to the Democratic Party. In addition, Denise Rich contributed $450,000 to the Clinton Library, and Dozoretz pledged to raise $1 million for the Clinton Library. Both lobbied the President on the Rich pardon. Both have also invoked their Fifth Amendment rights rather than testify about their discussions with the President. ...

Denise Rich's special relationship with President Clinton was also manifested in her large contributions to the William J. Clinton Presidential Foundation, the charitable foundation responsible for building the Clinton Library. Between 1998 and 2000, Denise Rich gave $450,000 to the Clinton Library.[53]Among these contributions was a $250,000 gift in July 1998, which was one of the earliest large contributions to the Library, made during one of the darkest times in the Clinton presidency.[54] ...

One document suggests that Denise Rich was seeking 'help' from Dozoretz. On a note accompanying her $100,000 library contribution, Denise Rich wrote, 'Dear Beth, Thanks for your help, Lots of love, Denise'."[55]

As noted further in the Congressional report,

"The Marc Rich pardon is replete with evidence that a number of the major actors had improper motives. The first and most obvious piece of evidence is that the four major players in the Marc Rich case—Marc Rich, Pincus Green, Denise Rich, and Beth Dozoretz—have refused to discuss their involvement in the case, with two of them relying on their Fifth Amendment right against self-incrimination. The two people closest to President Clinton who lobbied him on the Rich and Green pardons-Denise Rich and Beth Dozoretz-have refused to testify about their discussions with the President without a grant of prosecutorial immunity. The consistent refusal of key witnesses to answer questions certainly raises concerns about their motives. ...

---

53   Congressional Report (2002), Original Footnote 436: See William J. Clinton Presidential Foundation Document Production WJCPF 0002 (Check from Denise Rich to the Clinton Library for $250,000 (July 15, 1998); William J. Clinton Presidential Foundation Document Production WJCPF 0008 (Check from Denise Rich to the Clinton Library for $100,000 (August 7, 1999); William J. Clinton Presidential Foundation Document Production WJCPF 0031 (Check from Denise Rich to the Clinton Library for $100,000 (May 11, 2000) (Exhibit 74).

54   Congressional Report (2002), Original Footnote 437: Id.

55   Congressional Report (2002), Original Footnote 438: William J. Clinton Presidential Foundation Document Production WJCPF 0037 (Note from Denise Rich to Beth Dozoretz, former finance chair, Democratic National Committee; Exhibit 75).

The clear factual record established by the report demonstrates that there was no reasonable explanation for the Marc Rich and Pincus Green pardons. All of the explanations offered to date by the President are factually inaccurate or totally irrelevant."

The Congressional report goes further to say this:

"It apparently does not concern the President that he has pardoned two of the largest tax cheats and most wanted international fugitives in U.S. history. It apparently is not a matter of concern that a man who traded oil with (and thus has financially supported) terrorist regimes ranging from Ayatollah Khomeini's Iran to Saddam Hussein's Iraq has escaped any punishment from the U.S. legal system. President Clinton is apparently unconcerned that a man who attempted to renounce his citizenship to escape the law and was described as a 'traitor' by his own attorney is now free to return to the United States. President Clinton is apparently not troubled that he has undermined U.S. efforts to apprehend criminals abroad by pardoning two of the FBI's most wanted fugitives."

Additionally, it has been reported that Beth Dozoretz was a board member in a small publicly traded company, U.S. Technologies, which is now all but insolvent and the company and its chief executive, C. Gregory Earls, are facing suits by investors who say they were defrauded of millions of dollars, with the misconduct said to have occurred in late 2001 and 2002. While the investigation (and the suits) over U.S. Technologies relate to Mr. Earls (the company's chairman and chief executive), it has been reported that Mr. Earls is the one who recruited Mr. Webster and other prominent Washington figures, including George Mitchell, the former Senate majority leader, and Beth Dozoretz, the former finance chairwoman of the Democratic National Committee, to serve on the board of U.S. Technologies and invest in the company.[56]

---

56   'S.E.C. Orders Investigation Into Webster Appointment, by Stephen Labaton', — http://www.nytimes.com/2002/10/31/business/01CND-ACCO. html?pagewanted=all#h; https://www.justice.gov/archive/dag/cftf/chargingdocs/ earlsindictment.pdf

Given this context, and in the light of her repeated assertions about rooting out corruption in high places, it is truly surprising that Hillary Clinton chooses to use Beth Dozoretz as a Hillblazer. This is especially surprising, after the serious comments made in the report titled, "Justice Undone: Clemency Decisions In The Clinton White House, Second Report, By The Committee On Government Reform, Volume 1 Of 3, United States HOUSE OF REPRESENTATIVES,107th CONGRESS, Washington, 2002."

In fact, when Hillary Clinton talks so much about rooting out corruption in high places, does that not require that she be seen in the company of people devoid of (any kind of) controversy? And given what has been said about Beth Dozoretz in the Congressional report mentioned above, and given what has been written about and discussed in the newspapers,[57] is it not prudent for the Hillary Clinton campaign to avoid using such people as bundlers or Hillblazers to raise campaign contribution money? It is worthy noting that the Hillary Clinton website thanks the Hillblazers[58] for helping to raise $100,000 or more in primary election contributions and espouses gratitude for their support to Hillary Clinton. One is forced to wonder if Hillary Clinton actually wants to be seen expressing gratitude to convicts like Paul Adler or to people like Beth Dozoretz (also a Hillblazer), who have had serious remarks made against them in a Congressional hearing report.

The Case of James Simons

The third case that I report on is that of James Harris Simons, who is a well known American mathematician, hedge fund manager, and philanthropist. The Forbes hedge fund list had his name listed against a company called Renaissance Technologies (RenTec), a New York-based hedge fund.

The reason I took up James Simons and RenTec as my first Wall Street case study was the fact that employees and executives of RenTec

---

57   'Bill Clinton's pardon of fugitive Marc Rich continues to pay big' — http://nypost.com/2016/01/17/after-pardoning-criminal-marc-rich-clintons-made-millions-off-friends/

58   https://www.hillaryclinton.com/about/hillblazers/

had supposedly made nearly $13.8 million in campaign contributions over the three cycles, more than any other high frequency trading company.[59] As per this report, RenTec contributed $692,300 during the 2008 cycle and nearly $11.8 million during the 2012 cycle, a 1,600 percent increase. Incidentally, the net worth of James H. Simons stands at about $15.5 billion, according to the Bloomberg Billionaires Index.[60]

Curious, I started digging deeper and came across a website[61] that stated Dr. James H. Simons is President of Euclidean Capital, supposedly a "family office." Such organizations that handle the financial wealth and affairs of a single family are not required[62] to disclose any details to the U.S. Securities and Exchange Commission (SEC). The website also mentioned that Dr. James Simons is the board chair of Renaissance Technologies LLC, a highly quantitative investment firm engaged in algorithmic trading from which he supposedly retired in 2009 after serving several years as CEO.[63]

A look at the FEC data[64] reveals that James Simons of Euclidean Capital contributed $2,700 to Hillary Clinton for the 2016 presidential election cycle. Incidentally, his former wife, Barbara Simons, a computer scientist, has also made a $2,700 contribution to Hillary Clinton. I found two more names associated with Renaissance Technologies: Francesco Scattone and Vincent Dellapietra. Both have contributed $2,700 and $2,600 respectively to the Hillary Clinton campaign as per the FEC website. All of these are individual contributions.

A closer look at various political action committees (PACs) supporting Hillary Clinton led me to focus on a very interesting group called "Priorities USA Action."[65]

---

59   http://www.citizensforethics.org/page/-/PDFs/Reports/5_13_13_high_ frequency_trading_report.pdf?nocdn=1

60   http://www.bloomberg.com/billionaires/2016-05-03/cya

61   https://tiger21.com/presenter-bio/1735

62   'Private Investment Firms Win the Right to Keep Money in the Family'— http://www.bloomberg.com/news/articles/2015-02-10/meryl-streep-money-stays-with-simon-family-as-sec-grants-in-laws

63   https://tiger21.com/presenter-bio/1735

64   www.fec.gov

65   http://prioritiesusaaction.org/about/

Their website is in very clear support of Hillary Clinton for President and it argues that "Priorities USA Action" is supporting Hillary Clinton because they believe that, among other reasons, she is the candidate best suited to advance the interests and well being of the middle class.[66]

A quick check of the FEC website for the names of the donors to this PAC was revealing to say the least!

Table 2.2: Priorities USA Action pro-Clinton PAC						
Contributor Name	Employer	Occupation	City	State	Zip	Amount (in $)
Simons, James	Euclidean Capital	Philanthropist	New York	NY	10010	3,500,000
Simons, James	Euclidean Capital	Philanthropist	New York	NY	10010	3,500,000
Source: Data from Federal Election Commission, http://www.fec.gov/						

Throughout the current presidential campaign season, I have observed that hedge fund managers have increasingly contributed to Priorities USA Action, the PAC supporting former Secretary of State Hillary Clinton. They have also contributed to the "Hillary Victory Fund." Therefore, in some ways, it is not surprising that Dr. James Simons has donated large sums of money to the Hillary Clinton campaign. That said, Simons' contributions have not been quite enough to put him past George Soros, another hedge fund manager, as Hillary Clinton's leading supporter in terms of PAC contributions.[67]

At this point, I would like to reemphasize the fact that Dr. James H. Simons is not only President of Euclidean Capital, but is also <u>still</u> the

---

66   http://prioritiesusaaction.org/about/

67   As of May 28, 2016, both George Soros and James Simons have reportedly been surpassed by Haim Saban, the media mogul, whose family and institutions have provided more than $10 million to the Hillary Clinton campaign directly and through pro-Clinton PACs. See, 'The Top Donors Backing Hillary Clinton's Super PAC' — http://www.forbes.com/sites/ivonaiacob/2016/05/27/top-donors-hillary-clinton-superpac/#3434fc0e2740

Board Chair of Renaissance Technologies LLC (RenTec), from which he retired in 2009 after many years as CEO.[68]

Given the fact that James Simons was one of the largest donors to the Hillary Clinton campaign, I decided to delve deeper into his companies. I came across a very interesting and high profile report on RenTec[69] that included significant comments on the practices within the company with regard to long — and short-term capital gains and avoidance of taxes. The report that I refer to is called, "Abuse of Structured Financial Products: Misusing Basket Options to Avoid Taxes and Leverage Limits."[70] by United States Senate PERMANENT SUBCOMMITTEE ON INVESTIGATIONS (JULY 22, 2014).

What follows is an excerpt from the above report[71] of the U.S. Senate Permanent Subcommittee on Investigations on Renaissance Technologies LLC (RenTec):

"For the last decade, the U.S. Senate Permanent Subcommittee on Investigations has presented case histories showing how financial institutions, law firms, accountants, and others have designed and implemented complex financial structures to take advantage of and, at times, abuse or violate U.S. tax statutes, securities regulations, and accounting rules."[72]

---

68 https://tiger21.com/presenter-bio/1735
69 'Senate: Renaissance Hedge Fund Avoided $6 Billion in Taxes in Bogus Scheme With Banks' — http://wallstreetonparade.com/2014/07/senate-renaissance-hedge-fund-avoided-6-billion-in-taxes-in-bogus-scheme-with-banks/
70 Report: Abuse Of Structured Financial Products: Misusing Basket Options to Avoid Taxes and Leverage Limits (July 22, 2014) (805.6 KB) — http://www.hsgac.senate.gov/download/report-abuse-of-structured-financial-products-misusing-basket-options-to-avoid-taxes-and-leverage-limits
71 Report: Abuse Of Structured Financial Products: Misusing Basket Options to Avoid Taxes and Leverage Limits (July 22, 2014) (805.6 KB) — http://www.hsgac.senate.gov/download/report-abuse-of-structured-financial-products-misusing-basket-options-to-avoid-taxes-and-leverage-limits
72 Abuse of Structured Financial Products Report (Basket Options) (2014), Original Footnote 1: See, e.g., U.S. Senate Permanent Subcommittee on Investigations reports and hearings, 'Fishtail, Bacchus, Sundance, and Slapshot: Four Enron Transactions Funded and Facilitated by U.S. Financial Institutions,' S. Prt. 107-

The final phrase is the key stating that they have attempted to "abuse or violate U.S. tax statutes, securities regulations, and accounting rules" and needs to be carefully noted. The above report further states:

> "This investigation offers yet another detailed case study of how two financial institutions — Deutsche Bank AG and Barclays Bank PLC — developed structured financial products called MAPS and COLT, two types of basket options, and sold them to one or more hedge funds, including Renaissance Technologies LLC (RenTec) and George Weiss Associates, that used them to avoid federal taxes and leverage limits on buying securities with borrowed funds. While that type of option product was identified as abusive in a public memorandum by the Internal Revenue Service (IRS) in 2010, taxes have yet to be collected on many of the basket option transactions and its use to circumvent federal leverage limits has yet to be analyzed or halted."[73]

As the U.S. Senate report further observes:

> "The basket option contracts examined by the Subcommittee investigation were used by at least 13 hedge funds to conduct over $100 billion in securities trades, most of which were short-term transactions and some of which lasted only seconds."[74]

---

82 (1/2/2003); 'U.S. Tax Shelter Industry: The Role of Accountants, Lawyers, and Financial Professionals,' S. Hrg. 108-473 (11/18 and 20/2003); 'Tax Haven Abuses: The Enablers, The Tools and Secrecy,' S. Hrg 109-797 (8/1/2006); 'Repatriating Offshore Funds: 2004 Tax Windfall for Select Multinationals,' S. Prt. 112-27 (10/11/2011); 'Offshore Profit Shifting and the ;U.S. Tax Code — Part 1 (Microsoft and Hewlett-Packard),' S. Hrg. 112-781 (9/20/2012); and 'Offshore Profit Shifting and the U.S. Tax Code — Part 2 (Apple Inc.),' S. Hrg. 113-90 (5/13/2013).

73   Report: Abuse Of Structured Financial Products: Misusing Basket Options to Avoid Taxes and Leverage Limits (July 22, 2014) (805.6 KB) — http://www.hsgac. senate.gov/download/report-abuse-of-structured-financial-products-misusing-basket-options-to-avoid-taxes-and-leverage-limits

74   Report: Abuse Of Structured Financial Products: Misusing Basket Options to Avoid Taxes and Leverage Limits (July 22, 2014) (805.6 KB) — http://www.hsgac. senate.gov/download/report-abuse-of-structured-financial-products-misusing-basket-options-to-avoid-taxes-and-leverage-limits

Please note that the U.S. Senate report clearly specifies that most of the transactions were short-term transactions that lasted a mere few seconds and as the report further notes:

"Yet the resulting short-term profits were frequently cast as long-term capital gains subject to a 20% tax rate (previously 15%) rather than the ordinary income tax rate (currently as high as 39%) that would otherwise apply to investors in hedge funds engaged in daily trading. ... specific data supplied by the banks with respect to RenTec, the largest basket option user, suggests that the basket options may have been used to treat short-term capital gains as long-term capital gains, resulting in estimated tax avoidance of more than $6 billion. ... Over a fourteen-year period from 1999 to 2013, one hedge fund, Renaissance Technologies LLC, held 60 basket option contracts... [and] ...used them to carry out an investment strategy utilizing hundreds of millions of trades, virtually all of which lasted less than 12 months, and characterized the vast majority of the resulting $34 billion in trading profits as long-term capital gains."[75]

This certainly needs serious consideration as this action perhaps caused a huge loss to the United States (tax) exchequer by the hedge funds concerned. As is clear, Renaissance Technologies LLC (RenTec) is one of the major hedge funds explored in the U.S. Senate report.

In fact, the aforementioned Senate report unequivocally argues and settles the debate as follows:

"While the banks styled the trading arrangement as an 'option' under which profits from short-term trades would be treated as long-term capital gains, in essence, the banks loaned the hedge funds money to finance their trading and allowed them to trade for themselves in highly leveraged positions in the banks' proprietary accounts and reap the resulting profits. The banks offering the 'options' benefited from the

---

75   Report: Abuse Of Structured Financial Products: Misusing Basket Options to Avoid Taxes and Leverage Limits (July 22, 2014) (805.6 KB) — http://www.hsgac. senate.gov/download/report-abuse-of-structured-financial-products-misusing-basket-options-to-avoid-taxes-and-leverage-limits

financing, trading, and other fees charged to the hedge funds initiating the trades. In the end, the trading conducted by the hedge funds using the basket option accounts was virtually indistinguishable from the trading conducted by hedge funds using their own brokerage accounts, and provided no justification for treating the resulting short-term trading profits as long-term capital gains."[76]

The report also notes a second issue related to these events and it pertains to "circumventing Federal Leverage Limits." As the report argues,

"In addition to using basket options to reduce taxes on their short-term capital gains, the hedge funds used them to obtain financing for securities trades far in excess of what federal leverage limits allow. Federal leverage limits were established in response to the stock market crash of 1929, when securities purchased on borrowed funds magnified stock market losses and caused failures of, not only the stock speculators, but also the banks and broker-dealers that lent them money. Federal 'margin rules' were enacted to impose a leverage limit of 2:1 on brokerage accounts opened by U.S. broker dealers for their customers. In contrast, because the participating banks seemingly lent money to their own accounts, the basket option accounts examined by the Subcommittee provided the hedge fund option holders with leverage ratios as high as 20:1. RenTec indicated in one document that it had been unable to attain such high leverage levels in any other setting."[77]

The seriousness of the issue has been underlined by the financial crisis of 2008 and I quote from the FCIC report,[78] in which it is argued that:

---

76 Report: Abuse Of Structured Financial Products: Misusing Basket Options to Avoid Taxes and Leverage Limits (July 22, 2014) (805.6 KB) — http://www.hsgac. senate.gov/download/report-abuse-of-structured-financial-products-misusing-basket-options-to-avoid-taxes-and-leverage-limits

77 Report: Abuse Of Structured Financial Products: Misusing Basket Options to Avoid Taxes and Leverage Limits (July 22, 2014) (805.6 KB) — http://www.hsgac. senate.gov/download/report-abuse-of-structured-financial-products-misusing-basket-options-to-avoid-taxes-and-leverage-limits

78 Final Report Of The National Commission On The Causes Of The Financial And

"We conclude a combination of excessive borrowing, risky investments, and lack of transparency put the financial system on a collision course with crisis. ...

In the years leading up to the crisis, too many financial institutions, as well as too many households, borrowed to the hilt, leaving them vulnerable to financial distress or ruin if the value of their investments declined even modestly. For example, as of 2007, the five major investment banks — Bear Stearns[79], Goldman Sachs, Lehman Brothers, Merrill Lynch, and Morgan Stanley — were operating with extraordinarily thin capital. By one measure, their leverage ratios were as high as 40 to 1, meaning for every $40 in assets, there was only $1 in capital to cover losses. Less than a 3% drop in asset values could wipe out a firm. To make matters worse, much of their borrowing was short-term, in the overnight market — meaning the borrowing had to be renewed each and every day. For example, at the end of 2007, Bear Stearns had $11.8 billion in equity and $383.6 billion in liabilities and was borrowing as much as $70 billion in the overnight market. It was the equivalent of a small business with $50,000 in equity borrowing $1.6 million, with $296,750 of that due each and every day. One can't really ask, 'What were they thinking?' when it seems that too many of them were thinking alike.

And the leverage was often hidden—in derivatives positions, in off-balance-sheet entities, and through 'window dressing' of financial reports available to the investing public." (FCIC Report[80])

Looks like history may repeat itself in terms of another financial crisis, if the above practice of "high leverage" through basket options is allowed to continue.

Economic Crisis In The United States, Submitted by The Financial Crisis Inquiry Commission, Pursuant to Public Law 111-21, January 2011 — http://fcic-static. law.stanford.edu/cdn_media/fcic-reports/fcic_final_report_full.pdf

79   It must be noted that Bear Stearns and RenTec worked closely for several years!

80   http://fcic-static.law.stanford.edu/cdn_media/fcic-reports/fcic_final_report_full. pdf

That said, in summary, the report of the U.S. Senate Permanent Subcommittee on Investigations notes the following:

"Although Deutsche Bank and Barclays established proprietary accounts for the basket options, purportedly to hold assets that would serve as a hedge to cover the option payoffs, those accounts actually functioned as if they were RenTec's own prime brokerage trading accounts, with RenTec acting in the role of trader rather than option holder. The facts show RenTec had active and total control over the trading strategy and executions. ...

The resulting rapid asset turnover in the various option accounts meant that the options purchased by RenTec had no fixed assets and did not function as true options. The accounts existed simply to carry out RenTec's algorithmic trading strategy.

In the end, for all practical purposes, the accounts functioned as over-leveraged prime brokerage accounts controlled by the hedge fund...to produce trading profits rather than as accounts controlled by the banks to provide a hedge against an option contract. ...

This RenTec's control over the trading strategy and related activities, high-volume trading and account turnover, integration of the accounts into a larger investment strategy, and use of the accounts to produce regular cash payments supporting its business operations, contradict a depiction of RenTec as a passive option holder awaiting derivative gains. The option structure functioned instead as a vehicle for RenTec to conduct direct trades with leverage at much higher levels than available in normal margin accounts, to aggregate and defer its gains, and to avoid billions of dollars in short-term capital gains taxes."[81]

---

81   Report: Abuse Of Structured Financial Products: Misusing Basket Options to Avoid Taxes and Leverage Limits (July 22, 2014) (805.6 KB) — http://www.hsgac.senate.gov/download/report-abuse-of-structured-financial-products-misusing-basket-options-to-avoid-taxes-and-leverage-limits

Consequent to the 2014 report by the Senate Permanent Subcommittee on Investigations, reportedly[82] hedge funds like RenTec that used the basket option strategy to avoid billions of dollars in tax faced new scrutiny from the government, in accordance with guidelines issued by the Internal Revenue Service (IRS).

According to the new IRS guideline, basket options — that allowed companies like RenTec to bypass taxes on short-term trades — were to be labeled listed transactions. What this meant was that anyone using the options strategy had to declare them on their tax returns. Failure to do so meant they ran the risk of penalty.

What is even more interesting is the fact that the new IRS guidance was made retroactive, applying to all transactions from January 1, 2011. A fact that brought within its ambit transactions by companies like RenTec, which according to a 2014 report by the Senate Permanent Subcommittee on Investigations,[83] was able to avoid more than $6 billion in taxes over a decade through the use of the basket option strategy.

In fact, commenting on the activities, two Democrats reportedly supported the IRS action. Carl Levin, a Michigan Democrat, and chairman of the 2014 Senate Permanent Subcommittee on Investigations supposedly said that the investigations showed that banks and hedge funds used "dubious structured financial products, costing the Treasury billions and bypassing safeguards that protect the economy from excessive bank lending for stock speculation." He added that the amount of money that hedge funds like Renaissance Technology were able to keep back by strategizing and not paying the required taxes, was a very significant amount, even by Washington standards. Likewise, Senator Ron Wyden of Oregon, the ranking Democrat on the Finance Committee, said he was all for the IRS action to crack down on these types of basket option products.[84]

---

82   'IRS Cracks Down on Hedge Fund Tax Strategy' — http://www.nytimes.com/2015/07/09/business/dealbook/irs-cracks-down-on-hedge-fund-tax-strategy.html?_r=0

83   'Senate Inquiry Faults Hedge Funds' Tax Strategy' — http://dealbook.nytimes.com/2014/07/21/senate-inquiry-faults-hedge-funds-tax-strategy/

84   Summarized from 'IRS Cracks Down on Hedge Fund Tax Strategy' — http://www.nytimes.com/2015/07/09/business/dealbook/irs-cracks-down-on-hedge-fund-tax-strategy.html?_r=0

In light of all this, it is baffling how the presumptive Democratic nominee for the U.S. presidential elections, Hillary Clinton, who promises to reign in Wall Street and who has also vowed to penalize (corporate) tax evaders, has no qualms in accepting campaign money from a company like RenTec and its founder and current chairman, James Simons.[85]

This is because, as noted earlier, according to the 2014 report of the U.S. Senate Permanent Subcommittee on Investigations, RenTec used the basket option structure with hundreds of millions of trades (virtually all of which lasted less than 12 months) and characterized the vast majority of the resulting $34 billion in trading profits as long-term capital gains and thereby avoided (paying) billions of dollars in taxes — which the Senate Permanent Subcommittee has estimated as amounting to over $6 billion, a huge number by any standards!

I wonder what the American people think of this juxtaposed against Hillary Clinton's promises with regard to reigning in Wall Street and penalizing tax evaders. Whether she can walk the talk on reigning in Wall Street and penalizing tax evaders, is something that only time can answer.

The Case of David Elliot Shaw (D. E. Shaw)

David Elliot Shaw (born 1951) is an American computer scientist and computational biochemist who founded D. E. Shaw & Co., a hedge fund company in 1988. The *Fortune* magazine called it "the most intriguing and mysterious force on Wall Street."[86] Employing algorithmic trading, it is reported that D. E. Shaw, "made $530 million in 2014 in comparison to James H. Simons of Renaissance

85   It must be emphasized that James Simons is the founder of RenTec and serves as the company's current chairman. Therefore, whether he donates from RenTec or another company that he runs — Euclidean Capital, which is a family office — is immaterial. In addition, it must be clearly noted that James Simons was CEO of RenTec for much of the period when RenTec used the basket option strategy with Deutsch Bank and Barclays Bank!

86   http://ftalphaville.ft.com/2007/01/31/2195/the-25-most-intriguing-hedge-funds/

Technologies who is said to have made $1.2 billion. Incidentally, both contributors to the Hillary Clinton campaign, D. E. Shaw and James H. Simons were said to be among the top 25 earners in the hedge fund industry."[87] As noted above, D. E. Shaw, like James Simons, is a major contributor to the Clinton campaign. Not only has he contributed the maximum $2,700 as his individual contribution, D. E. Shaw has also contributed significantly to pro-Clinton PACs as summarized below:

Table 2.3: D. E. Shaw's Contributions to PACs Supporting Hillary Clinton				
Contributor Name	Employer	Occupation	City	Amount (in $)
Priorities USA Action				
Shaw, David E.	D. E. Shaw Research	Founder And Chief Scientist	New York	750,000
Shaw, David E.	D. E. Shaw Research	Bio-Medical Research	New York	750,000
Hillary Victory Fund				
E. Shaw, David	D. E. Shaw Research	Bio-Medical Research	New York	33,400
E. Shaw, David	D. E. Shaw Research	Bio-Medical Research	New York	33,400
Ready PAC				

---

87   https://en.wikipedia.org/wiki/David_E._Shaw

Table 2.3: D. E. Shaw's Contributions to PACs Supporting Hillary Clinton				
Contributor Name	Employer	Occupation	City	Amount (in $)
E. Shaw, David	D. E. Shaw Research	Bio-Medical Research	New York	25,000
E. Shaw, David	D. E. Shaw Research	Bio-Medical Research	New York	25,000
Source: Data from Federal Election Commission, http://www.fec.gov/				

Additionally, Beth (David E. Shaw's spouse[88]) and David Shaw have also donated in the range of $500,001 to $1,000,000 to the Clinton Foundation.[89]

Many of the employees in Shaw's firms/companies have also donated to the Hillary Clinton campaign as noted below:

Table 2.4: Individual Contribution of Staff From The D. E. Shaw Group/Company to The Hillary Clinton Campaign				
Contributor Name	Employer	Occupation	City	Amount (in $)
Beck, Andrew E.	D. E. Shaw & Co.	Managing Director	New York	2,700
Bradbury, Darcy	The D. E. Shaw Group	Finance	New York	2,700

---

88   https://en.wikipedia.org/wiki/David_E._Shaw

89   This is given in the Clinton Foundation donor website — https://www. clintonfoundation.org/contributors. The website does not provide the exact amount donated. Rather, it specifies only a range given by the contributor.

Table 2.4: Individual Contribution of Staff From The D. E. Shaw Group/Company to The Hillary Clinton Campaign				
Contributor Name	**Employer**	**Occupation**	**City**	**Amount (in $)**
Crnkovic, Cedomir	D. E. Shaw & Co.	Finance	New York	2,700
Gnepp, Andrei	D. E. Shaw & Co.	Programmer	New York	2,700
Gnepp, Andrei	D. E. Shaw & Co.	Programmer	New York	2,700
Reff, Jeremy	D. E. Shaw & Co.	Financial Analyst	Brooklyn	2,700
Shaw, David	D. E. Shaw Research	Bio-medical Research	New York	2,700
Tang, Donald	D. E. Shaw & Co. (Asia Pacific)	CEO	Arcadia	2,700
Stern, Janna	The D. E. Shaw Group	Attorney	New York	1,000
Source: Data from Federal Election Commission, http://www.fec.gov/				

While all this data is indeed enlightening, what is even more so is the Securities and Exchange Commission order, under the Securities Exchange Act of 1934 (Release No. 70396 / September 16, 2013) and Administrative Proceeding (File No. 3-15476)[90] which instituted "cease-and-desist proceedings... pursuant to Section 21C of the Securities Exchange Act of 1934 ('Exchange Act'), against D. E. Shaw & Co., L.P. ('D. E. Shaw' or 'Respondent')." The SEC order[91] notes,

90   https://www.sec.gov/litigation/admin/2013/34-70396.pdf
91   https://www.sec.gov/litigation/admin/2013/34-70396.pdf

"**1.** These proceedings arise out of violations of Rule 105 of Regulation M of the Exchange Act by D. E. Shaw, a New York-based registered investment adviser. Rule 105 prohibits buying an equity security made available through a public offering, conducted on a firm commitment basis, from an underwriter or broker or dealer participating in the offering after having sold short the same security during the restricted period as defined therein.

2. On five occasions, from May 2010 through March 2012, D. E. Shaw bought offered shares from an underwriter or broker or dealer participating in a follow-on public offering after having sold short the same security during the restricted period. The violations resulted in profits of $447,794."

The SEC[92] further notes,

"Accordingly, it is hereby ORDERED that:

A. Pursuant to Section 21C of the Exchange Act, Respondent D. E. Shaw cease and desist from committing or causing any violations and any future violations of Rule 105 of Regulation M of the Exchange Act;

B. D. E. Shaw shall within fourteen (14) days of the entry of this Order, pay disgorgement of $447,794 prejudgment interest of $18,192.37, and a civil money penalty in the amount of $201,506.00 (for a total of $667,492.37) to the United States Treasury. If timely payment is not made, additional interest shall accrue pursuant to SEC Rule of Practice 600."

This is not the only issue with D. E. Shaw and company.

Along with several other funds, D. E. Shaw has participated in the management of the $7 billion Employee Retirement System of the State

---

92   Ibid.

of Rhode Island, which is embroiled in a huge controversy as noted below.

In an article titled "Rhode Island Public Pension 'Reform' Looks More Like Wall Street Feeding Frenzy," Edward Siedle succinctly notes[93] that Rhode Island Treasurer, Gina Raimondo's changes to the investment portfolio of the $7 billion Employee Retirement System of the State of Rhode Island will undoubtedly cause a huge increase not just in fees paid to the (eclectic) Wall Street-based investment managers (read hedge funds and private equity companies), but will also result in a significant enhancement of the risk of the pension fund portfolio. This in effect seems to indicate that while the alternative investment strategy pursued by Gina Raimondo would increase the risk several fold, the returns will also be lower because the fees would be much higher — clearly, if this is true, then, something is amiss here.

It must be noted that Gina Raimondo is now Governor of Rhode Island. A close associate of Hillary Rodham Clinton,[94] she has even been mentioned as a possible running mate for Hillary Clinton.[95]

Siedle further argues that the key problem in the Rhode Island Public Pension Reform controversy is the payment of "undisclosed and/or illegal placement agent fees" related to alternative investments by the new fund managers. This, he emphasizes, should be investigated by the SEC. While claiming he is all for public pension reform that calls for proper, safe, and prudent investing coupled with sustainable returns, he says he just cannot sit quiet while Wall Street takes control of a huge state pension fund and recklessly dumps such hard earned money into very high cost, alternative, and risky investments, all of which, he says, will simply erode the workers'

---

93   'Rhode Island Public Pension 'Reform' Looks More Like Wall Street Feeding Frenzy' — http://www.forbes.com/sites/edwardsiedle/2013/04/04/rhode-island-public-pension-reform-looks-more-like-wall-street-feeding-frenzy/#e5aea312db00

94   'Hillary Clinton stumps for R.I. governor candidate Raimondo, "one of best choices in the country"' — http://www.ginaraimondo.com/news-clips/hillary-clinton-stumps-ri-governor-candidate-raimondo-%E2%80%98one-best-choices-country

95   'Governor Raimondo Mentioned As Possible Hillary Clinton VP' — http://www.thenewportbuzz.com/governor-raimondo-mentioned-as-possible-hillary-clinton-vp/7893

benefit. He signs off by calling this pension reform, initiated by Gina Raimondo, as nothing but a money grab[96]. In fact, Siedle claims he has asked for an FBI, SEC, and DoJ investigation.[97]

The data on fees[98] released by Raimondo has been cast into a table for easy reading below:

Table 2.5: Management and Performance Fees in Rhode Island Public Pension Fund		
Type of Fees	**General Norms for Fees (Industry Data)**	**Fees in Rhode Island Public Pension Fund after Alternative Investment Using Hedge Funds**
Management Fees	1.5 to 2% of money invested. Industry norm is 2%	• 10 funds charge 1.5%, 8 charge 2% and D.E. Shaw charges 2.5% which is the highest
Performance Fees	Generally, 20% of any gains	• 16 funds charge 20% of any gains and this is deducted once a year • 2 funds take 17.5% • D.E. Shaw and Brevan Howard take 25% each, which is among the highest

---

96   'Rhode Island Public Pension "Reform" Looks More Like Wall Street Feeding Frenzy' — http://www.forbes.com/sites/edwardsiedle/2013/04/04/rhode-island-public-pension-reform-looks-more-like-wall-street-feeding-frenzy/#e5aea312db00 or http://ricouncil94.org/Portals/0/Uploads/Documents/Public/2013ForbesSiedleMediaCoverage2.pdf

97   'Will Rhode Island Pension Looters Be Prosecuted?' — http://www.forbes.com/sites/edwardsiedle/2015/12/16/will-sec-fbi-and-doj-prosecute-any-hedge-fund-and-private-equity-looting-of-rhode-island-pension/#29e451e9596f

98   'R.I. treasurer Raimondo releases data about pension hedge funds' — http://www.providencejournal.com/article/20130523/BUSINESS/305239879

Table 2.5: Management and Performance Fees in Rhode Island Public Pension Fund		
Type of Fees	**General Norms for Fees (Industry Data)**	**Fees in Rhode Island Public Pension Fund after Alternative Investment Using Hedge Funds**
Sample of Combined Fees for a year[99] with over $ 1 million	-	• OZ Domestic partners — $1.9 million • D. E Shaw — $1.8 million • Viking Global — $1.5 million • Elliot — $1.3 million • Davidson Kempner[100] — $1.1 million • Brevan Howard $1 million

Two observations gleaned from the above data must be shared:

(1) three of the above funds have contributed to the Hillary Clinton campaign[101] and D. E. Shaw is the major contributor; and

---

99   "Rhode Island paid 6 of its 20 hedge-fund managers more than $1 million each in fees last year, and a total of $15.9 million on its $1 billion hedge-fund portfolio. Those numbers reflect only about six months of the 2012 fiscal year — which ended June 30, 2012 — because the State Investment Commission didn't start moving money into hedge funds until November 2011, building them up to 15 percent of the state's $7.7 billion pension fund." — http://www.providencejournal.com/article/20130523/BUSINESS/305239879

100   Davidson Kempner Capital Management is a global institutional investment management firm reported to have $25.4 billion in assets under management (as of March 2015). The firm was founded in 1983 by Marvin H. Davidson and is led by Thomas L. Kempner, Jr., who has contributed to the Hillary Clinton campaign (see Appendix for details). Thus, this is yet another large hedge fund where the senior management has contributed to Hillary Clinton campaign. What is interesting is that Thomas Kempner has not contributed to any other candidate and Hillary Clinton seems to be the preferred choice of Wall Street firms and hedge funds undoubtedly.

101   The three funds that participate in the management of the $7 billion Employee Retirement System of the State of Rhode Island and have contributed to the Hillary Clinton campaign, are OZ Domestic Partners via its parent company (Och-Ziff), Davidson Kempner and D. E. Shaw. There are several issues with

(2)　the management and performance fees charged by D. E. Shaw are among the highest.

In fact, the level of fees paid has reportedly prompted the Rhode Island Retired Teachers Association (RIRTA) to retain Edward Siedle to "bring potential civil and criminal malfeasance"[102] suits in relation to the Employees' Retirement System of Rhode Island (ERSRI). Siedle claims that he has investigated this so as to provide base information for the benefit of the FBI, SEC, and DOJ so that they can further investigate and prosecute, if required.[103] He also notes that he has "sent a letter to key officials at these agencies on RIRTA's behalf."[104] Siedle further emphasizes that the potential legal violations elaborated on in his letter would also impact other stakeholders in ERSRI, such as taxpayers and general participants.

In fact, it has been reported that the impact of Gina Raimondo's pension wealth transfer scheme that "cut workers' 3 percent COLAs to pay 4 percent to Wall Street hedge fund and private equity managers"[105] supposedly amounted to a reduction of "$1 million a day or $1.4 billion."[106] Again, a claim worthy of investigation by the SEC, FBI, and DoJ!

Therefore, given the above context of the Rhode Island Public Pension Reform controversy, which is, indeed serious if found to be true, and also given the SEC violation committed by D. E. Shaw and Company, I wonder, how comfortable Hillary Clinton is with taking

---

regard to the Och-Ziff as well including very serious allegations against it under the Foreign Corrupt Practices Act (FCPA). It must also be noted that Och-Ziff Capital Management Group has also donated $10,001 to $25,000 to the Clinton Foundation.

102　'Will Rhode Island Pension Looters Be Prosecuted?' — http://www.forbes.com/sites/edwardsiedle/2015/12/16/will-sec-fbi-and-doj-prosecute-any-hedge-fund-and-private-equity-looting-of-rhode-island-pension/#53e85695596f

103　Ibid.

104　Ibid.

105　'Rhode Island Retired Teachers Association Turns Up the Heat on Pension Looting' — http://www.forbes.com/sites/edwardsiedle/2015/11/20/rhode-island-retired-teachers-association-turning-up-the-heat-on-pension-looting/#5192917f7170

106　Ibid.

(huge) campaign contributions from the founder of The D. E. Shaw Group/D. E. Shaw and Company[107] directly and through PACs that support her. Would this not contribute to the American public viewing her campaign finance strategy with suspicion? Without a doubt, a potential conflict of interest has been created here.

Come next year, as President of The United States, Hillary Clinton may have to take (strong) action to protect the peoples' (pension) money in the $7 billion Employee Retirement System of the State of Rhode Island. How can she do this when the fund is managed by D. E. Shaw (and others) from whom she has received huge campaign contributions? More importantly, how can she do what needs to be done given that her close associate (and possible Vice President pick) Gov. Raimondo may be one of those Hillary will have to take action against after all? There are indeed serious questions that require a clear and transparent answer from Hillary Clinton.

The Case of George Soros

One of the highest contributors to the 2016 Hillary Clinton campaign is the Hungarian-American businessman George Soros. An investor, philanthropist and author of Jewish-Hungarian ancestry, Soros is said to hold dual citizenship (Hungary and the United States). He is the Chairman of Soros Fund Management and figures in the list of the world's top thirty rich men. A supporter of American progressive and American liberal political causes, Soros is reported to have donated more than $11 billion to various philanthropic causes between 1979 and 2015[108].

Given below are the details of contributions made by George Soros to pro-Hillary Clinton PACs in the 2016 presidential election cycle:

107   With regard to D. E. Shaw and Company, it has also been reported, as follows — "The $24bn fund recently made headlines when it hired Lawrence Summers, former Treasury Secretary with the Clinton administration" — Stacy-Marie Ishmael (January 31, 2007), 'The 25 Most Intriguing Hedge Funds', http://ftalphaville.ft.com/2007/01/31/2195/the-25-most-intriguing-hedge-funds/

108   https://en.wikipedia.org/wiki/George_Soros

Table 2.6: Contributions of George Soros to pro-Clinton PACs						
Contributor Name	Employer	Occupation	City	State	Zip	Amount (in $)
Hillary Victory Fund						
Soros, George	Soros Fund Management	Business Executive	New York	NY	10106	343,400
Priorities USA Action						
Soros, George	Soros Fund Management	Chairman	New York	NY	10106	6,000,000
Soros, George	Soros Fund Management	Chairman	New York	NY	10106	1,000,000
Ready PAC						
Soros, George	Soros Fund Management	Chairman	New York	NY	10106	25,000
Source: Data from Federal Election Commission, http://www.fec.gov/						

He has also contributed the maximum of $2,700 to Hillary Clinton's campaign directly (as an individual) and the Soros Foundation has donated in the range of $500,001 to $1,000,000 to the Clinton Foundation.[109]

While there seems to be a running competition between mathematician James Simons, (Euclidean Capital and RenTech Chair) and George Soros for the honor[110] of being the highest contributor to the Hillary Clinton campaign, it appears that they have yet another pertinent fact in common - allegations of tax avoidance. RenTec, founded by James Simons who is still the Chairman, was named in a

---

109   This is given in the Clinton Foundation donor website — https://www. clintonfoundation.org/contributors. The website does not provide the exact amount donated. Rather, it specifies only a range given by the contributor.

110   As of May 28, 2016, both Soros and James Simons have been reportedly surpassed by Haim Saban, the media mogul, whose family and institutions have provided more than $10 million to the Hillary Clinton campaign directly and through pro-Clinton PACs. See, 'The Top Donors Backing Hillary Clinton's Super PAC' — http://www.forbes.com/sites/ivonaiacob/2016/05/27/top-donors-hillary-clinton-superpac/#3eda84a82740

Congressional report for supposedly having evaded tax to the tune of a cool six billion dollars.

Likewise, *Fox News* reported that George Soros could face a $7 billion tax bill, after delaying payment for years.[111] The article also strongly points out that, despite Soros having argued for higher taxes for the super-rich, he himself, a very wealthy billionaire, has used a loophole in the U.S. law and thereby, delayed paying his own taxes on client fees. The article further notes that as this loophole was closed by the Congress in 2008, Soros may have to deal with a tax bill close to a whopping $7 billion.

Additionally, George Soros, was convicted[112] of insider trading on the French stock market. "His insider-trading conviction was upheld by the highest court in France on June 14, 2006.[113] In December 2006, he appealed to the European Court of Human Rights on various grounds including that the 14-year delay in bringing the case to trial precluded a fair hearing.[114] On the basis of Article 7 of the European Convention on Human Rights, stating that no person may be punished for an act that was not a criminal offense at the time that it was committed, the court agreed to hear the appeal.[115] In October 2011, the court rejected

---

111 'George Soros reportedly could face up to $7B tax bill, after delaying payment for years' — http://www.foxnews.com/politics/2015/05/01/george-soros-reportedly-could-face-up-to-7b-tax-bill-after-delaying-payment-for.html. I was however unable to get any further information on this matter!

112 A Paris-based prosecutor reopened the case against Soros and two other French businessmen, disregarding the COB's (the French stock exchange regulatory authority) findings. This resulted in Soros's 2005 conviction for insider trading by the Court of Appeals (he was the only one of the three to receive a conviction). The French Supreme Court confirmed the conviction on June 14, 2006, but reduced the penalty to €940,000.

113 Cited from Soros, Wikipedia, Original Footnote 60: 'Insider trading conviction of Soros is upheld'. *International Herald Tribune.* June 14, 2006.

114 Cited from Soros, Wikipedia, Original Footnote 62: Lichfield, John (December 22, 2002). 'Financier Soros fined £1.4m for insider trading'. *The Independent* (London). Retrieved October 12, 2011.

115 Cited from Soros, Wikipedia, Original Footnote 63: Saltmarsh, Matthew (September 15, 2010). 'Soros to Get a Day in Court Over Insider Trading Case'. *The New York Times.* Retrieved September 18, 2011.

his appeal in a 4–3 decision, saying that Soros had been aware of the risk of breaking insider trading laws."[116, 117]

Likewise, it has also been reported that on September 16, 1992, called Black Wednesday, the short selling of more than $10 billion pounds was done by the Soros Fund,[118] which essentially profited from the British government's inability and/or reluctance to either raise its interest rates[119] or to float its currency. Reportedly, the UK finally withdrew from the European Exchange Rate Mechanism, devaluing the pound. It was estimated that Soros's profit on the bet was a whopping $1 billion — really huge money at that time.[120] This led to his being called "the man who broke the Bank of England."[121] It has been reported that the (estimated) cost of Black Wednesday to the UK Treasury was approximately £3.4 billion.[122]

The icing on the cake is what Nobel Prize winning economist, Paul Krugman said about the "Soros's effect" on financial markets:

"[N]obody who has read a business magazine in the last few years can be unaware that these days there really are investors who not only move money in anticipation of a currency crisis, but actually do their best to trigger that crisis for fun and profit. These new actors on the scene do not yet have a standard name; my proposed term is 'Soroi'."[123]

---

116   Cited from Soros, Wikipedia, Original Footnote 64: Smith, Heather (October 6, 2011). 'Soros Loses Case Against French Insider-Trading Conviction'. *Bloomberg L.P.* Retrieved October 9, 2011.

117   Wikipedia — https://en.wikipedia.org/wiki/George_Soros

118   Wikipedia — https://en.wikipedia.org/wiki/George_Soros, "George Soros". Retrieved November 25, 2011.

119   When I talk of raising interest rates, I am making a specific reference to levels comparable to those of other European Exchange Rate Mechanism countries.

120   Wikipedia — https://en.wikipedia.org/wiki/George_Soros, Mallaby, Sebastian, *More Money Than God*, Penguin, 2010, p. 167.

121   Litterick, David (September 13, 2002), 'Billionaire who Broke the Bank of England', *The Telegraph.*

122   Johnston, Philip (September 10, 2012). 'Black Wednesday: The Day that Britain went over the Edge'. *The Telegraph.* Retrieved April 13, 2015.

123   Cited from Soros, Wikipedia — https://en.wikipedia.org/wiki/George_Soros, Krugman, Paul (1999). *The Accidental Theorist: And Other Dispatches from the Dismal Science.* New York: W.W. Norton & Company. p. 160.

In an effort to understand the seriousness of the allegations against Soros and his subsequent conviction, it would be interesting to recall the case of Rajat Gupta, convicted of insider trading in the U.S. stock markets. Gupta was a powerful man, with far-reaching influence. He served as McKinsey and Company's managing director (worldwide) until his retirement in 2007 and has been on the board of many of today's influential corporations and banks, including most prominently, Goldman Sachs.

Gupta was charged with leaking information from his position on the board of Goldman Sachs, to hedge fund investor Raj Rajaratnam (currently serving an 11-year prison sentence) about internal transactions at Goldman, including Warren Buffet's $5 billion bailout at the height of the crisis. This prompted Rajaratnam, to hedge himself against the coming fluctuations in the stock price. Gupta wasn't believed to have had any realistic financial gain and his attorneys say the two friends were discussing the deal in their position as investors themselves. Nevertheless, the timing of it and the fact that the information was revealed before the public announcement, told a more sinister story.

The case was deemed the big scalp for the US Federal Reserve in its crusade against insider trading. It was touted as the tale of how public service could not be used as an excuse for white-collar crimes, of boardroom influences not reaching far enough (to ultimately save oneself). Some might call the case an example of persecution, others might call it profiling by race, but it is above all an example of the sentiment worldwide about Wall Street — the protests, the disillusions, the many accusations of corruption and desire for quick fast money driven by simple greed. It is the tale of a prosperous environment gone terribly wrong and a stark wake-up call to correct it if indeed we are to make an attempt to revive the faltering world economy at all.

Given this context, it is apparent that insider trading is a huge breach of trust after all, irrespective of conviction or sentencing. Moreover, the same set of standards must be used to judge persons held guilty of the crime, whether in the United States of America or outside of it. If Rajat Gupta, convicted of insider trading and sentenced to two years' imprisonment and a fine of five million dollars for being compliant to insider trading, should rightly be regarded as an untouchable in terms of political association, the same standards have to be applied to George Soros.

The argument against association with Soros is further strengthened by latest reports that have emerged indicating that three offshore investment vehicles controlled by him "are catalogued in the Panama Papers."[124] One is Soros Finance, Inc. incorporated in Panama; another is Soros Holdings Limited that was set up in the British Virgin Islands and the third is a limited partnership called Soros Capital that was created in Bermuda[125]. The details of two of these entities are given in the table below:

Table 2.7: Entities of Soros Named in The Panama Papers		
Name	Soros Finance Inc.	Soros Holdings Limited
Category	Entity	Entity
Incorporation Date	December 27, 1979	December 10, 1996

---

124 'Panama Papers reveal George Soros' deep money ties to secretive weapons, intel investment firm' — http://www.foxnews.com/world/2016/05/16/panama-papers-reveal-george-soros-deep-money-ties-to-secretive-weapons-intel-firm.html

125 'Soros Capital as a major investor and corporate officer of AIF (Indonesia) Limited. AIF combines private investments with public funding contributed by Asian governments to develop massive infrastructure projects. The database links Soros Capital to Dongya Ports Limited, owned by a tangle of offshore entities.' — Panama Papers reveal George Soros' deep money ties to secretive weapons, intel investment firm — http://www.foxnews.com/world/2016/05/16/panama-papers-reveal-george-soros-deep-money-ties-to-secretive-weapons-intel-firm.html. As the *Fox News* article notes, an additional point to note here is that the laws of Panama, Bermuda, the British Virgin Islands and a score of "tax havens" allow foreign firms to shroud (their) ownership of cash, real estate and/or other assets from securities regulators, tax collectors in the countries that they are physically headquartered.

Table 2.7: Entities of Soros Named in The Panama Papers		
Name	**Soros Finance Inc.**	**Soros Holdings Limited**
Address	Mr. George de Geofroy 5, Avenue Miremont 1206 Geneva Switzerland	Management Trustees Group S.A. Rue du Consail General 14 1205 Geneve Switzerland
Country of Incorporation	Panama	British Virgin Islands
Linked Countries	Switzerland	Switzerland
Agent	Mossack Fonseca	Mossack Fonseca
Source: The Panama Papers Data Base, https://offshoreleaks.icij.org/		

To sum up, the achievements of Soros, a global newsmaker are as follows:

- In 1992, Soros is said to have nearly bankrupted the Bank of England through price manipulation of the pound.

- In 1997 or thereabouts, Soros reportedly betted against Thai and Malaysian currencies and thereby accelerated a regional economic crisis.

- In 2010, Soros invested in the Indian micro-finance institution SKS Microfinance Ltd (SKSML). It has been reported that SKSML had been involved in a spate of controversies including suicides of poor borrowers in Andhra Pradesh, coercive tactics to recover loans from such poor people and several corporate governance/other violations.

- Indeed, Soros has built a vast empire of off-shore funds with its humongous profits. He is the sole proprietor of Manhattan-based Soros Fund Management LLC, which controls this offshore empire.

- In July 2011, Soros reportedly moved to becoming a family office by closing the multibillion-dollar fund to all but immediate family members — this has enabled him to escape disclosure requirements stipulated by the Dodd-Frank Act mandate for hedge funds.

- In 2011, Soros also lost the final appeal of his 2002 (insider trading) conviction by a French court.

- In 2013, it was reported that Soros may end paying $7 billion in taxes that he may have deferred using a loophole in the U.S. law, which the Congress (reportedly) plugged in 2008.[126]

- In 2016, Soros has made it to the 'Panama Papers' expose charts, having been named in the ICIJ database.

Despite the series of controversies over his investments, Soros has continued to remain a strong political force. While Soros' companies may not be entirely paying their share of U.S. taxes,[127] he still donates huge amounts to Democrat lawmakers including those who contested against George Bush in 2004. The FEC data shows he contributed significantly to President Obama's campaign. It must be noted that, as of the date of publication of this book, as per FEC data on individual and pro-Clinton PAC contributions, he is among the largest donors to Hillary Clinton's 2016 Presidency run, having donated close to $7.5 million. If you search the Clinton Foundation website, it shows that he contributed up to $1 million to the Clinton Foundation.

Fox News reports that, "Secretary of State Clinton's emails reveal that Soros has lobbied her on behalf of his interests, which encircle the globe, mostly in the dark."[128]

---

126 'George Soros reportedly could face up to $7B tax bill, after delaying payment for years' — http://www.foxnews.com/politics/2015/05/01/george-soros-reportedly-could-face-up-to-7b-tax-bill-after-delaying-payment-for.html

127 'George Soros reportedly could face up to $7B tax bill, after delaying payment for years' — http://www.foxnews.com/politics/2015/05/01/george-soros-reportedly-could-face-up-to-7b-tax-bill-after-delaying-payment-for.html

128 'Panama Papers reveal George Soros' deep money ties to secretive weapons, intel

Given that the 2016 U.S. presidential campaign is being fought on the issues of "big money in politics" and a "corrupt campaign finance system," continued association with and acceptance of money from a Wall Street player convicted for insider trading in France and also facing mounting allegations of financial deceit — irrespective of who the person is and how wealthy he may be — is tantamount to compromising the very values the current political battle is being fought on! This is something that Hillary needs to ponder over.

---

investment firm' — http://www.foxnews.com/world/2016/05/16/panama-papers-reveal-george-soros-deep-money-ties-to-secretive-weapons-intel-firm.html

Chapter 3

The Wall Street Speeches

The Clintons have had a fairy packed schedule of speaking assignments across the globe in the last decade or so, especially during times when either or both of them have not held any political office. A brief analysis of the 39 speeches given by Bill Clinton and Hillary Clinton[1] over the years to six big banks and numerous large Wall Street firms is given below.

Of the 39 speeches given to big banks and Wall Street firms, 8 speeches were delivered by Hillary (2013–2014) and 31 by Bill (2001–2015). While Hillary received $1,835,000 for her 8 speeches, Bill was paid $5,910,000 for his 31 speeches. Together, Bill and Hillary made about a total of $7.75 million from the 39 speeches that were delivered to the 6 big banks and large Wall Street firms. Further, Hillary Clinton made a total of $21.14 million from 91 speeches[2] (given to 84 organisations)

---

1   The website, http://www.releasethetranscripts.com/ provides a complete listing of all 91 speeches given by Hillary Clinton to 84 organizations after she left the position of Secretary of State in 2013. A full listing of the 39 speeches that Hillary and Bill Clinton delivered to 6 large banks and Wall Street firms can be found in the article — '$153 million in Bill and Hillary Clinton speaking fees, documented' — http://edition.cnn.com/2016/02/05/politics/hillary-clinton-bill-clinton-paid-speeches/ and http://citizenuprising.com/hillary-clintons-speaking-fees-2013-2015/

2   This figure includes her 8 Wall Street speeches given above for which she received $1.835 million — See '$153 million in Bill and Hillary Clinton speaking fees, documented' — http://edition.cnn.com/2016/02/05/politics/hillary-clinton-bill-clinton-paid-speeches/ and http://citizenuprising.com/hillary-clintons-speaking-fees-2013-2015/

that she delivered post her laying down office as Secretary of State in 2013.

In terms of individual institutions, Goldman Sachs (12 speeches) and UBS (10 speeches) had the maximum number. Interestingly, 5 out of the 6 institutions listed — Citigroup, Goldman Sachs, Morgan Stanley, Bank of America/Merrill Lynch and Deutsch Bank[3] — were involved and in some ways responsible for the 2008 financial crisis. Most of these institutions were also recipients of the Unites States taxpayer bailout.

Another interesting fact is that all of these institutions were lobbying with various government departments in the United States and several of them had issues and cases pending with the SEC, IRS and other departments at various points in time. It must also be mentioned that all the speeches made by Bill and Hillary Clinton to UBS, an organization that ran into severe problems with the IRS, for example happened at a time when either the IRS problem persisted or after it had been resolved. As per the official lobbying database, these 6 institutions had directly lobbied the government 2,411 times during a 16-year period[4] (1999–2015), spending over $400 million.[5] This does not include what

---

3   All the five institutions have donated significant amounts to the Clinton Foundation. The Foundation has only indicated the range of the donations made on their website and not the exact amounts. They are as follows: Citigroup Inc. — $500,001 to $1,000,000, Goldman Sachs Group, Inc. — $1,000,001 to $5,000,000, Goldman Sachs Philanthropy Fund — $250,001 to $500,000, Bank of America — $100,001 to $250,000, Bank of America Foundation — $500,001 to $1,000,000, Merrill Lynch & Company Foundation, Inc. — $100,001 to $250,000, UBS AG — $50,000 to $100,000, UBS Wealth Management USA — $500,001 to $1,000,000, Morgan Stanley — $100,001 to $250,000, Morgan Stanley Global Impact Funding Trust — $250,001 to $500,000, Morgan Stanley Bank AG — $10,001 to $25,000, Deutsche Bank AG — $250,001 to $500,000, Deutsche Bank Americas — $250,001 to $500,000. Please see https://www.clintonfoundation.org/contributors

4   Data is not uniformly available across the years and therefore, taking the number of years as 16 is indeed an overestimate. In reality, the number of years for which data is available would be closer to 10 years! This data comes from just one database — http://soprweb.senate.gov/index.cfm?event=selectfields

5   It must be noted that many of the entries in the lobbying database had blank entries for expenses!

their trade associations lobbied nor does it include the money each of their employees had contributed to PACs and campaign financing, nor the money that they had paid for celebrity speeches and the like. This is also the number that is officially reported to the lobbying database[6] and it is expected that the actual figures could have been even higher. Please note that[7] from 1999 to 2008, the financial sector is said to have expended $2.7 billion in reported federal lobbying expenses and individuals/political action committees in the financial sector made more than $1 billion in campaign contributions.

Similarly, the 84 organisations[8], to whom Hillary Clinton delivered 91 speeches (since she moved on from her position as Secretary of State in 2013), had directly lobbied the government on 11,628 occasions, spending about $1.95 billion[9], which is an incredible amount by any standards. Taken together, the above data clearly indicate that the influence of corporate America in lobbying the government should not be underestimated in any way. Their power to influence is huge indeed.

There have been several demands, by Bernie Sanders and others, asking Hillary Clinton, to immediately release the transcripts of these Wall Street speeches, most notably the ones made to Goldman Sachs. While there have been arguments for and against this practice (of releasing speech transcripts), it is about time that we looked objectively at this issue from a larger standpoint. To do so, we need to understand the context of the 2008 financial crisis better and this chapter is devoted to that even as it tries to answer the question of whether or not Hillary

---

6   http://soprweb.senate.gov/index.cfm?event=selectfields

7   Final Report Of The National Commission On The Causes Of The Financial And Economic Crisis In The United States, Submitted by The Financial Crisis Inquiry Commission, Pursuant to Public Law 111-21, January 2011 — http://fcic-static. law.stanford.edu/cdn_media/fcic-reports/fcic_final_report_full. pdf

8   This includes the 8 speeches by Hillary Clinton to the 6 big banks and large Wall Street firms.

9   The time period is 1999–2015. However, data is not uniformly available across the years and therefore, taking the number of years as 16 is indeed an overestimate. In reality, the number of years for which data is available would be closer to 10 years! This data comes from just one database — http://soprweb.senate.gov/index. cfm?event=selectfields

Clinton is duty-bound to release the transcripts of her speeches.

If there is one thing that stands out about the 2008 financial crisis, it is the fact that weak, lax and laissez-faire regulation — caused by lobbying, PACs, campaign financing, and the power of Wall Street to influence policy makers, regulators and others — served as an important factor that triggered off the meltdown. There are no two opinions on this and this is what the Financial Crisis Inquiry Commission (FCIC) Final Report[10] dated January 2011 has said over and over again.

Just to understand the context,

> "The Financial Crisis Inquiry Commission was created to 'examine the causes of the current financial and economic crisis in the United States.' In this report, the Commission presents to the President, the Congress, and the American people the results of its examination and its conclusions as to the causes of the crisis. ...
>
> The Commission was established as part of the Fraud Enforcement and Recovery Act (Public Law 111-21) passed by Congress and signed by the President in May 2009. This independent, 10-member panel was composed of private citizens with experience in areas such as housing, economics, finance, market regulation, banking, and consumer protection. Six members of the Commission were appointed by the Democratic leadership of Congress and four members by the Republican leadership."

What exactly did the FCIC say in its final report and what is the connection with the requests by Bernie Sanders and others urging Hillary Clinton to immediately release the transcripts of her Goldman Sachs speech?

Transparency and accountability in public life and electoral

---

10   Final Report Of The National Commission On The Causes Of The Financial And Economic Crisis In The United States, Submitted by The Financial Crisis Inquiry Commission, Pursuant to Public Law 111-21, January 2011 — http://fcic-static. law.stanford.edu/cdn_media/fcic-reports/fcic_final_report_full. pdf

politics are at the root of a healthy democracy and they call for sharing of information (with the electorate) in a clear manner by all potential law makers[11] now and in the future. That is precisely why Hillary Clinton needs to release her Wall Street speeches immediately. Without a doubt, she owes this disclosure to the American people.[12] What she told Wall Street during her speeches has huge ramifications for the future of financial regulation in America (including that of Wall Street firms), which, in turn, will have a significant bearing on what happens in the global economy — in reality, I don't think that any of us want another financial crisis[13] caused by Wall Street ... period!

In addition, it goes without saying that much water has flown under the Wall Street bridge over the years and the regulation and orderly growth of Wall Street firms (including investment banks, commercial banks, financial conglomerates etc.) indeed has a very important stake in the American Presidency with gigantic implications for the global economy. And financial regulation — especially regulation of Wall Street — has therefore become as important a topic as campaign financing, foreign policy, trade and jobs, homeland security and terrorism (and the like) in the American Presidential election. Therefore, if any of the candidates have delivered speeches at Wall Street, be it Hillary Clinton, Bernie Sanders, or Donald Trump, they better provide full and complete disclosure on these paid/unpaid speeches that they have made to Wall Street firms as well as other corporations. This is an imperative from the point of view of "good" electoral and political governance that calls for minimum standards in transparency and accountability.

Please see what the Financial Crisis Inquiry Commission (FCIC)

---

11   A candidate who could get elected as The President of the Unites States is a potential lawmaker.

12   Her refusal to release the speeches would only make the American people more curious and perhaps, even a tad suspicious!

13   This is because lax and laissez-faire regulation and supervision (due to conflicts of interests) resulted in the financial crisis in 2008, which had global ramifications as well!

Final Report[14] (January 2011) says about the 2008 financial crisis and its causes (including the role of Wall Street firms). Then decide on whether or not, Hillary Clinton, who is the presumptive Democratic presidential nominee, is correct in refusing to release the text of speeches made by her at Wall Street firms (like Goldman Sachs etc.). You can see multiple references to Goldman Sachs and other Wall Street firms in the FCIC report as it dwells on the causes that led to the financial crisis of 2008.

If one looks closely at many of the past financial crisis situations (like the 2008 global financial crisis fuelled by the U.S. sub-prime), it is clear that they can be linked to lax and laissez-faire regulatory and supervisory frameworks. These frameworks were either developed by industry insiders with commercial interests or created with significant input from such insiders — both with a view to benefit the overall financial industry concerned.

In other words, these regulatory and supervisory frameworks had serious "conflict of interest situations" that led to such lax and laissez-faire regulatory and supervisory frameworks being developed in the first place. In effect, they were regulating their own industry! There can be no doubt that this was conflict of interest at its worst.

Despite all that has happened, even today, there is a puzzling lack of attention given to the role played by conflicts of interest in the corruption saga and especially with regard to the larger financial sector. Look at the United Nations Convention Against Corruption (UNCAC). Even the UNCAC only makes a fleeting mention of the role played by conflicts of interests, despite it being the very important keystone to unearthing corruption and supporting the structure to fight against corruption worldwide.

It is not just my opinion but many scholars, academics, economists, politicians, and business people worldwide also agree that the close regulation and monitoring of conflicts of interest are of great importance

---

14   Final Report Of The National Commission On The Causes Of The Financial And Economic Crisis In The United States, Submitted by The Financial Crisis Inquiry Commission, Pursuant to Public Law 111-21, January 2011 — http://fcic-static. law.stanford.edu/cdn_media/fcic-reports/fcic_final_report_full. pdf

to regulatory ethics. Moreover, this is something that all of us need to note with urgency because, if not eliminated, these conflict of interest situations could spell disaster for the larger financial sector as they will inevitably lead to corruption and ultimately, lead to financial crisis caused by laissez-faire regulation and supervision.

That said, let us now look at what is meant[15] by "conflict of interest." A "conflict of interest" is a conflict between the duty, roles, responsibilities, and private interests of any official that could improperly and unfairly influence the performance of his/her official roles and responsibilities.

By private interests, I mean the following: Private interests include financial, pecuniary and other interests[16] which generate a direct personal benefit to the public official as also personal affiliations, associations, and family ties, that could (practically be considered as likely to) improperly and unfairly influence the official's performance of his/her roles, duties and responsibilities.

Defined in this way, conflict of interest has the potential to undermine the proper functioning of institutions (public, private, not-for-profit), governments and the like by:

- Weakening adherence by officials to the ideals of impartiality, objectivity, fairness, and legitimacy, in decision making, and

- Distorting the rule of law, the development and application of policy, the functioning of organizations and markets, as well as the allocation of resources.

Indeed, what is the difference between conflict of interest and corruption?

---

15   These definitions have been compiled from several sources including OECD and other material found on the web, which are far too numerous to quote. These are gratefully and sincerely acknowledged.

16   The negotiation of future employment by an official (for himself/family/friends) prior to his leaving his present office is one example here and there is many more examples that I could provide. This is like negotiating a job with a vendor. For example, an official may say, "I will make rules governing X and Y situations very lenient provided you make my nephew the CEO in another project of yours."

Conflict of interest situations exist where officials, because of their position, have the *opportunity* to abuse the power and authority of their position for personal and private gain. On the other hand, corruption exists where officials *have abused* their position for personal and private gain. Put differently, conflicts of interest situations do not always lead to corruption. However, where there is corruption, you can be sure that conflicts of interest indeed exist.

Why do we need to attach so much importance to conflicts of interest with regard to regulation and supervision in the financial sector? Because if conflicts of interest are not entirely eliminated and/or at least properly monitored by independent bodies or reduced, the situation can easily lead to corruption in regulation and supervision and thereby threaten the entire financial system.

This is not new. This is what past crisis situations have taught us. In fact, if there is a single most recurring theme in financial crises and scandals globally, it is the failure to manage conflicts of interest. The following are some well-known examples.

Let us look at this with regard to the larger financial sector in the United States, which provides a very useful learning with regard to conflicts of interest and their relationship to crisis situations. They hold very important lessons for how the United States politicians, including Hillary Clinton, deal with Wall Street.

As described[17] by former SEC Chairman Arthur Levitt:

> "Bank involvement in the securities markets came under close scrutiny after the 1929 market crash. The Pecora hearings of 1933 …uncovered a wide range of abusive practices on the part of banks and bank affiliates. These included a variety of conflicts of interest; the underwriting of unsound securities in order to pay off bad bank loans; and 'pool operations' to support the price of bank stocks."

In fact, as Levitt has further argued,[18] and please note this carefully, it

---

17   http://www.sec.gov/news/testimony/testarchive/1995/spch029.txt
18   http://www.sec.gov/news/testimony/testarchive/1995/spch029.txt

is the significant revelations of "uncontrolled conflicts of interest" that provided the basis and rationale for the passing of many subsequent regulations — the Securities Act (1933), the Securities Exchange Act (1934), and the Glass-Steagall Banking Act (1933). In fact, it appears that conflicts of interest were also the major reason for the enactment of the Investment Company Act (1940) and the Investment Advisor Act (1940).

Closer to the 1990s, I see numerous examples of conflicts of interest that led directly to financial crisis:

- The insider trading scandals (such as, the Ivan Boesky and Dennis Levine scandals in the 1980s), the closure of Drexel Burnham Lambert (the investment bank) and the associated (criminal) conviction of its famous employee (Michael Milken) are still fresh in my memory.

- Later, there were more financial scandals in the early 2000s — for example, the internet bubble in 2000/2001 exposed problems with dubious high-flying research analysts (with very significant conflicts of interest), whose reports were in fact, influenced by their own institutions' investment banking interests. This, in fact, led to specific provisions in the Sarbanes-Oxley Act that dealt with this conflict of interest issue.

- Then, just over a decade ago, in 2003, the SEC found that the use of brokerage commissions to facilitate the sales of fund shares [was] widespread among funds that relied on broker-dealers to sell fund shares. This led to the adoption of new rules to prohibit funds from this practice.[19]

Then, even closer to home, we had the mother of all financial crises in recent times — the financial crisis of 2008 that started in America

---

19　Prohibition on the Use of Brokerage Commissions to Finance Distribution, Investment Company Act Release 26591 (Sept. 2, 2004), 69 Fed. Register 54728, 54728 (September 9, 2004) — http://www.sec.gov/rules/final/ic-26591.pdf

and spread worldwide — which was again based on significant conflicts of interest in many areas and I quote from the FCIC report hereafter which identifies several key aspects that caused the 2008 financial crisis including conflicts of interest.

1st Cause: The first key point from the FCIC report is given below:

(a) "The captains of finance and the public stewards of our financial system ignored warnings and failed to question, understand, and manage evolving risks within a system essential to the well-being of the American public. Theirs was a big miss, not a stumble. ...

The prime example is the Federal Reserve's pivotal failure to stem the flow of toxic mortgages, which it could have done by setting prudent mortgage-lending standards. The Federal Reserve was the one entity empowered to do so and it did not. The record of our examination is replete with evidence of other failures: financial institutions made, bought, and sold mortgage securities they never examined, did not care to examine, or knew to be defective; firms depended on tens of billions of dollars of borrowing that had to be renewed each and every night, secured by subprime mortgage securities; and major firms and investors blindly relied on credit rating agencies as their arbiters of risk. What else could one expect on a highway where there were neither speed limits nor neatly painted lines?" (FCIC Report[20])

The reader will note the emphasis on the "pivotal failure" of the regulator — the Federal Reserve. The reader will also note that the FCIC report mentions the fact that:

"financial institutions made, bought, and sold mortgage securities they never examined, did not care to examine, or knew to be defective; firms depended on tens of billions of dollars of borrowing that had

---

20   http://fcic-static.law.stanford.edu/cdn_media/fcic-reports/fcic_final_report_full. pdf

to be renewed each and every night, secured by subprime mortgage securities; and major firms and investors blindly relied on credit rating agencies as their arbiters of risk."(FCIC Report[21])

And surely, as the FCIC report argues in the next point (given below), policy- and law-makers and regulators, for reasons best known to them, did have a huge say in creating such a "highway where there were neither speed limits nor neatly painted lines"[22] and where reckless driving was the norm (rather than the exception).

Given the above, you will now understand why it is important that current as well as future law — and policy-makers and politicians, who participate in the American electoral process and especially compete for the office of the President of the Unites States, must come clean on their relationships with Wall Street firms. There should be no question about this.

2nd Cause: Let us move to the next key point identified by FCIC:

(b) **"We conclude widespread failures in financial regulation and supervision proved devastating to the stability of the nation's financial markets.** The sentries were not at their posts, in no small part due to the widely accepted faith in the self-correcting nature of the markets and the ability of financial institutions to effectively police themselves. More than 30 years of deregulation and reliance on self-regulation by financial institutions, championed by former Federal Reserve chairman Alan Greenspan and others, supported by successive administrations and Congresses, and actively pushed by the powerful financial industry at every turn, had stripped away key safeguards, which could have helped avoid catastrophe. This approach had opened up gaps in oversight of critical areas with trillions of dollars at risk, such as the shadow banking system and

---

21   http://fcic-static.law.stanford.edu/cdn_media/fcic-reports/fcic_final_report_full.pdf

22   http://fcic-static.law.stanford.edu/cdn_media/fcic-reports/fcic_final_report_full.pdf

over-the-counter derivatives markets. In addition, the government permitted financial firms to pick their preferred regulators in what became a race to the weakest supervisor. ...

Changes in the regulatory system occurred in many instances as financial markets evolved. Nevertheless, as the report will show, the financial industry itself played a key role in weakening regulatory constraints on institutions, markets, and products. It did not surprise the Commission that an industry of such wealth and power would exert pressure on policy makers and regulators. From 1999 to 2008, the financial sector expended $2.7 billion in reported federal lobbying expenses; individuals and political action committees in the sector made more than $1 billion in campaign contributions. What troubled us was the extent to which the nation was deprived of the necessary strength and independence of the oversight necessary to safeguard financial stability." (FCIC Report[23])

Please note the comment on failure of financial regulation and supervision in causing the crisis as well as the reference to lobbying expenses, campaign contributions and the power and wealth of Wall Street to "exert pressure on policy makers and regulators." For a moment I thought that it was Bernie Sanders who had written this report but I was mistaken. These words appear in the final report of the FCIC, the Statutory Commission that inquired into the financial crisis of 2008. Now, tell me whether, as an American, you feel comfortable when a potential law/policy maker talks of reigning in Wall Street but refuses to release the paid speeches that she made to a key Wall Street firm like Goldman Sachs, which has been repeatedly cited in the FCIC report!

3rd **Cause:** Alright, let us move on to the next point cited by FCIC and it is about self-regulation — an idea sold by large Wall Street Firms, Financial Conglomerates, Big Banks and Corporations to Law/Policy

---

23   http://fcic-static.law.stanford.edu/cdn_media/fcic-reports/fcic_final_report_full. pdf

Makers and Regulators, who readily bought this idea and faced the
consequences via the financial crisis of 2008:

(c) **"We conclude dramatic failures of corporate governance and
     risk management at many systemically important financial
     institutions were a key cause of this crisis.** There was a view that
     instincts for self-preservation inside major financial firms would
     shield them from fatal risk-taking without the need for a steady
     regulatory hand, which, the firms argued, would stifle innovation.
     Too many of these institutions acted recklessly, taking on too much
     risk, with too little capital, and with too much dependence on short-
     term funding. In many respects, this reflected a fundamental change
     in these institutions, particularly the large investment banks and
     bank holding companies, which focused their activities increasingly
     on risky trading activities that produced hefty profits. They took
     on enormous exposures in acquiring and supporting subprime
     lenders and creating, packaging, repackaging, and selling trillions of
     dollars in mortgage-related securities, including synthetic financial
     products. Like Icarus[24], they never feared flying ever closer to the
     sun.

     Many of these institutions grew aggressively through poorly
     executed acquisition and integration strategies that made effective
     management more challenging. The CEO of Citigroup told the
     Commission that a $40 billion position in highly rated mortgage
     securities would 'not in any way have excited my attention,' and
     the co-head of Citigroup's investment bank said he spent 'a small

---

24   In Greek mythology, Icarus is the son of the master craftsman Daedalus, the creator
      of the Labyrinth. Icarus and his father attempted to escape from Crete by means
      of wings that his father had constructed from feathers and wax. Icarus's father
      warns him first of complacency and then of hubris, asking that he fly neither too
      low nor too high, so the sea's dampness would not clog his wings or the sun's heat
      melt them. Icarus ignored his father's instructions not to fly too close to the sun,
      whereupon the wax in his wings melted and he fell into the sea. — Paraphrased
      from https://en.wikipedia.org/wiki/Icarus

fraction of 1%' of his time on those securities. In this instance, too big to fail meant too big to manage.

Financial institutions and credit rating agencies embraced mathematical models as reliable predictors of risks, replacing judgment in too many instances. Too often, risk management became risk justification.

Compensation systems — designed in an environment of cheap money, intense competition, and light regulation — too often rewarded the quick deal, the short-term gain — without proper consideration of long-term consequences. Often, those systems encouraged the big bet — where the payoff on the upside could be huge and the downside limited. This was the case up and down the line — from the corporate boardroom to the mortgage broker on the street.

Our examination revealed stunning instances of governance breakdowns and irresponsibility. You will read, among other things, about AIG senior management's ignorance of the terms and risks of the company's $79 billion derivatives exposure to mortgage-related securities; Fannie Mae's quest for bigger market share, profits, and bonuses, which led it to ramp up its exposure to risky loans and securities as the housing market was peaking; and the costly surprise when Merrill Lynch's top management realized that the company held $55 billion in 'super-senior' and supposedly 'super-safe' mortgage-related securities that resulted in billions of dollars in losses." (FCIC Report[25])

Yet the law/policy makers and regulators swore by self-regulation. Why were they so dogmatic and short-sighted? First of all, self-regulation is an oxy-moron and has never worked ... ever! It pushes people to fly like Icarus who did not fear flying closer to the sun

---

25   http://fcic-static.law.stanford.edu/cdn_media/fcic-reports/fcic_final_report_full.
      pdf

and simply perished. Now, this again, is a clear failure on the part of policy- and law-makers who were convinced by these large Wall Street firms, financial conglomerates, banks and corporations to bring in the paradigm of self-regulation as a key component of the regulatory and supervisory process. Again, as before, the cost of this decision was very high and it resulted in the financial crisis of 2008, the impact of which, we are still feeling today.

4th, 5th and 6th Causes: The FCIC report talks of three more critical aspects that led to the financial crisis of 2008 and each of these are highlighted below:

(d) **"We conclude a combination of excessive borrowing, risky investments, and lack of transparency put the financial system on a collision course with crisis.** Clearly, this vulnerability was related to failures of corporate governance and regulation, but it is significant enough by itself to warrant our attention here.

In the years leading up to the crisis, too many financial institutions, as well as too many households, borrowed to the hilt, leaving them vulnerable to financial distress or ruin if the value of their investments declined even modestly. For example, as of 2007, the five major investment banks — Bear Stearns, Goldman Sachs, Lehman Brothers, Merrill Lynch, and Morgan Stanley — were operating with extraordinarily thin capital. By one measure, their leverage ratios were as high as 40 to 1, meaning for every $40 in assets, there was only $1 in capital to cover losses. Less than a 3% drop in asset values could wipe out a firm. To make matters worse, much of their borrowing was short-term, in the overnight market — meaning the borrowing had to be renewed each and every day. For example, at the end of 2007, Bear Stearns had $11.8 billion in equity and $383.6 billion in liabilities and was borrowing as much as $70 billion in the overnight market. It was the equivalent of a small business with $50,000 in equity borrowing $1.6 million, with $296,750 of that due each and every day. One can't really ask,

"What were they thinking?" when it seems that too many of them were thinking alike." (FCIC Report[26])

Anyone with financial sense will argue that such leverage is ridiculous, and yet it was consciously allowed by the powers that be. Where were regulators and the policy- and law-makers? I don't know. No one seems to know!

(e) **"We conclude over-the-counter derivatives contributed significantly to this crisis.** The enactment of legislation in 2000 to ban the regulation by both the federal and state governments of over-the-counter (OTC) derivatives was a key turning point in the march toward the financial crisis. ...

OTC derivatives contributed to the crisis in three significant ways. First, one type of derivative — credit default swaps (CDS) — fuelled the mortgage securitization pipeline. CDS were sold to investors to protect against the default or decline in value of mortgage-related securities backed by risky loans. Companies sold protection — to the tune of $79 billion, in AIG's case — to investors in these newfangled mortgage securities, helping to launch and expand the market and, in turn, to further fuel the housing bubble.

Second, CDS were essential to the creation of synthetic CDOs. These synthetic CDOs were merely bets on the performance of real mortgage-related securities. They amplified the losses from the collapse of the housing bubble by allowing multiple bets on the same securities and helped spread them throughout the financial system.

Goldman Sachs alone packaged and sold $73 billion in synthetic CDOs from July 1, 2004, to May 31, 2007. Synthetic CDOs created by Goldman referenced more than 3,400 mortgage securities, and

---

26   http://fcic-static.law.stanford.edu/cdn_media/fcic-reports/fcic_final_report_full.
      pdf

610 of them were referenced at least twice. This is apart from how many times these securities may have been referenced in synthetic CDOs created by other firms. ...

While financial institutions surveyed by the FCIC said they do not track revenues and profits generated by their derivatives operations, some firms did provide estimates. For example, Goldman Sachs estimated that between 25% and 35% of its revenues from 2006 through 2009 were generated by derivatives, including 70% to 75% of the firm's commodities business, and half or more of its interest rate and currencies business. From May 2007 through November 2008, $133 billion, or 86%, of the $155 billion of trades made by Goldman's mortgage department were derivative transactions."[27] (FCIC Report[28])

Here we go once again with another example where regulation was banned by legislation and as the FCIC report argues, and I quote, "the enactment of legislation in 2000 to ban the regulation by both the federal and state governments of over-the-counter (OTC) derivatives was a key turning point in the march toward the financial crisis."

Why on earth would the Federal Government ban regulation with legislation and thereby purchase a crisis? The answer eludes me. I simply don't understand why this happened or how it could happen! Was no one watching? Was it lobbying, friendly relationships between policy- and law-makers with Wall Street firms, paid speeches, and/or campaign donations that did the trick? I'm not sure, and I simply cannot fathom why this banning of regulation happened in the year 2000! Now, you will understand why people like Bernie Sanders and others are asking for Hillary Clinton's paid speeches to be released and why I fully support this demand.

---

27   FCIC Report (2011), Original Footnote 57: Data provided to the FCIC by Goldman Sachs.

28   http://fcic-static.law.stanford.edu/cdn_media/fcic-reports/fcic_final_report_full. pdf

(f) "Removing barriers helped consolidate the banking industry. Between 1990 and 2005, 74 'megamergers' occurred involving banks with assets of more than $10 billion each. Meanwhile the 10 largest jumped from owning 25% of the industry's assets to 55%. From 1998 to 2007, the combined assets of the five largest U.S. banks — Bank of America, Citigroup, JP Morgan, Wachovia, and Wells Fargo — more than tripled, from $2.2 trillion to $6.8 trillion.[29] And investment banks were growing bigger, too. Smith Barney acquired Shearson in 1993 and Salomon Brothers in 1997, while Paine Webber purchased Kidder, Peabody in 1995. Two years later, Morgan Stanley merged with Dean Witter, and Bankers Trust purchased Alex. Brown & Sons. The assets of the five largest investment banks — Goldman Sachs, Morgan Stanley, Merrill Lynch, Lehman Brothers, and Bear Stearns — quadrupled, from $1 trillion in 1998 to $4 trillion in 2007.[30]

In the spring of 1996, after years of opposing repeal of Glass-Steagall, the Securities Industry Association — the trade organization of Wall Street firms such as Goldman Sachs and Merrill Lynch — changed course. Because restrictions on banks had been slowly removed during the previous decade, banks already had beachheads in securities and insurance. Despite numerous lawsuits against the Fed and the OCC, securities firms and insurance companies could not stop this piecemeal process of deregulation through agency rulings.[31] Edward Yingling, the CEO of the American Bankers Association (a lobbying organization), said, 'Because we had

---

29   FCIC Report (2011), Original Footnote 2: These were the largest banks as of 2007. See FCIC, "Preliminary Staff Report: Too-Big-to-Fail Financial Institutions," August 31, 2010, p. 14.

30   FCIC Report (2011), Original Footnote 3: Data from SNL Financial (www.snl. com/).

31   FCIC Report (2011), Original Footnote 12: Securities Industry Association v. Board of Governors of the Federal Reserve System, 627 F. Supp. 695 (D.D.C. 1986); Kathleen Day, "Reinventing the Bank; With Depression-Era Law about to Be Rewritten, the Future Remains Unclear," *Washington Post*, October 31, 1999.

knocked so many holes in the walls separating commercial and investment banking and insurance, we were able to aggressively enter their businesses — in some cases more aggressively than they could enter ours. So first the securities industry, then the insurance companies, and finally the agents came over and said let's negotiate a deal and work together.'[32]

The new regime encouraged growth and consolidation within and across banking, securities, and insurance. The bank-centered financial holding companies such as Citigroup, JP Morgan, and Bank of America could compete directly with the 'big five' investment banks — Goldman Sachs, Morgan Stanley, Merrill Lynch, Lehman Brothers, and Bear Stearns — in securitization, stock and bond underwriting, loan syndication, and trading in over-the-counter (OTC) derivatives. The biggest bank holding companies became major players in investment banking. The strategies of the largest commercial banks and their holding companies came to more closely resemble the strategies of investment banks. Each had advantages: commercial banks enjoyed greater access to insured deposits, and the investment banks enjoyed less regulation. Both prospered from the late 1990s until the outbreak of the financial crisis in 2007. However, Greenspan's 'spare tire' that had helped make the system less vulnerable would be gone when the financial crisis emerged — all the wheels of the system would be spinning on the same axle." (FCIC Report[33])

Again, the above represents a classic case where, in the name of innovation and consolidation, regulatory safeguards were removed, resulting in the system being more vulnerable when the financial crisis actually emerged (as all the wheels of the system were indeed spinning on the same axle, which eventually broke under the load). Please note

---

32   FCIC Report (2011), Original Footnote 13: Edward Yingling, quoted in "The Making of a Law," *ABA Banking Journal*, December 1999.

33   http://fcic-static.law.stanford.edu/cdn_media/fcic-reports/fcic_final_report_full. pdf

that, as the FCIC report argues very clearly, the financial crisis was essentially caused by a regulatory and policy failure that occurred because regulation and supervision were either lax and/or regulatory safeguards had been removed through lobbying, legislation and the like. We simply cannot afford more of this in the future. That is why, with the backdrop of the 2008 financial crisis (and its aftermath) and the role played by Wall Street (including investment banks, commercial banks, financial conglomerates etc.) in creating and sustaining this crisis, we simply cannot have presidential nominees cosy up to Wall Street and refuse to release transcripts of their paid for speeches. Sorry, but that is unacceptable and is not good electoral governance in any form or manner . . . anywhere!

7th Cause: Let us move further on and get to the governance of compensation, which played a very important role in the 2008 financial crisis. Indeed, compensation is one factor among many that contributed to the financial crisis in the United States, and elsewhere. Moreover, the FCIC report has also mentioned the same and this is quoted below:

(g) "Both before and after going public, investment banks typically paid out half their revenues in compensation. For example, Goldman Sachs spent between 44% and 49% a year between 2005 and 2008, when Morgan Stanley allotted between 46% and 59%. Merrill paid out similar percentages in 2005 and 2006, but gave 141% in 2007 — a year it suffered dramatic losses.[34]

As the scale, revenue, and profitability of the firms grew, compensation packages soared for senior executives and other key employees. John Gutfreund, reported to be the highest-paid executive on Wall Street in the late 1980s, received $3.2 million in 1986 as CEO of Salomon Brothers.[35] Stanley O'Neal's package

---

34   FCIC Report (2011), Original Footnote 63: Goldman Sachs, 2006 and 2009 10-K; Morgan Stanley, 2008 10-K; Merrill Lynch, 2005 and 2008 10-K.

35   FCIC Report (2011), Original Footnote 64: "Gutfreund's Pay Is Cut," *New York Times*, December 23, 1987.

was worth more than \$91 million in 2006, the last full year he was CEO of Merrill Lynch.[36] In 2007, Lloyd Blankfein, CEO at Goldman Sachs, received \$68.5 million;[37] Richard Fuld, CEO of Lehman Brothers, and Jamie Dimon, CEO of JPMorgan Chase, received about \$34 million and \$28 million, respectively.[38] That year Wall Street paid workers in New York roughly \$33 billion in year-end bonuses alone.[39] Total compensation for the major U.S. banks and securities firms was estimated at \$137 billion.[40]" (FCIC Report[41])

In effect, in all these firms, the focus was on the short-term performance, incentives, and compensation when, in reality, the risks (which existed) were mostly, medium and/or long-term. Of course, the regulator and policy- and law-makers sat and watched as compensation soared way beyond acceptable levels and firms started paying as high as 50% of their revenues in compensation. Did not the regulators and policy — and law-makers find it strange that:

(a) Goldman Sachs spent between 44% and 49% of its revenue per year on compensation (during the years 2005 to 2008);

(b) Morgan Stanley allotted between 46% and 59%; and

---

36   FCIC Report (2011), Original Footnote 65: Merrill Lynch, "2007 Proxy Statement," p. 38.

37   FCIC Report (2011), Original Footnote 66: Goldman Sachs, "Proxy Statement for 2008 Annual Meeting of Shareholders," March 7, 2008, p. 16: Blankfein received \$600,000 base salary and a 2007 year-end bonus of \$67.9 million.

38   FCIC Report (2011), Original Footnote 67: Lehman Brothers, "Proxy Statement for Year-end 2007," p. 28; JP Morgan Chase, "2007 Proxy Statement," p. 16.

39   FCIC Report (2011), Original Footnote 68: New York State Office of the State Comptroller, "New York City Securities Industry Bonus Pool," February 23, 2010. The bonus pool is for securities industry (NAICS 523) employees who work in New York City.

40   FCIC Report (2011), Original Footnote 69: "Banks Set for Record Pay, Top Firms on Pace to Award \$145 Billion for 2009, Up 18%, WSJ Study Finds," WSJ.com, January 14, 2010.

41   http://fcic-static.law.stanford.edu/cdn_media/fcic-reports/fcic_final_report_full.pdf

(c) Merrill paid out similar percentages in 2005 and 2006, and more importantly, gave as high as 141% in 2007 (a year in which it suffered dramatic losses).

What, on earth, were the regulators and policy — and law-makers doing? This is where, again, it is very important for a presidential candidate to forego any close relationships with Wall Street. As the 2008 financial crisis has clearly demonstrated, there is no free lunch!

8th Cause: Basically, as the FCIC report correctly argues, a lot of this happened because conflicts of interest were at play and they were, in a big measure, responsible for the financial crisis of 2008. While there are innumerable examples from the FCIC report that I could cite as evidence of conflicts of interest that were responsible for the financial crisis of 2008, one very relevant example from the SEC[42] is given below:

(h) "Another high profile example of conflict of interest in the recent years is the settlement that the SEC reached with Goldman Sachs, in which that firm paid $550 million to settle charges filed by the Commission, and acknowledged that disclosures made in marketing a subprime mortgage product contained incomplete information as they did not disclose the role of a hedge fund client who was taking the opposite side of the trade in the selection of the CDO."[43]

And I quote:

"Goldman acknowledges that the marketing materials for the ABACUS 2007-ACI transaction contained incomplete information. In particular, it was a mistake for the Goldman marketing materials to state that the reference portfolio was 'selected by' ACA Management LLC without disclosing the role of Paulson & Co.

---

42   Conflicts of Interest and Risk Governance — https://www.sec.gov/News/Speech/Detail/Speech/1365171491600

43   Ibid.

Inc. in the portfolio selection process and that Paulson's economic interests were adverse to CDO investors. Goldman regrets that the marketing materials did not contain that disclosure."[44]

Before I close this chapter, I would like to quote the FCIC report one last time and I do so below:

(i) "Goldman Sachs: 'Multiplied the Effects of the Collapse in Subprime'

Henry Paulson, the CEO of Goldman Sachs from 1999 until he became secretary of the Treasury in 2006 testified to the FCIC that by the time he became secretary many bad loans already had been issued — 'most of the toothpaste was out of the tube' — and that 'there really wasn't the proper regulatory apparatus to deal with it.'[45] Paulson provided examples: 'Subprime mortgages went from accounting for 5 percent of total mortgages in 1994 to 20 percent by 2006. . . . Securitization separated originators from the risk of the products they originated.' The result, Paulson observed, 'was a housing bubble that eventually burst in far more spectacular fashion than most previous bubbles.'[46]

Under Paulson's leadership, Goldman Sachs had played a central role in the creation and sale of mortgage securities. From 2004 through 2006, the company provided billions of dollars in loans to mortgage lenders; most went to the subprime lenders Ameriquest, Long Beach, Fremont, New Century, and Countrywide through

---

44   http://www.sec.gov/litigation/litreleases/2010/consent-pr2010-123.pdf, Page 2, point 3

45   FCIC Report (2011), Original Footnote 96: Henry M. Paulson Jr., testimony before the FCIC, Hearing on the Shadow Banking System, day 2, session 1: Perspective on the Shadow Banking System, May 6, 2010, transcript, p. 22.

46   FCIC Report (2011), Original Footnote 97: Henry M. Paulson Jr., written testimony for the FCIC, Hearing on the Shadow Banking System, day 2, session 1: Perspective on the Shadow Banking System, May 6, 2010, p. 2.

warehouse lines of credit, often in the form of repos.[47] During the same period, Goldman acquired $53 billion of loans from these and other subprime loan originators, which it securitized and sold to investors.[48] From 2004 to 2006 Goldman issued 318 mortgage securitizations totalling $184 billion (about a quarter were subprime), and 63 CDOs totalling $32 billion; Goldman also issued 22 synthetic or hybrid CDOs with a face value of $35 billion between 2004 and June 2006."[49]

To summarize, the FCIC report cites the following as among the key causes for the financial crisis of 2008:

(a) the lack of proper regulation and supervision;

(b) the lax and laissez-faire attitude of the regulators and policy- and law-makers (due to conflicts of interests);

(c) the reckless ride that many Wall Street firms (including investment banks, commercial banks, financial conglomerates etc.) took down a highway with no speed limits;

(d) the poor operational practices, weak financial condition, and huge compensation packages at many of these Wall Street firms (including investment banks, commercial banks, financial conglomerates etc.);

(e) the conflicts of interest that were prevalent in the larger policy, business, and political environment and so on.

Given all of this, the question that begs asking is whether Hillary Clinton is right in refusing to release speeches made by her to these same Wall Street firms. When a future policy — and law-maker, and

---

47   FCIC Report (2011), Original Footnote 98: Goldman Sachs, 2005 and 2006 10-K (Appendix 5a to Goldman's March 8, 2010, letter to the FCIC).

48   FCIC Report (2011), Original Footnote 99: Appendix 5c to Goldman's March 8, 2010, letter to the FCIC.

49   FCIC Report (2011), Original Footnote 100: Goldman's March 8, 2010, letter to the FCIC, p. 28 (subprime securities).

potential President refuses to release her speeches made to Wall Street firms in private, what signals are being sent to the American people and society at large? Whether Hillary's stance is proper or not, is something for the people to decide, but I strongly believe that given the demands of transparency and accountability in public life and electoral politics, that Hillary Clinton must come clean on this matter and release her speech transcripts immediately.

Without a doubt, the paid speeches delivered by Hillary Clinton to Wall Street firms create huge areas of conflict of interest. This is especially true given what happened in the late 1990s, when Bill Clinton was President, i.e., unregulated and unmonitored conflicts of interest that directly led to rampant deregulation, thereby resulting in the financial crisis of 2007/2008. Therefore, it is imperative that Hillary Clinton release the transcripts of her speeches immediately and before the general election so that the American people and society at large can make an objective judgment on this hugely important matter once and for all!

Chapter 4

Corporate Crime[1], Tax Evasion, Paid Speeches and Conflicts of Interest!

If campaign contributions are one way of creating conflicts of interest, accepting paid speaking engagements with organizations could potentially be another. Potentiality may well get converted to actuality when said organizations are involved in corporate crime.

It has been long argued that just as donations to presidential PACs, lobbying and campaign contributions could create conflicts of interest, paid speeches given by potential presidential candidates to entities involved in serious corporate crime could also result in conflicts of interest. This chapter applies the same yardstick to the Hillary Clinton candidature and details a series of instances, just as has been done in the case of campaign financing. These cases assume greater significance in the context of Hillary Clinton coming down heavily on President Obama for his perceived softness on corporate crime.[2] Fair point — all

---

1   Any violation of the law, whether through a civil or criminal act and/or caused by violation of specific 'legal acts'/rules/regulations is regarded as a crime in the context of this book.

2   She has talked of this several times on the campaign trail. See 'Clintons And Foundation Raked In Cash From Banks That Admitted Wrongdoing' — http://www.ibtimes.com/clintons-foundation-raked-cash-banks-admitted-wrongdoing-2010404; 'Hillary Clinton Denounces Corporate Crime While Accepting Cash From Blackstone, Firm Sanctioned By SEC' — http://www.ibtimes.com/political-capital/hillary-clinton-denounces-corporate-crime-while-accepting-cash-blackstone-firm

the more reason that we should look at Hillary Clinton's track record on paid speeches to see if any conflicts of interest have been created with regard to corporate crime.

Hillary Clinton made a total of 91 speeches[3] after she relinquished office as Secretary of State in 2013. It must be noted that Hillary Clinton reportedly received a total of $21.14 million from these 91 speeches[4] she gave to various organizations. We will now look at some of the individual cases — that could create a potential conflict of interest — in a sequential manner!

On January 22, 2015, just a few months before she officially announced her 2016 presidential bid, Hillary Clinton reportedly delivered a paid speech at the Canadian Imperial Bank of Commerce (CIBC) in Whistler, Canada. She is said to have been paid $150,000 for her speech.

CIBC is an interesting case in point for a variety of reasons. It has been embroiled with the IRS on issues of abetting tax evasion as espoused by the official communication from the Department of Justice, United States, which noted as follows in a release[5] dated April 30, 2013:

> "The Justice Department announced that a federal court in San Francisco entered an order authorizing the Internal Revenue Service (IRS) to serve a John Doe summons seeking information about U.S. taxpayers who may hold offshore accounts at 'Canadian Imperial Bank

---

3   A full listing of all 91 speeches given by Hillary Clinton to 84 organizations (between 2013–2015) is given on the website — http://www.releasethetranscripts. com/. Also see '$153 million in Bill and Hillary Clinton speaking fees, documented' — http://edition.cnn.com/2016/02/05/politics/hillary-clinton-bill-clinton-paid-speeches/ and http://releasethetranscripts.com/

4   This figure includes her 8 Wall Street speeches given above for which she received $1.835 million — see http://releasethetranscripts.com/ and other sources listed in the footnote above.

5   'Court Authorizes Service of John Doe Summons Seeking the Identities of U.S. Taxpayers with Offshore Accounts at Canadian Imperial Bank of Commerce's FirstCaribbean International Bank', Department of Justice Office of Public Affairs, April 30, 2013 — https://www.justice.gov/opa/pr/court-authorizes-service-john-doe-summons-seeking-identities-us-taxpayers-offshore-accounts

of Commerce FirstCaribbean International Bank' (CIBC FCIB). The order was signed by Senior District Judge Thelton E. Henderson. The IRS summons seeks records of FCIB's United States correspondent account at Wells Fargo N.A., which will allow the IRS to identify U.S. taxpayers who hold or held interests in financial accounts at FCIB and other financial institutions that used FCIB's Wells Fargo correspondent[6] account."[7]

The release[8] notes that, according to a statement filed by the IRS Revenue Agent Cheryl R. Kiger in support of the petition, FCIB is based out of Barbados with branches in 18 countries in the Caribbean. While it does not reportedly have any U.S. branches, it has a correspondent account in the United States at Wells Fargo Bank N.A. In addition "as alleged in Agent Kiger's declaration, the IRS learned that U.S. taxpayers were using FCIB to help them keep their offshore accounts undetected by the IRS and not pay U.S. federal income tax on money placed in those offshore accounts." [9]

Kiger's declaration is indeed very significant as it describes

---

6   A correspondent account is a bank deposit account maintained by one bank for another bank. Financial transactions involving U.S. dollars flow through U.S. banks. Therefore, foreign banks that do business in U.S. dollars, but have no office in the U.S., obtain a correspondent account at a U.S. bank in order to engage in such transactions. These transactions leave a trail in the U.S. that the IRS can access through the records of the correspondent bank accounts. These correspondent bank accounts have records of money deposited, money paid out through checks and money moved through the correspondent account by wire transfers. All of this information the IRS can obtain through a John Doe summons issued to the U.S. bank holding the correspondent account — Paraphrased from https://www.justice.gov/opa/pr/court-authorizes-service-john-doe-summons-seeking-identities-us-taxpayers-offshore-accounts

7   'Court Authorizes Service of John Doe Summons Seeking the Identities of U.S. Taxpayers with Offshore Accounts at Canadian Imperial Bank of Commerce's FirstCaribbean International Bank', Department of Justice, Office of Public Affairs, April 30, 2013 — https://www.justice.gov/opa/pr/court-authorizes-service-john-doe-summons-seeking-identities-us-taxpayers-offshore-accounts

8   Ibid.

9   Ibid.

her review of the information submitted by more than 120 FCIB customers who participated in the IRS's Offshore Voluntary Disclosure Program. It reportedly alleges that many of the FCIB customers in the John Doe class may have been "under-reporting income, evading income taxes, or otherwise violating the internal revenue laws of the United States."[10]

Readers should also note that U.S. tax law "requires U.S. taxpayers to pay taxes on all income earned worldwide. U.S. taxpayers must also report foreign financial accounts if the total value of the accounts exceeds $10,000 at any time during the calendar year. A deliberate failure to report a foreign account can result in a penalty of up to 50 percent of the amount in the account at the time of the violation."[11]

It is worth recalling here that, on January 28, 2013, in a very similar case,

> "the U.S. District Court for the Southern District of New York entered an order authorizing the IRS to serve a John Doe summons on UBS AG, seeking records of Swiss bank Wegelin & Co.'s United States correspondent account at UBS, which will allow the United States to determine the identity of U.S. taxpayers who hold or held interests in financial accounts at Wegelin and other Swiss financial institutions to evade federal income taxes."[12]

The above apart, it must be noted that the CIBC has been charged with other violations as well, including fraud:

> "1. CIHI (Canadian Imperial Holdings Inc.) and World Markets, which are subsidiaries of Canadian Imperial Bank of Commerce, Inc. (CIBC), participated in a scheme to defraud numerous mutual

---

10   Ibid.

11   Ibid.; '2012 Offshore Voluntary Disclosure Program' — https://www.irs.gov/uac/2012-offshore-voluntary-disclosure-program

12   Department of Justice, Office of Public Affairs Release — https://www.justice.gov/usao-sdny/pr/court-authorizes-irs-seek-records-ubs-relating-us-taxpayers-swiss-bank-accounts

funds and their shareholders through late trading and deceptive market timing.

2. More specifically, CIHI and World Markets engaged in three types of conduct that violated the federal securities laws: a) CIHI financed hedge fund customers while knowing the hedge funds would use the leverage to late trade and deceptively market time mutual funds; b) CIHI provided, and World Markets arranged, improper financing for market timing hedge fund customers in violation of the margin and extension of credit requirements; and c) a team of World Markets registered representatives (RR) enabled numerous customers to late trade and deceptively market time mutual funds.

3. With respect to the financing, CIHI provided funds to at least two hedge fund customers knowing those hedge funds would use the leverage to late trade and market time through Security Trust Corporation (STC), a Trust Company in Phoenix, Arizona. A CIHI Managing Director wrote a due diligence memorandum to CIBC's Credit Department in which he explicitly stated that STC's ability to allow late trades provided 'significant benefits to our customers.' Moreover, in addition to late trading, numerous CIHI officials understood that the hedge funds they were leveraging, in executing their market timing strategy, had to 'hide' their activity, use 'stealth' tactics, and otherwise 'stay under the radar' of the mutual funds. By leveraging these entities while knowing they were engaged in deceptive market timing and late trading, CIHI participated in a scheme to defraud mutual funds and their long term shareholders, thus violating the antifraud provisions of the federal securities laws.

4. Moreover, CIHI provided leverage to its hedge fund customers that violated the margin requirements. CIHI financed market timing hedge funds purportedly through the use of total return swaps (TRSs). These TRSs were extensions of credit in excess of 50% of the margin stock's value. Thus, CIHI violated Section 7(d)

of the Exchange Act and Regulation U promulgated by the Federal Reserve Board. In addition, because World Markets helped arrange this financing, World Markets violated Section 7(c) of the Exchange Act and Regulation T promulgated by the Federal Reserve Board. Moreover, because World Markets effected transactions in mutual funds for hedge funds in connection with which it arranged this financing, World Markets violated Section 11(d) of the Exchange Act.

5.   Finally, from at least 1999 until January 2003, World Markets received over 1,000 letters and emails from mutual funds complaining about abusive trading by a team of RRs at World Markets. This team of RRs, led by an RR (hereinafter described as 'Broker Doe'), used, among other tactics, multiple accounts, multiple RR numbers, and small trade size broken up across related accounts to deceive mutual funds and 'stay under the radar' of the mutual funds' internal timing monitors. Senior World Markets officials knew about this team of RRs' deceptive market timing activities and took steps to assist them, ensuring that this team of significant business producers could continue to facilitate market timing. In addition, some of these RRs knowingly accepted numerous mutual fund orders from at least one of their timing customers after 4:00 p.m. ET, and processed those orders as though the customer had placed the order prior to 4:00 p.m. ET. As a result of these acts, World Markets violated the antifraud provisions of the federal securities laws and Rule 22c-1, as adopted under Section 22(c) of the Investment Company Act."[13]

In fact, based on the above, the SEC passed an order as follows:

"A. Respondents shall pay, on a joint and several basis, disgorgement and prejudgment interest in the amount of $100 million, and a civil money penalty in the amount of $25 million, for a total payment of $125 million; ...

---

13   https://www.sec.gov/litigation/admin/33-8592.pdf

D. Respondents shall, within 30 days of the entry of this Order, pay on a joint and several basis, disgorgement and prejudgment interest in the total amount of $100 million, and civil money penalties in the amount of $25 million, for a total payment of $125 million, to the United States Treasury." [14]

That is not all, there are other issues as well. SEC also

"instituted a settled enforcement proceeding against one of North America's largest financial institutions, Canadian Imperial Bank of Commerce (CIBC), for CIBC's role in Enron Corp.'s manipulation of its financial statements. The SEC also sued three of CIBC's executives, two of whom are settling. The Commission's complaint charges CIBC and the three executives with having helped Enron to mislead its investors through a series of complex structured finance transactions over a period of several years preceding Enron's bankruptcy. The Commission filed a civil injunctive action in U.S. District Court in Texas. CIBC consented to the entry of a final judgment in that action that (i) permanently enjoins CIBC from violating the antifraud, books and records, and internal control provisions of the federal securities laws, and (ii) orders CIBC to pay $80 million: $37.5 million in disgorgement, a $37.5 million penalty, and $5 million in prejudgment interest." [15]

Given these circumstances, Hillary Clinton's decision to accept a paid speaking assignment to address institutions such as CIBC or UBS certainly comes under a cloud. At a time when the IRS authorities were using all legal means to obtain information about the use of foreign tax heavens by U.S. nationals, and unearth potential tax evaders, it certainly was not appropriate for a former First Lady, former Secretary of State and presidential candidate (who contested the primaries in 2008 and is

---

14   https://www.sec.gov/litigation/admin/33-8592.pdf

15   'SEC Announces Agreement with Canadian Imperial Bank of Commerce and Two Executives to Settle Charges of Aiding and Abetting Enron Accounting Fraud', Press Release, Washington, D.C., December 22, 2003 — https://www.sec.gov/news/press/2003-180.htm

doing so now in 2016) to deliver a paid speech at CIBC, which has been served with a court order (regarding its subsidiary FCIB) and also has committed several violations in the past.

The same is true of UBS where the situation is actually much worse. Bill and Hillary Clinton delivered a total of 10 speeches between 2011–2015 to UBS, when it was embroiled in the IRS tax problem. While Bill Clinton made nine speeches, Hillary Clinton gave one speech. The key point to note here is that several of the speeches delivered by Bill Clinton were at a time when Hillary Clinton served as the Secretary of State. That creates a huge conflict of interest because of the kind of tax issues that UBS was facing with the IRS then.

Thus, given that Hillary and Bill Clinton received large sums of money to the tune of $2.065 million from UBS and CIBC for a total of 11 speeches during the period 2011–15, there is a huge conflict of interest. The above events cannot simply be wished away as merely poor judgment as it has occurred several times. In fact, there are more examples of organizations that had perhaps violated the law while Bill and Hillary Clinton gave speeches to these organizations, especially after these organizations had orders passed against them by relevant authorities like the SEC. I am not including the details here since the examples provided sufficiently illustrate the degree of conflict already.

As a former Senator, First Lady, and Secretary of State, what was the rationale behind Hillary Clinton accepting an invitation to speak at the Canadian Imperial Bank of Commerce? The bank had previously been indicted for several violations, including the CIHI, World Markets, and Enron cases, and against whose Caribbean operations (FirstCaribbean International Bank) the court had passed an order authorizing service of a John Doe summons seeking the identities of U.S. taxpayers with offshore accounts.

Likewise, what were Hillary and Bill Clinton telling UBS AG in private in their paid speeches after UBS AG had received a "summons requiring UBS AG to produce information about U.S. taxpayers holding accounts at the Swiss bank, Wegelin & Co. (Wegelin) and other banks based in Switzerland with a view to evade federal income taxes?"[16]

These are questions that the American public deserve an answer to, prior to exercising their right to franchise for or against Hillary Clinton. Even more so, given that Hillary Clinton has promised the strongest action against offshore accounts and tax evaders, a topic that is discussed in greater detail in the forthcoming chapter on the Panama Papers expose.

---

16   'Court Authorizes IRS To Seek Records From UBS Relating To U.S. Taxpayers With Swiss Bank Accounts' — https://www.justice.gov/usao-sdny/pr/court-authorizes-irs-seek-records-ubs-relating-us-taxpayers-swiss-bank-accounts

Panama Papers, Off-Shore Accounts, Tax Evasion and Contributions to the Hillary Campaign

One of the hotly debated topics in the run up to the 2016 U.S. presidential election has been the tax evasion issue and use of tax havens by the wealthy in the United States. The recent Panama Papers expose has certainly resulted in a significant increase in the decibel levels. The expose has already caused a few heads to roll including that of the Prime Minister of Iceland[1] and it is expected to topple a few more high profile personalities from their pedestals before it runs its course. Speaking on the topic of the Panama papers controversy on her campaign trail, Hillary Clinton[2] has declared emphatically,

"I'll shut down the private tax system for the wealthy."

Talking at the AFL-CIO convention in Philadelphia, Hillary Clinton is reported[3] to have referred to the "Panama Papers" that revealed

---

1   'Iceland PM steps aside after protests over Panama Papers revelations' — http://www.theguardian.com/world/2016/apr/05/iceland-prime-minister-resigns-over-panama-papers-revelations

2   'Clinton: I'll shut down the "private tax system" for the wealthy' — http://thehill.com/blogs/ballot-box/presidential-races/275368-clinton-ill-shut-private-tax-system-for-the-wealthy

3   Paraphrased from The Hill.com — http://thehill.com/blogs/ballot-box/presidential-races/275368-clinton-ill-shut-private-tax-system-for-the-wealthy

information about the outrageous financial dealings of super-rich politicians and public figures from around the globe. If elected President, she promised to shut down legal tax havens used by the ultra-wealthy, by eliminating the loopholes in the tax system. She sounded the bugle on illegal tax havens and emphatically stated, "Anyone who violates the law anywhere should be held accountable." She wound up her speech saying that she will go after all these scams and ensure that everyone pays their fair share of due taxes in America.

While on the topic of the Panama papers expose, it is important that a cross reference is made to the U.S.–Panama Trade Promotion Agreement that came into force in 2012.[4] An interesting statement was made by Hillary Clinton, who was Secretary of State at the time when the agreement was signed. This is what she said:

"The Free Trade Agreements passed by Congress tonight will make it easier for American companies to sell their products to South Korea, Colombia, and Panama, which will create jobs here at home. The Obama administration is constantly working to deepen our economic engagement throughout the world and these agreements are an example of that commitment.

"The stakes are not just economic. South Korea, Colombia, and Panama are three important partners in strategically vital regions. With the passage of these agreements, America has delivered for our friends and allies. I want to thank Presidents Lee, Santos, and Martinelli for their patience and willingness to partner with the Obama Administration as these agreements moved through Congress.

"But our work is not yet done. We will not be content until these agreements are fully implemented so that American exporters can reap the benefits as soon as possible."[5]

---

4   https://ustr.gov/trade-agreements/free-trade-agreements/panama-tpa
5   'Passage of Colombia, Panama, and South Korea Trade Agreements' — https://blogs.state.gov/stories/2011/10/13/passage-colombia-panama-and-south-korea-trade-agreements#sthash.ZloicUCP.dpuf

Again, I would be remiss if I did not make a mention of a Bernie Sanders speech made in the U.S. Senate in 2011 on the Panama free trade agreement. It was a speech that displayed remarkable foresight, especially seen now from the context of the Panama papers expose. I quote:

> "Finally, Mr. President, let's talk about the Panama Free Trade Agreement. Panama's entire annual economic output is only $26.7 billion a year, or about two-tenths of one percent of the U.S. economy. No-one can legitimately make the claim that approving this free trade agreement will significantly increase American jobs. Then, why would we be considering a stand-alone free trade agreement with this country?

> Well, it turns out that Panama is a world leader when it comes to allowing wealthy Americans and large corporations to evade U.S. taxes by stashing their cash in offshore tax havens. And, the Panama Free Trade Agreement would make this bad situation much worse. Each and every year, the wealthy and large corporations evade $100 billion in U.S. taxes through abusive and illegal offshore tax havens in Panama and other countries. According to Citizens for Tax Justice, 'A tax haven . . . has one of three characteristics: It has no income tax or a very low-rate income tax; it has bank secrecy laws; and it has a history of non-cooperation with other countries on exchanging information about tax matters. Panama has all three of those. ... They're probably the worst.'

> Mr. President, the trade agreement with Panama would effectively bar the U.S. from cracking down on illegal and abusive offshore tax havens in Panama. In fact, combating tax haven abuse in Panama would be a violation of this free trade agreement, exposing the U.S. to fines from international authorities.

> In 2008, the Government Accountability Office said that 17 of the 100 largest American companies were operating a total of 42 subsidiaries in Panama. This free trade agreement would make it easier for the wealthy and large corporations to avoid paying U.S. taxes and it must be defeated.

At a time when we have a record-breaking $14.7 trillion national debt and an unsustainable federal deficit, the last thing that we should be doing is making it easier for the wealthiest people and most profitable corporations in this country to avoid paying their fair share in taxes by setting-up offshore tax havens in Panama.

Adding insult to injury, Mr. President, the Panama FTA would require the United States to waive Buy America requirements for procurement bids from thousands of foreign firms, including many Chinese firms, incorporated in this major tax haven. That may make sense to China, it does not make sense to me.

Finally, Panama is also listed by the State Department as a major venue for Mexican and Colombian drug cartel money laundering. Should we be rewarding this country with a free trade agreement? I think the answer should be a resounding no."[6]

It is common knowledge that interested parties lobby with the government for the passage of important legislation and the U.S.-Panama Trade Promotion Agreement is no exception.

In the context of the U.S.–Panama Trade Promotion Agreement, the lobbying database[7] revealed that Goldman Sachs had lobbied with the U.S. House of Representatives in 2011 (3rd quarter, months 7–9) on "Issues related to consideration of pending free trade agreements (South Korea, Colombia, Panama) — Proposed legislation re these issues; Executive Branch action re these issues." The same form also lists that Goldman Sachs lobbied on budgetary issues with the State Department, when Hillary Clinton was Secretary of State.

---

6   https://www.youtube.com/watch?v=LrsI0Sw2hq8 and Senate Speech by Sen. Bernie Sanders on Unfettered Free Trade (2011) — http://www.sanders. senate.gov/newsroom/press-releases/senate-speech-by-sen-bernie-sanders-on-unfettered-free-trade — U.S. Senate speech by Bernie Sanders dated 2011. This speech made in the United States Senate is in the public domain.

7   The lobbying database — http://soprweb.senate.gov/index.cfm?event=selectfields. See book website for specific lobbying form related to lobbying by Goldman Sachs with regard to the free trade agreements.

Goldman Sachs had in turn used the services of The Duberstein Group, Inc., (2100 Pennsylvania Avenue, NW, Suite 500, Washington, D.C. 20037 USA) for this purpose. Six people represented this lobbying firm and their names are given below:

Table 5.1: Lobbyists Listed in the Goldman Sachs Form[8]	
First Name	**Last Name**
Michael	Berman
Steven	Champlin
Kenneth	Duberstein
Brian	Griffin
Daniel	Meyer
Marti	Thomas
Source: The Lobbying Database, http://soprweb.senate.gov/index. cfm?event=selectfields	

The key person appears to be Michael S. Berman (Mike Berman), whose name is given as the contact of the lobbying firm. What acquires great significance here is the fact that Mike Berman, Steven Champlin, and Brian Griffin have each contributed the maximum individual contribution of $2,700 to the Hillary Clinton 2016 presidential campaign. Mike Berman is also said to have contributed $10,001 to $25,000 to the Clinton Foundation. However, more than the financial contributions made, it is Mike Berman's background, and his close links to the Clintons that deserve closer scrutiny. As Berman's statement from "Remembrance of Campaigns Past" reveals:

"I met the Clintons in the mid-70s. In 1992, when Bill got nominated, I began working closely with them. After the convention I spent two-

---

8   With regard to Lobbying House of representatives in 2011, 3rd quarter, months 7–9, on pending free trade agreements — South Korea, Colombia, Panama

thirds of my time in Little Rock working on the campaign. ... After the Clinton campaign I went on to work on inaugural celebrations. I ended up being closer to Mrs. Clinton than to the President. ...I also worked with the Clintons in the 1996 reelection campaign. Hillary has true affection for the people that work for her. She has loyalty towards them and that goes both ways."[9]

Given his self-admitted proximity to the Clintons and the fact that the lobbying took place while Hillary Clinton was serving as Secretary of State in the first Obama administration, it is without doubt a case of conflict of interest. A further perusal of the State Department blog reveals that even while the Obama administration (including President and Secretary of State etc.) was talking of cracking down on tax havens and the wealthy who were evading taxes, they had simultaneously pushed the Panama[10] and other free trade agreements and got them signed.

And as the *International Business Times* notes,

"Even while Obama championed his commitment to raise taxes on the wealthy, he pursued and eventually signed the Panama agreement in 2011."[11]

We already saw what Hillary Clinton, as Secretary of State, said after the trade agreement with Panama was ratified by the Congress:

"The Free Trade Agreements passed by Congress tonight will make it easier for American companies to sell their products to South Korea, Colombia and Panama, which will create jobs here at home. The Obama Administration is constantly working to deepen our economic

---

9   http://www.d.umn.edu/external-affairs/homepage/07/berman.html
10   'Panama Papers: Obama, Clinton Pushed Trade Deal Amid Warnings It Would Make Money Laundering, Tax Evasion Worse' — http://www.ibtimes.com/panama-papers-obama-clinton-pushed-trade-deal-amid-warnings-it-would-make-money-2348076
11   Ibid.

engagement throughout the world and these agreements are an example of that commitment." [12]

It has to be said here that all of this sends severely contradictory signals: The Obama administration (which included President Obama and Secretary Clinton) had promised a crackdown on the rich, wealthy American tax evaders operating from tax havens; yet the same administration had also pushed the Panama and other trade agreements and got them signed; there were firms like Goldman Sachs which had actively lobbied for the trade agreements through a lobbying firm (with staff) close to Hillary Clinton and after the signing of the Panama agreement, Secretary Clinton came out and issued a hugely positive statement.

As I continued my research into the Panama Papers controversy, I came across one more interesting name who has not only been linked to off-shore entities and named in the Panama Papers but who is also a vociferous supporter of the Hillary Clinton campaign — Donald Sussman. While Sussman has contributed $2,700 to Hillary Clinton directly as an individual, he has also given huge donations (in excess of $4.7 million) to pro-Clinton PACs that are supporting her campaign as per details given below.

Table 5.2: Contribution of Donald Sussman to pro-Clinton PACs						
Contributor Name	Employer	Occupation	City	State	Zip	Amount (in $)
Priorities USA Action						
Sussman, Donald	Paloma Partners Advisors, Inc.	President	Rye Brook	NY	10573	1,500,000

---

12   'Passage of Colombia, Panama, and South Korea Trade Agreements' — https://blogs.state.gov/stories/2011/10/13/passage-colombia-panama-and-south-korea-trade-agreements#sthash.ZloicUCP.dpuf

Table 5.2: Contribution of Donald Sussman to pro-Clinton PACs						
Contributor Name	Employer	Occupation	City	State	Zip	Amount (in $)
Sussman, Donald	Paloma Partners Advisors, Inc.	President	Rye Brook	NY	10573	1,500,000
Sussman, Donald	Paloma Partners Advisors, Inc.	President	Rye Brook	NY	10573	1,000,000
Hillary Victory Fund						
Sussman, S. Donald	Paloma Partners Advisors	Investment Advisor	Rye Brook	NY	10573	343,400
Sussman, S. Donald	Paloma Partners Advisors	Investment Advisor	Rye Brook	NY	10573	343,400
Correct The Record						
Sussman, Donald	Paloma Partners Advisors, Inc.	President	Fort Lauderdale	FL	33301	100,000
All Total						4,786,800
Source: Data from Federal Election Commission, http://www.fec.gov/ as of April 1, 2016						

Additionally, the Sussman Family Foundation has also donated between $50,000 and $100,000 to the Clinton Foundation.

Recently, Sussman was named in the Panama Papers[13] and he has been linked to Simply Radiant Ltd. incorporated in the British Virgin Islands as a director. Paloma Partners LP is listed as a shareholder

---

13   https://offshoreleaks.icij.org/search?utf8=%E2%9C%93&q=Sussman+&e= &commit=Search; 'Major Hillary Clinton Donor Caught Up in Fresh Panama Papers Scandal' — http://www.telesurtv.net/english/news/Major-Clinton-Donor-Caught-Up-in-Fresh-Panama-Papers-Scandal-20160510-0033.html

of Simply Radiant Ltd. and Paloma Partners International Investors Corp is listed as an intermediary of Simply Radiant Ltd. This Paloma Partners International Investors Corp. (incorporated in the United States) is linked to another Paloma Partners International Investors Corp. whose jurisdiction is unknown. His daughter, Selwyn Donald Sussman,[14] has been linked to New China Technology Licensing Inc., which is also incorporated in the British Virgin Islands and she is listed as a director.

This apart, there is another interesting and related issue with regard to Donald Sussman as revealed by a *New York Times* article[15] titled "Tax Break Bringing Businesses, and Fraud, to the Virgin Islands" (by Stephanie Strom and Lynnley Browning). According to the article, the principal threat to the United States mainland tax coffers could come from the emigration of extremely well compensated hedge fund managers — such as Donald Sussman, the founder of Paloma Partners of Greenwich which manages capital of about $3 billion — who had started claiming tax benefits under the Virgin Island program.

The above aspects apart, it must also be noted that Sussman, in September 1997 as per a Securities and Exchange Commission order under the Investment Advisers Act of 1940 (Release No. 1653 / September 2, 1997), accounting and auditing enforcement (Release No. 948 / September 2, 1997) and administrative proceeding (File No. 3-9382) has been charged with several violations.

"C. Sussman violated Section 206(2) in the following manner. As to 99 River Road, Sussman failed to disclose the Initial Loan that enabled him to buy 99 River Road for his wholly-owned corporation and the potential conflicts of interest that resulted. Sussman's interests were in potential conflict with those of his clients in that the documentation concerning the building indicated that Sussman was now Paloma

---

14   https://offshoreleaks.icij.org/search?utf8=%E2%9C%93&q=Sussman+&e= &commit=Search

15   'Tax Break Bringing Businesses, and Fraud, to the Virgin Islands' — http://www. nytimes.com/2004/09/18/us/tax-break-bringing-businesses-and-fraud-to-the-virgin-islands.html

Limited's landlord and stood to profit on any resale of the building, even though Paloma Limited had loaned to Sussman, interest free, the money needed to purchase the building.

This conflict created a risk that Sussman's decisions regarding 99 River Road would not be disinterested and that the arrangement at 99 River Road might as a result be less favorable to Paloma Limited than an arrangement reached at arms' length with a third party would be. Sussman should have disclosed these potential conflicts to the limited partners of Paloma Limited. Sussman's subsequent statement in the Paloma Limited financial statements that he intended for the limited partners to benefit on resale did not inform them that there were no formal documents legally binding Sussman to provide them with this benefit. Sussman also failed to inform the limited partners that they were at a risk of loss if there were insufficient funds from a resale to enable Lamda Holdings to repay the mortgage or the Lamda Receivable. Information concerning these potential conflicts of interest and Sussman's use of Paloma Limited's funds for his own benefit would be material to a limited partner.

D. With respect to the bonus expense accounting, Sussman violated Section 206(2) by failing to charge $3.35 million in expenses in 1992, which resulted in a 36% understatement of operating expenses. If it had been charged in 1992, it would have reduced the investors' rate of return for the year from 11% to 10.6%.

As a result of the foregoing, Sussman willfully violated Section 206(2) of the Advisers Act.

Accordingly, IT IS HEREBY ORDERED that Sussman:

A.   shall cease and desist from committing or causing any violation and any future violation of Section 206(2) of the Advisers Act;

B.   shall, within ten days of any sale of 99 River Road, disgorge to Paloma Limited any net profits earned on such sale;

C. shall comply with his undertakings, as specified in his Offer of Settlement:

1. not to impose on Paloma Limited any losses incurred in connection with the resale of 99 River Road;

2. not to impose on Paloma Limited any future costs of future capital improvements, if any, to 99 River Road; and

3. within ten days of any sale of 99 River Road, to pay any remaining indebtedness due from Lamda Holdings to Paloma Limited; and

D. shall, within ten days of the date of this Order, pay a civil money penalty in the amount of $40,000 to the United States Treasury."[16]

Leaving Sussman aside for a moment, let us look at yet another high profile contributor to the Clinton campaign — Haim Saban, who is an Israeli and American media mogul, investor, philanthropist, musician, record, film and television producer. Saban is said to be a very accomplished businessman with wide-ranging business interests — from financial services to entertainment, media, and so on. His estimated net worth is $3 billion and he has been a major donor to the U.S. Democratic Party.[17]

Cheryl and Haim Saban have in fact been very close to the Clintons and specifically, they and The Saban Family Foundation have made donations ranging from $10,000,001 to $25,000,000 to the Clinton Foundation. That is indeed a huge donation by any standards. Apart from making individual contributions to Hillary Clinton's campaign, the Sabans have generously donated to the pro-Clinton PACs. As per data, they are the single highest contributing family to the Hillary Clinton campaign with contributions to PACs exceeding $10 million.[18]

---

16   https://www.sec.gov/litigation/admin/ia1653.txt

17   https://en.wikipedia.org/wiki/Haim_Saban

18   As of May 27, 2016, they have exceeded the contributions of George Soros and James Simons to the Hillary Clinton campaign! See, 'The Top Donors Backing Hillary Clinton's Super PAC' — http://www.forbes.com/sites/ivonaiacob/2016/05/27/top-donors-hillary-clinton-superpac/#51fe34412740

Table 5.3: Contribution of Haim Saban to pro-Clinton PACs						
Contributor Name	Employer	Occupation	City	State	Zip	Amount (in $)
Priorities USA Action						
Saban, Haim	Saban Entertainment	Chairman & Chief Executive Officer	Los Angeles	CA	90067	1,500,000
Saban	Saban Entertainment	Chairman & Chief Executive Officer	Los Angeles	CA	90067	1,000,000
Saban	Saban Entertainment	Chairman & Chief Executive Officer	Los Angeles	CA	90067	1,000,000
Saban, Cheryl	Self-Employed	Philanthropist	Los Angeles	CA	90067	1,500,000
Saban, Cheryl	Self-Employed	Philanthropist	Los Angeles	CA	90067	1,000,000
Saban, Cheryl	Self Employed	Philanthropist	Los Angeles	CA	90067	1,000,000
Hillary Victory Fund						
Saban, Haim	Saban Capital Group Inc.	Executive	Los Angeles	CA	90067	343,400
Saban, Haim	Saban Capital Group Inc.	Executive	Los Angeles	CA	90067	353,400
Saban, Cheryl	Self-Employed	Author/ Producer	Los Angeles	CA	90067	353,400
Saban, Cheryl	Self-Employed	Author/ Producer	Los Angeles	CA	90067	353,400
All Total						8,403,600
Source: Data from Federal Election Commission, http://www.fec.gov/ (This data is as of April 1, 2016.)						

Saban however, has not been without his share of controversies, especially with regard to tax evasion. The United States Senate, Permanent Subcommittee On Investigations, Committee on Homeland Security and Governmental Affairs with Norm Coleman, Chairman and Carl

Levin, Ranking Minority Member released a report titled: "Tax Haven Abuses: The Enablers, The Tools And Secrecy", Minority & Majority Staff Report by the Permanent Subcommittee on Investigations. This report was released in conjunction with the Permanent Subcommittee on Investigations August 1, 2006 hearing. The report dated 2007 observes the following:

> **"POINT: Offshore Securities Portfolio.** This case history examines a complex securities transaction used to shelter over $2 billion in capital gains from U.S. taxes, relying in part on offshore secrecy to shield its workings from U.S. law enforcement. In contrast to the case histories examining offshore structures used over a period of years, this inquiry focuses on the use of offshore secrecy jurisdictions to facilitate one-time tax shelter transactions. The tax shelter was designed, promoted, and implemented by a Seattle-based securities firm, Quellos Group, LLC, (Quellos), with the assistance of lawyers, bankers, and other professionals. Quellos sold the shelter, called POINT (Personally Optimized INvestment Transaction), to six wealthy clients in six separate transactions. Together, the tax shelters were used in an effort to erase over $2 billion in capital gains that would otherwise have been taxed, costing the U.S. Treasury lost revenue of about $300 million.
>
> The Subcommittee found that the POINT tax strategy was based upon billions of dollars' worth of fake securities transactions that were used to generate billions of dollars in fake capital losses to offset real taxable capital gains of U.S. taxpayers so they could avoid paying taxes to the U.S. Treasury. The fake securities transactions were undertaken by two offshore shell corporations in the Isle of Man, Jackstones and Barnville, whose ownership has been kept secret.
>
> The transactions were carried out by compliant offshore administrators and trustees, since the corporations had no employees of their own. Using circular transactions and offsetting payments that cancelled each other out, these offshore corporations created a paper portfolio of over $9 billion in U.S. high tech stocks that appeared to suffer price drops

and generated the fake capital losses used in the POINT transactions. The fees charged by Quellos depended upon the amount of tax loss generated in each transaction for the taxpayer who bought the shelter; the more money the taxpayer 'lost' from the transaction, the more Quellos charged for the scheme.

Six U.S. taxpayers, including Haim Saban and Robert Wood Johnson IV, purchased the tax shelter, paying fees totaling approximately $65 million. Prominent law firms, such as Cravath, Swaine & Moore and Bryan Cave, provided written tax opinion letters affirming that it was 'more likely than not' that the Quellos plan would produce the favorable tax consequences promised, and collaborated with Quellos on its design or implementation. The factual statements used to support the legal analysis in the opinion letters inaccurately described the nature of the securities transactions generating the capital losses. The law firms accepted the representations of Quellos on these matters without inquiring behind them. Prominent U.S. and foreign financial institutions, including HSBC Bank, provided financing for the POINT transactions, without conducting adequate due diligence into the underlying transactions."

These are indeed grave observations on tax haven abuses[19] and coming from the United States Senate, they are even more serious. It is perplexing to think that Hillary Clinton did not take cognizance of this while taking such huge contributions from Haim Saban. As mentioned earlier, in May 2016, he has become the single largest contributor to the Hillary Clinton campaign by giving over $10 million thereby overtaking both George Soros and James Simons.

---

19   In a related suit, Matthew Krane claimed that, "Saban defrauded the government out of tax money when he sold his company to the Walt Disney Company in October 2001 for $5.3 billion. Saban demanded Krane put together a tax plan to ensure that Saban would pay $0 on his $1.5 billion profit from the impending sale," the suit alleges. "The plan thus saved Defendants $150,000,000 or more in tax benefits while, at the same time, placing $60,000,000 in potential stock profit at Saban's disposal." — 'Haim Saban Loses Court Round; Former Tax Lawyer Can Sue Him' — http://www.thewrap.com/haim-saban-loses-court-round-former-tax-lawyer-can-sue-him-26386/

Now, irrespective of whatever the exact tax situation is with regard to Sussman or Saban, the larger question that becomes relevant is how Clinton can crack down on potential tax evaders(s) or tax shifters (to tax havens), when people supporting her and stakeholders close to her are perhaps doing the same thing.

In this context, it must be noted that the names of Gabriella Fialkoff,[20] Hillary Clinton's former finance director in the 2000 Senate campaign, and her brother and late father have also been listed in the Panama papers disclosures. Their names have been associated with UPAC Holdings Ltd. (a British Virgin Islands offshore company), a company incorporated in June 2012.

While Gabriella has contributed the maximum permitted of an individual ($2,700), it is important to note that she shares a very close relationship with Hillary, having served as the finance director of Clinton's 2000 Senate bid when the present New York Mayor, de Blasio, was in charge of Hillary's Senate campaign. Incidentally, even now Gabriella Fialkoff continues to work[21] with Mayor de Blasio, yet another big supporter of Hillary Clinton.

What is really important to note is that Gabriella Fialkoff, her brother Bret Fialkoff, and late father Frank Fialkoff are all mentioned as beneficiaries *and* shareholders in relation to UPAC Holdings Ltd. Interestingly, the address given for all the three Fialkoffs is the address of their Shop[22] in New York (Flagship Store, Robert Lee Morris, 390 Fifth Ave, 2nd Floor, New York NY 10018 with tel: 212.764.3332 and press inquiries — hfialkoff@robertleemorris.com).

Thus, the aforementioned examples of Donald Sussman,[23] Haim Saban and Gabriella Fialkoff are fairly telling. All of their names have

---

20   'Inside Panama Papers: Multiple Clinton Connections' — www.mcclatchydc.com/
      news/politics-government/election/article72215012.html
21   See Gabrilla Fialkoff's LinkedIn profile — https://www.linkedin.com/in/gabrielle-
      fialkoff-8ab84a68. She now serves as Advisor to the Mayor of New York.
22   https://www.robertleemorris.com/pages/contact
23   'Tax Break Bringing Businesses, and Fraud, to the Virgin Islands' — http://www.
      nytimes.com/2004/09/18/us/tax-break-bringing-businesses-and-fraud-to-the-
      virgin-islands.html

been linked to offshore companies in tax havens and there is no denying that they share close proximity with the Clintons! While Sussman and Saban have contributed millions to the Hillary Clinton campaign, Gabriella Fialkoff has provided the maximum permitted of individuals ($2,700) but is a former associate, having served on Hillary's campaign staff back in 2000. She has also donated to the Clinton Foundation.[24]

After all that Hillary Clinton has said with regard to tax evasion and the use of tax havens, it remains to be seen how she will justify accepting huge contributions from people like Sussman and Saban, who have been "called out" for doing exactly the same.

My further research into the SEC filing database revealed interesting information about a fund called "The Eaglevale Partners Offshore Fund, Ltd." incorporated in Cayman Islands. It has a New York address (1330 Avenue of the Americas, 22nd Floor, New York, NY — 10019 with phone number 212-621-4500). The following names have been provided in the filed documents[25] as its directors:

Table 5.4: Directors in Eaglevale Partners Offshore Fund Ltd			
Name of Person	Title	Address	Name of the Fund
Kenneth Mark Mallon II	Director	1330 Avenue of the Americas, 22nd Floor, New York, NY — 10019	Eaglevale Partners Offshore Fund, Ltd
Ernest A. Morrison	Director	c/o Cox Hallett Wilkinson Limited, Cumberland House, 9th Fl, 1 Victoria St., Hamilton, BERMUDA — HM FX	Eaglevale Partners Offshore Fund, Ltd

---

24   'Hillary Clinton Donors Implicated In Panama Papers — Decades Of Dark Money' — http://trofire.com/2016/04/21/hillary-clinton-donors-implicated-panama-papers/

25   Please see website — http://www.madampresident2016.net/ and also the websites given in the tables.

Table 5.4: Directors in Eaglevale Partners Offshore Fund Ltd			
Name of Person	Title	Address	Name of the Fund
Geoff Ruddick	Director	c/o Int'l Management Services Ltd, Harbour Centre, P.O. Box 61, George Town, Grand Cayman, CAYMAN ISLANDS — KY1-1102	Eaglevale Partners Offshore Fund, Ltd
Source: https://www.sec.gov/Archives/edgar/data/1546868/000091957412002861/xslFormDX01/primary_doc.xml			

As per other filings with SEC,[26] another fund called The Eaglevale Partners Fund LP, which was incorporated in Delaware (in year 2011), has three executive officers as per details given hereafter:

Table 5.5: Executive Officers in Eaglevale Partners Fund LP			
Name of Person	Title	Address	Name of the Fund
Bennett G. Grau	Executive Officer	c/o Eaglevale Partners GP LLC, 1330 Avenue of the Americas, 22nd Floor, New York, New York — 10019	Eaglevale Partners Fund LP
Kenneth Mark Mallon II	Executive Officer	c/o Eaglevale Partners GP LLC, 1330 Avenue of the Americas, 22nd Floor, New York, New York — 10019	Eaglevale Partners Fund LP

---

26   Please see website — http://www.madampresident2016.net/ and also the websites given in the tables.

Table 5.5: Executive Officers in Eaglevale Partners Fund LP			
Marc M. Mezvinsky	Executive Officer	c/o Eaglevale Partners GP LLC, 1330 Avenue of the Americas, 22nd Floor, New York, NY — 10019	Eaglevale Partners Fund LP
Source: https://www.sec.gov/Archives/edgar/data/1546867/000091957415002867/ xslFormDX01/primary_doc.xml			

The name of Kenneth Mark Mallon II (1330 Avenue of the Americas, 22nd Floor, New York, NY — 10019 and the following telephone number 212-621-4500) appears in both tables 5.3 and 5.4. In other words, while he is a director in the Cayman Islands incorporated Eaglevale Partners Offshore Fund Ltd., he is an executive officer in Eaglevale Partners Fund LP headquartered in the United States.

What is of significance here is that Hillary Clinton's son-in-law Marc M. Mezvinsky is also listed as "executive officer" under Eaglevale Partners Fund LP (Table 5.4). As revealed above, his fellow "executive officer" in Eaglevale Partners Fund LP, Kenneth Mark Mallon II, is also listed as a director in the Cayman Islands incorporated Eaglevale Partners Offshore Fund Ltd. This is an interesting discovery no doubt.

It must also be noted that the person who has signed all three SEC filings is Gary G. Tynes and he is listed as Chief Financial Officer (CFO)/Chief Operating Officer (COO) in the 2015 filing of Eaglevale Partners Fund LP (incorporated in U.S.A.), CFO in 2012 filing of Eaglevale Partners Fund LP (incorporated in U.S.A.) and CFO/Partner in 2012 filing of Eaglevale Partners Offshore Fund Ltd. (incorporated in Cayman Islands). Again, a very interesting finding.

Furthermore, Marc M. Mezvinsky and Gary Tynes — the signatory to all the Eaglevale funds companies' filings, including that of the offshore fund — have contributed individually to the Hillary Clinton campaign as shown below in addition to a partner, Michael Fox.

Table 5.6: Staff of Eaglevale Partners Who Contributed to Hillary Clinton						
Contributor Name	Employer	Occupation	City	State	Zip	Amount (in $)
Fox, Michael	Eaglevale Partners LP	Partner	New York	NY	10010	2,700
Mezvinsky, Marc	Eaglevale Partners	Partner	New York	NY	10019	2,700
Mezvinsky, Marc	Eaglevale Partners	Partner	New York	NY	10019	2,700
Tynes, Gary	Eaglevale Partners LP	CFO	Dix Hills	NY	11746	2,102
Tynes, Gary	Eaglevale Partners	CFO	New York	NY	10024	636
Total						10,838
Source: Data from Federal Election Commission, http://www.fec.gov/						

One other fact must be mentioned here. Marc Mezvinsky's colleagues in the Eaglevale Partners Fund LP, Bennett G. Grau and Kenneth Mark Mallon II, are both former Goldman Sachs employees, where Marc Mezvinsky had also worked in the past.

While Hillary Clinton speaks of the wrong behavior of corporate America, legally as well as otherwise, fleeing U.S.A. to avoid taxation by incorporating in foreign lands, how does she explain her son-in-law, Marc M. Mezvinsky, being a part of an entity that shares a related person, address, telephone number and signatory with an offshore fund incorporated in Cayman Islands with a hugely similar sounding name? Hillary Clinton certainly needs to provide answers on what is the relationship between her son-in-law Marc M. Mezvinsky and the Cayman Islands incorporated Eaglevale Partners Offshore Fund Ltd., which has an officer and a signatory in common with Eaglevale Partners Fund LP, which is incorporated in the United States and where Mezvinsky himself is an executive officer. Without a credible explanation, her statements about penalizing tax evaders, especially those who fly away (legally and/or otherwise) to tax havens (like Cayman Islands, Panama etc.) seems to amount to nothing more than mere rhetoric.

Chapter 6

Climate Change and Contributions By Energy, Fossil Fuel, and Fracking Companies

In February 2012, Hillary Clinton, as the U.S. Secretary of State, reportedly arrived in Sofia, the Bulgarian capital, to hold discussions with the country's top political leaders, including Prime Minister Boyko Borissov. The focus of their talks was apparently fracking given that the Bulgarian government had, in the previous year, signed a five-year, $68 million agreement that gave U.S. oil giant Chevron[1] access to several million acres in shale gas concessions. The Bulgarian people were apparently enraged by this and it is reported that just before Clinton arrived, large numbers of protesters (literally, thousands) took over the streets with placards that supposedly read "Stop fracking with our water" and "Chevron go home." The Bulgarian parliament had to acknowledge public sentiment and voted overwhelmingly in favor of a moratorium on fracking.[2]

---

[1]   As per available FEC data, Hillary Clinton has indeed received campaign contributions from Chevron staff totaling $22,647 in individual contributions. According to other unconfirmed sources, her bundlers have also reportedly received money from Chevron employees! Harris, Victoria, Chevron Corporation, contributed in 2015, $1,000 to the Hillary Victory Fund super PAC. Additionally, Chevron Corporation has donated between $500,001 and $1,000,000 to the Clinton Foundation.

[2]   Paraphrased from 'How Hillary Clinton's State Department Sold Fracking to the

Clinton had supposedly travelled to Sofia in a bid to urge Bulgarian officials to give fracking one more chance — she agreed to fly in the world's "best specialists" on fracking, so that the Bulgarian people could better understand the benefits. Nevertheless, local resistance only grew and grew. The subsequent month proved even more eventful. In adjoining Romania, large numbers of people gathered to protest yet another Chevron fracking project, even as Romania's parliament began weighing its own shale gas moratorium. Again, reportedly, Clinton is said to have intervened by sending Richard Morningstar[3] to backtrack on the fracking bans.[4]

Apparently, the State Department's lobbying effort at the highest levels culminated in late May 2012 — when Morningstar is said to have had meetings with high ranking Bulgarian and Romanian officials on the subject of fracking. Morningstar is also reported to have praised the technology in a Bulgarian national radio interview, specifically arguing that fracking could result in a huge price drop for natural gas. It is no surprise that the Romanian parliament backtracked on its proposed ban on fracking while Bulgaria undid its moratorium.[5]

Thus, as reported, Hillary Clinton had undoubtedly achieved her purpose of actively selling fracking[6] to the world despite its known negative impacts — drinking-water contamination, instigation of

---

World' — http://www.motherjones.com/environment/2014/09/hillary-clinton-fracking-shale-state-department-chevron

3   Clinton's special envoy for energy in Eurasia.

4   Paraphrased from 'How Hillary Clinton's State Department Sold Fracking to the World' — http://www.motherjones.com/environment/2014/09/hillary-clinton-fracking-shale-state-department-chevron

5   Paraphrased from 'How Hillary Clinton's State Department Sold Fracking to the World' — http://www.motherjones.com/environment/2014/09/hillary-clinton-fracking-shale-state-department-chevron

6   "Fracking refers to the procedure of creating fractures in rocks and rock formations by injecting fluid into cracks to force them further open. The larger fissures allow more oil and gas to flow out of the formation and into the wellbore, from where it can be extracted." — http://www.investopedia.com/terms/f/fracking.asp?layout=orig

earthquakes, and so on.[7] Given the above strategic context, this chapter attempts to take a closer look at fracking, the fossil fuel industry, and its contribution to Hillary Clinton's campaign.

Let us start with the case of Franklin Square Capital Partners (FSCP), which has not only contributed significantly to the Hillary Clinton campaign,[8] but also raised money[9] for her from big Wall Street firms. It should also be noted that the individual contributions[10] from senior management and other staff of FSCP to the Hillary Clinton campaign are in excess of $57,500.

What makes the FSCP example interesting is the fact that, one of its main funds, FS Energy and Power Fund, is said to be strongly and deeply invested in the fracking extraction of fossil fuels. In addition, let us not forget that fracking is an issue that will be hugely influenced by the 45th President of the United States, especially given the controversies associated with it. Moreover, therein lies a conflict of interest because FSCP, which is a significant investor in the fossil-fuel industry, especially fracking particularly concentrated in Pennsylvania, reportedly hosted a huge fundraiser for Hillary Clinton in Philadelphia at their headquarters.[11]

In fact, a closer look at the FS Energy & Power Fund, floated by FSCP, reveals that the fund is hugely invested in fossil fuel companies, offshore oil drilling, and fracking. As the prospectus of the FS Energy and Power Fund notes and I quote,

"Energy companies are subject to significant international, foreign, federal, state and local government regulation, including how facilities

---

7   'How Hillary Clinton's State Department Sold Fracking to the World' — http://www.motherjones.com/environment/2014/09/hillary-clinton-fracking-shale-state-department-chevron

8   www.fec.gov

9   'Hillary's coming! Because she loves Philadelphia...cash'— http://www.philly.com/philly/blogs/attytood/Yay-Hillary-loves-Philadelphiamoney.html

10   The maximum individual contributions is $2,700.

11   'Hillary's coming! Because she loves Philadelphia...cash'— http://www.philly.com/philly/blogs/attytood/Yay-Hillary-loves-Philadelphiamoney.html

are constructed, maintained and operated, environmental and safety controls, and the prices they may charge for the products and services they provide. Various governmental authorities have the power to enforce compliance with these regulations and the permits issued under them, and violators are subject to administrative, civil and criminal penalties, including civil fines, injunctions or both. For example, many state and federal environmental laws provide for civil penalties as well as regulatory remediation, thus adding to the potential liability an Energy company may face. More extensive laws, regulations or enforcement policies could be enacted in the future which would likely increase compliance costs and may adversely affect the financial performance of Energy companies in which we may invest. In particular, changes to laws and increased regulations or enforcement policies as a result of oil spills may adversely affect the financial performance of Energy companies. Additionally, changes to laws and increased regulation or restrictions on the use of hydraulic fracturing may adversely impact the ability of Energy companies to economically develop oil and natural gas resources and, in turn, reduce production for such commodities. Any such changes or increased regulations or policies may adversely affect the performance of Energy companies in which we may invest."[12]

The reader should note that the prospectus stresses the fact that "changes to laws and increased regulation or restrictions on the use of hydraulic fracturing may adversely impact" the fund's performance.[13]

So, surely, there is an inherent conflict of interest in receiving support from Franklin Square Capital Partners and I wonder how and why Hillary Clinton did that? Moreover, the issue becomes even more serious as the FS Energy and Power Fund of Franklin Square Capital Partners is reported to have invested in many of the heavy

---

12   http://mediacenter.merrillcorp.com/interface/viewer. asp?LocationID=6585560&ClientID=63&Purpose=HUMAN_ VIEW&Caller=RETRIEVE_FILE — see prospectus in pdf form, page 64.

13   http://mediacenter.merrillcorp.com/interface/viewer. asp?LocationID=6585560&ClientID=63&Purpose=HUMAN_ VIEW&Caller=RETRIEVE_FILE — see prospectus in pdf form, page 64

Pennsylvania frackers.[14]

In Table 6.1 below the inserts marked in bold and italics indicates a company that runs fracking wells in Pennsylvania. Eclipse Resources is a Pennsylvania-based company with fracking operations in Ohio. The other companies listed are industry service companies with business in Pennsylvania, including pipelines, trucking, chemicals, and power plants. Murray Energy runs coal-mining operations in Pennsylvania.

Table 6.1: Franklin Square Companies[15] in the Pennsylvania Fracking Industry	
✓ Ameriforge Group	✓ Exterran Partners
✓ *Atlas Resource Partners (HRC)*	✓ Gardner Denver
	✓ Global Partners
✓ Cactus Wellhead	✓ Gruden Acquisition
✓ Calpine (HRC)	✓ Kenan Advantage Group
✓ *Chief Oil & Gas*	✓ Moxie Liberty
✓ Cimarron Energy	✓ Murray Energy Corp
✓ Crestwood"	✓ PeroxyChem
✓ Dynegy	✓ *Vantage Energy*
✓ *Eclipse Resources*	✓ *Warren Resources*
✓ *EV Energy Partners*	✓ Zachry Holdings

Let us look at an example from the above group where Franklin Square Capital Partners has invested. Global Partners LP is one such company. It is unique because reportedly it has evolved from being a very small single truck, privately owned business in Dorchester to a large FORTUNE 500 company. While the story of Global Partners LP is interesting, it must be remembered that they are part of the distribution process for

---

14   'On Eve of Caucuses, Clinton Rakes in Fracking Cash'—http://www.huffingtonpost. com/entry/on-eve-of-caucuses-clinto_b_9117712.html?section=india

15   'On Eve of Caucuses, Clinton Rakes in Fracking Cash'—http://www.huffingtonpost. com/entry/on-eve-of-caucuses-clinto_b_9117712.html?section=india

oil that is produced through fracking. In addition, Richard B. Slifka, the company Chairman, is a contributor to Hillary Clinton's campaign and he has given the maximum $2,700 permitted to a candidate by an individual. Richard B. Slifka also contributed $33,400 to the Hillary Victory Fund super PAC in 2015.

Let us now turn our attention to the Avenue Capital Group run by "fracking-fund billionaire Marc Lasry," who is also a top Clinton advisor and fundraiser.[17]

A word about Lasry first. Lasry, the founder and chair of the Avenue Capital Group, in 2014, is said to have raised $1.3 billion specifically for a fund that supposedly bought debt of distressed energy companies, which later became worthless. Apparently, the Avenue Energy Opportunities Fund used $200 million that belonged to the Pennsylvania Public School Employees' Retirement System. Of course, Lasry has dismissed questions on the losses, arguing that he is sure that the frackers will do well again[18].

In fact, Marc Lasry, his wife Cathy, and son Alex are all top Hillary Clinton fundraisers called as "Hillblazers". As the Hillblazers site notes, Hillblazers "are individuals who have helped raise $100,000 or more in primary election contributions ... We are grateful for their support of Hillary for America."[19]

In fact, not only have Marc Lasry and the Avenue Capital Group raised money for the Hillary Clinton campaign, several of the Avenue Capital Group staff have also contributed individually to the Hillary Clinton campaign (as shown hereafter). Additionally, Marc Lasry's wife,

16   Compiled from 'On Eve of Caucuses, Clinton Rakes in Fracking Cash' — http://www.huffingtonpost.com/entry/on-eve-of-caucuses-clinto_b_9117712. html?section=india

17   https://www.hillaryclinton.com/about/hillblazers/; 'Fracking-Fund Billionaire Marc Lasry Is a Top Clinton Advisor and Fundraiser' — http://www.huffingtonpost. com/entry/frackingfund-billionaire-_b_9611512.html?section=india

18   'Fracking-Fund Billionaire Marc Lasry Is a Top Clinton Advisor and Fundraiser' — http://www.huffingtonpost.com/entry/frackingfund-billionaire-_b_9611512. html?section=india

19   https://www.hillaryclinton.com/about/hillblazers/

Cathy, and son, Alexander, have also contributed to the Hillary Clinton campaign.

Table 6.2: Individual Contribution of Avenue Capital Group Staff and Marc Lasry's Family to Hillary Clinton's Campaign					
Contributor Name	Employer	Occupation	City	Zip	Amount (in $)
Foley, Michael	Avenue Capital Group	Senior Portfolio Manager	New York	10024	2,700
Furst, Richard	Avenue Capital Group	CIO, Head of Europe Strategy	Westfield	N/A	2,700
Gardner, Sonia	Avenue Capital Group	Senior Managing Partner	New York	10024	2,700
Gellert, Edward	Avenue Capital Group	Investment Professional	Harrison	10528	2,700
Lasry, Marc	Avenue Capital Group	CEO	New York	10021	2,700
Steinberg, Ruth C.	Avenue Capital	Attorney	Scarsdale	10583	2,700
Wolfman, Alexander	Avenue Capital Group	Investment Management	New York	10038	2,700
Wolfman, Alexander	Avenue Capital Group	Investment Management	New York	10038	2,700
Kimble, Matthew	Avenue Capital	Finance	White Plains	10604	1,350
Lasry, Cathy	Home Maker	Home Maker	New York	10021	2,700
Lasry, Alexander	Milwaukee Bucks	Vice-President	New York	10021	2,700

Table 6.2: Individual Contribution of Avenue Capital Group Staff and Marc Lasry's Family to Hillary Clinton's Campaign					
Contributor Name	Employer	Occupation	City	Zip	Amount (in $)
Total					28,350
Source: Data from Federal Election Commission, http://www.fec.gov/					

In addition, Marc and Cathy Lasry have given $33,400 each to the super PAC, Hillary Victory Fund as shown in Table 6.3 below.

Table 6.3: Marc Lasry, Contribution to Super PAC						
Contributor Name	Employer	Occupation	City	State	Zip	Amount (in $)
Hillary Victory Fund						
Lasry, Marc	Avenue Capital Group	Chief Executive Officer	New York	NY	10021	33400
Lasry, Cathy	N/A	Home Maker	New York	NY	10021	33400
Total						66,800
Source: Data from Federal Election Commission, http://www.fec.gov/						

It must also be noted that the Avenue Capital Management II, L.P. has also donated $50,000 to $100,000 to the Clinton Foundation while Marc Lasry has himself donated between $100,001 to $250,000 to the Clinton Foundation.

While several examples have been shared in this section, the cases of Marc Lasry (Avenue Capital Group) and Franklin Square Capital Partners standout because they are both, not only ardent supporters of Hillary Clinton helping funnel significant contributions to her campaign, but are also heavily invested in the energy, fossil fuel, and fracking industries. Moreover, the fortunes of their companies and themselves would, in many ways, depend on how well these industries do, which, in turn, will also depend on the regulatory environment in the future.

Therefore, there is no doubt that, as the 45th President of the United

States, if and when she actually does assume that office, Hillary Clinton will have to decide on a range of urgent climate change and environment related issues that could put these very industries at huge risk. The question is, will she do that? The positive answer becomes even more doubtful considering the fact that:

(a) she has close ties to these industries; and

(b) two of her strongest Wall Street backers[20] have deep-rooted ties to these industries and most importantly, their fortunes depend on these industries.

A critical question indeed, but one that only time will answer.

In fact, the key question here is, in the event of Hillary Clinton becoming the 45th President of the United States, will she look to support her campaign financers or save mother Earth? Without a doubt, looking at Hillary Clinton's past record as Secretary of State when her state department reportedly sold fracking to the world,[21] the question does seem an extremely pertinent and legitimate one.

---

20 It has also been reported that "In 2011, Marc Lasry and Goldman Sachs CEO Lloyd Blankfein invested in Eaglevale Partners, the hedge fund set up by Marc Mezvinsky, Chelsea Clinton's husband. Lasry invested $1 million. The fund 'underperformed'." Hillary Clinton thus has another linkage that reinforces the inherent conflicts of interest that she has with the Avenue Capital Group and Marc Lasry — 'Fracking-Fund Billionaire Marc Lasry Is a Top Clinton Advisor and Fundraiser' — http://www.huffingtonpost.com/entry/frackingfund-billionaire-_b_9611512.html?section=india

21 'How Hillary Clinton's State Department Sold Fracking to the World' — http://www.motherjones.com/environment/2014/09/hillary-clinton-fracking-shale-state-department-chevron

Chapter 7

The Foreign Corrupt Practices Act, Campaign Contributions and Related Issues

Pat Stryker and her brother, Jon Stryker are two interesting names on the list of contributors to the Hillary Clinton campaign — both are the grandchildren of the famous Homer Stryker, surgeon and founder of Stryker Corporation, a medical technology company.

According to *Forbes*, Patricia Stryker, is an American businesswoman whose estimated net worth is around $1.6 billion (March 2013) and much of it is said to have come from the Stryker Corporation mentioned above. Pat Stryker, who was born in Michigan, reportedly now lives in Fort Collins, Colorado. She is also the owner of Bohemian Companies which is a diversified group engaged in venture capital, real estate, and other industries. She has floated the Bohemian Foundation, which works with youth and has community programs.[1]

Pat Stryker has contributed significantly to the Hillary Clinton campaign as noted hereafter:

---

1   Paraphrased from http://www.forbes.com/profile/pat-stryker/, 'Pat Stryker Net Worth' — http://www.therichest.com/celebnetworth/celebrity-business/women/pat-stryker-net-worth/ and 'The World's Billionaires' — http://www.forbes.com/profile/pat-stryker/

| Table 7.1: Pat Stryker's Contribution to PACs Supporting Hillary Clinton |||||||
Contributor Name	Employer	Occupation	City	State	Zip	Amount (in $)
Priorities USA Action						
Stryker, Pat	Bohemian	Chairman	Fort Collins	CO	80524	5,00,000
Stryker, Pat	Bohemian	Chairman	Fort Collins	CO	80524	5,00,000
Stryker, Pat	Bohemian	Chairman	Fort Collins	CO	80524	5,00,000
Correct The Record						
Stryker, Pat A.	Self Employed	Philanthropist	Fort Collins	CO	80524	250,000
Stryker, Pat A.	Self Employed	Philanthropist	Fort Collins	CO	80524	250,000
Hillary Victory Fund						
Stryker, Patricia A.	Self Employed	Philanthropist	Fort Collins	CO	80524	150,000
Stryker, Patricia A.	Self Employed	Philanthropist	Fort Collins	CO	80524	150,000
Stryker, Patricia A.	N/A	Philanthropist	Fort Collins	CO	80524	150,000
Stryker, Patricia A.	N/A	Philanthropist	Fort Collins	CO	80524	150,000
Stryker, Patricia A.	Self Employed	Philanthropist	Fort Collins	CO	80524	33,400
Total						**2,633,400**
Source: Data from Federal Election Commission, http://www.fec.gov/ (As of April 1, 2016)						

Likewise, Jon Stryker[2] self-employed, architect, said to be worth $2.1 billion, has given $1 million to Priorities USA Action, the PAC supporting Hillary Clinton. He has also made other contributions as outlined in Table 7.2 below.

---

2   Jon L. Stryker & Slobodan Randjelovic have also donated between $250,001 and $500,000 to the Clinton Foundation. See Clinton Foundation donor page.

Table 7.2: Jon Stryker's Contribution to Super PACs Supporting Hillary Clinton						
Contributor Name	Employer	Occupation	City	State	Zip	Amount (in $)
Correct The Record						
Stryker, Jon	Self Employed	Architect	Kalamazoo	MI	49005	100,000
Hillary Victory Fund						
Stryker, Jon	Self Employed	Architect	New York	NY	10014	153,500
Stryker, Jon	Self Employed	Architect	New York	NY	10014	75,000
Priorities USA Action						
Stryker, Jon L.	Self Employed	Architect	Kalamazoo	MI	49007	1,000,000
Total						1,328,500
Source: Data from Federal Election Commission, http://www.fec.gov/ (As of April 1, 2016)						

Both Pat and Jon Stryker have also directly contributed to Hillary Clinton, the maximum $2,700 allowed per person per candidate.

While Pat and Jon Stryker can be counted among Hillary Clinton's strongest supporters, Stryker Corporation, which they partly own[3] and derive their wealth from, is not without controversy.

Indeed, in 2013, the SEC charged Stryker Corporation under the Foreign Corrupt Practices Act (FCPA) for violations including bribery, which is a very serious matter.

In this context, it must be noted that the United States Foreign Corrupt Practices Act (FCPA) of 1977 is supposedly the most commonly and widely used anti-corruption law in the United States. Indeed, the

---

3   "Dr. Homer Stryker's three grandchildren — Jon, Pat, and Rhonda Stryker — are said to partly own the Stryker Corporation. Excluding other stock holdings, it has also been reported that the siblings have control over a trust that owns about 25% of the $6 billion company." See 'Medical supplier Stryker probed' — http://www.washingtontimes.com/news/2008/mar/11/medical-supplier-stryker-probed/?page=all

FCPA was the first law that introduced aspects such as corporate liability and third party responsibility along with extraterritoriality for corrupt practices and offences.

What this in effect means is that as per the FCPA, companies as well as individuals can be held accountable — both in a criminal and civil sense — for corrupt practices and offences that have been even committed outside of the United States.

It must be noted that the FCPA's anti-bribery provisions exclusively apply to three types of entities (including persons): a) issuers; b) domestic companies and c) certain persons and entities that fall under territorial jurisdiction.

These anti-bribery provisions specifically bar:

(a) US persons and companies including domestic concerns,

(b) companies that are organized as per US laws,

(c) companies whose principal place of business lies in the US,

(d) companies that are listed on stock exchanges within the US,

(e) companies that are mandated to file regular reports with the SEC (issuers), and

(f) certain types of foreign persons and businesses (when they are in the territory of the US — territorial jurisdiction) from making bribery (i.e., corrupt payments) to foreign stakeholders and officials to obtain, retain and/or expand business[4].

That said, getting back to Stryker Corporation, the SEC noted in a release[5] that:

"The Securities and Exchange Commission today charged a Michigan-based medical technology company with violating the Foreign Corrupt

---

4   The above discussion is paraphrased from 'US Foreign Corrupt Practices Act (FCPA)' — http://www.business-anti-corruption.com/resources/compliance-quick-guides/united-states.aspx

5   'SEC Charges Stryker Corporation with FCPA Violations' — https://www.sec.gov/News/PressRelease/Detail/PressRelease/1370540044262

Practices Act (FCPA) when subsidiaries in five different countries bribed doctors, health care professionals, and other government-employed officials in order to obtain or retain business.

An SEC investigation found that Stryker Corporation's subsidiaries in Argentina, Greece, Mexico, Poland, and Romania made illicit payments totaling approximately $2.2 million that were incorrectly described as legitimate expenses in the company's books and records. Descriptions varied from a charitable donation to consulting and service contracts, travel expenses, and commissions. Stryker made approximately $7.5 million in illicit profits as a result of the improper payments.

Stryker has agreed to pay more than $13.2 million to settle the SEC's charges. 'Stryker's misconduct involved hundreds of improper payments over a number of years during which the company's internal controls were fatally flawed,' said Andrew M. Calamari, director of the SEC's New York Regional Office. 'Companies that allow corruption to occur by failing to implement robust compliance programs will not be allowed to profit from their misconduct.'"

I wonder what the Hillary Clinton campaign was doing in accepting contributions from people who have inherited much of their wealth and also own a substantial portion of a **United States corporation that has been caught paying large and multiple bribes in many foreign countries to further its business and thereby make profits** — if this does represent the nexus between corruption and politics, I wonder what is? Unfortunately, Hillary Clinton's association with individuals and entities charged with FCPA violations does not end here.

Take the case of GE (General Electric), which is said to have donated from $1,000,001 to $5,000,000 to the Clinton Foundation. In addition, GE also invited Hillary Clinton for a speech on June 1, 2014 and reportedly paid her $225,000 for the appearance. As a corporation, GE was led by John Francis "Jack" Welch Junior, the legendary CEO (between 1981 and 2001) who catapulted GE to its current standing and fame. GE,[6] which is a classic American multinational conglomerate corporation, is incorporated in New York and headquartered in Fairfield, Connecticut. In 2011, GE figured in the Fortune 500 list as the 6th-largest firm in the U.S. by gross revenue, and the 14th most profitable.

While all of this reads well with regard to GE, it is also a fact that the SEC charged General Electric and two of its subsidiaries with FCPA violations as per a release dated 27 July 2010. Specifically,

> "The Securities and Exchange Commission charged the General Electric Company with violations of the Foreign Corrupt Practices Act (FCPA) for its involvement in a $3.6 million kickback scheme with Iraqi government agencies to win contracts to supply medical equipment and water purification equipment."[7]

According to the SEC release,

> "two other subsidiaries of public companies that have since been acquired by GE — made illegal kickback payments in the form of cash, computer equipment, medical supplies, and services to the Iraqi Health Ministry or the Iraqi Oil Ministry in order to obtain valuable contracts under the U.N. Oil for Food Program.

> GE agreed to pay $23.4 million to settle the SEC's charges against the company as well as the two subsidiaries for which GE assumed liability upon acquiring: Ionics Inc. and Amersham plc. The SEC charged GE, Ionics and Amersham with violating the books and records and internal controls provisions of the FCPA.

> 'Bribes and kickbacks are bad business, period,' said Robert Khuzami,

---

6   As of 2015, the company operates in the following sectors: Appliances, Power and Water, Oil and Gas, Energy Management, Aviation, Healthcare, Transportation, and Capital, which cater to the needs of Home Appliances, Financial Services, Medical Devices, Life Sciences, Pharmaceutical, Automotive, Software Development and Engineering Industries.

7   'SEC Charges General Electric and Two Subsidiaries with FCPA Violations' — https://www.sec.gov/news/press/2010/2010-133.htm

Director of the SEC's Division of Enforcement. 'This case affirms that law enforcement is active across the globe — offshore does not mean off-limits.'

Cheryl J. Scarboro, Chief of the SEC's Foreign Corrupt Practices Act Unit, added, 'GE failed to maintain adequate internal controls to detect and prevent these illicit payments by its two subsidiaries to win Oil for Food contracts, and it failed to properly record the true nature of the payments in its accounting records. Furthermore, corporate acquisitions do not provide GE immunity from FCPA enforcement of the other two subsidiaries involved.'[8]"

And that's not all. As per a release dated August 4, 2009,[9] the SEC also charged General Electric with accounting fraud and GE agreed to pay $50 million to settle the charges.

"'GE bent the accounting rules beyond the breaking point,' said Robert Khuzami, Director of the SEC's Division of Enforcement. 'Overly aggressive accounting can distort a company's true financial condition and mislead investors.'

David P. Bergers, Director of the SEC's Boston Regional Office, added, 'Every accounting decision at a company should be driven by a desire to get it right, not to achieve a particular business objective. GE misapplied the accounting rules to cast its financial results in a better light.'

The four accounting violations were:

- Beginning in January 2003, an improper application of the accounting standards to GE's commercial paper funding program to avoid unfavorable disclosures and an estimated approximately $200 million pre-tax charge to earnings.

---

8   'SEC Charges General Electric and Two Subsidiaries with FCPA Violations' — https://www.sec.gov/news/press/2010/2010-133.htm

9   'SEC Charges General Electric With Accounting Fraud' — http://www.sec.gov/news/press/2009/2009-178.htm

- A 2003 failure to correct a misapplication of financial accounting standards to certain GE interest-rate swaps.

- In 2002 and 2003, reported end-of-year sales of locomotives that had not yet occurred in order to accelerate more than $370 million in revenue.

- In 2002, an improper change to GE's accounting for sales of commercial aircraft engines' spare parts that increased GE's 2002 net earnings by $585 million."[10]

In effect, GE was charged not only under the FCPA, but also for huge accounting fraud.

Yet another example is Qualcomm Incorporated, which is a Delaware corporation headquartered in San Diego, California. It is involved in the design and sale of wireless telecommunication products.

Qualcomm invited Hillary Clinton to make a speech that reportedly was delivered in October 2014 and she was paid a fee for $335,000, a huge sum by any standards. Qualcomm has also donated $100,001 to $250,000 to the Clinton Foundation. Here, it must be mentioned that Qualcomm, way back in the mid-1990s were doing some fantastic and pioneering work related to wireless local loop (WLL). While one really appreciates the value created by Qualcomm to the wireless local loop industry, way back in 1990s, it is again unfortunate to note that Qualcomm is yet another corporation that violated the FCPA.

Specifically, as per the Securities and Exchange Commission release dated March 1, 2016,

> "Qualcomm Incorporated agreed to pay $7.5 million to settle charges that it violated the Foreign Corrupt Practices Act (FCPA) by hiring relatives of Chinese government officials deciding whether to select the

---

10   'SEC Charges General Electric With Accounting Fraud' — http://www.sec.gov/news/press/2009/2009-178.htm

company's mobile technology products amid increasing competition in the international telecommunications market."[11]

The release said that the "SEC investigation found that Qualcomm also provided gifts, travel, and entertainment to try to influence officials at government-owned telecom companies in China."[12] It also stated that "Qualcomm misrepresented in its books and records that the things of value provided to foreign officials were legitimate business expenses."[13]

According to Michele Wein Layne, Director of the SEC's Los Angeles Regional Office, "For more than a decade, Qualcomm went to extraordinary lengths to gain a business advantage with foreign officials deciding between Qualcomm's technology and its competitors."[14]

The above is a very serious statement indeed and given that it occurred for more than a decade, it says a lot about Qualcomm as a company. In fact, the SEC findings, which are very revealing in this regard, note:

"Several violations of the anti-bribery, books and records, and internal controls provisions of the Foreign Corrupt Practices Act (FCPA) by Qualcomm

1. From 2002 through 2012, Qualcomm provided things of value to foreign officials — including high-ranking employees of state owned enterprises (SOEs) and government ministers — to try to influence these decision makers to favor and/or promote Qualcomm-developed technology in an evolving international telecommunications market, thereby providing Qualcomm with a business advantage.

---

11 'SEC: Qualcomm Hired Relatives of Chinese Officials to Obtain Business' — https://www.sec.gov/news/pressrelease/2016-36.html
12 'SEC: Qualcomm Hired Relatives of Chinese Officials to Obtain Business' — https://www.sec.gov/news/pressrelease/2016-36.html
13 'SEC: Qualcomm Hired Relatives of Chinese Officials to Obtain Business' — https://www.sec.gov/news/pressrelease/2016-36.html
14 'SEC: Qualcomm Hired Relatives of Chinese Officials to Obtain Business' — https://www.sec.gov/news/pressrelease/2016-36.html

2. Qualcomm's extensive international operations accounted for more than 90% of the company's revenue. Even so, Qualcomm's internal controls were insufficient to prevent or detect improper payments to foreign officials. In several areas of its business operations, including hiring, hospitality planning, and business development, Qualcomm lacked an adequate oversight process to determine whether things of value that it provided to foreign officials were made with the intent to induce those officials to provide a business benefit to Qualcomm.

3. Qualcomm's insufficient internal controls resulted in books and records violations. Qualcomm misrepresented in its books and records that things of value provided to foreign officials were legitimate business expenses.

4. In sum, Qualcomm, through its agents and subsidiaries, violated Section 30A of the Exchange Act by providing things of value to foreign officials to obtain and retain business in China. Qualcomm also violated Section 13(b)(2)(B) of the Exchange Act by failing to devise and maintain internal accounting controls sufficient to provide reasonable assurance of preventing or detecting the authorization or payment of improper payments. Qualcomm violated Section 13(b)(2)(A) of the Exchange Act by having recorded improper payments to foreign officials in its books and records in a manner that failed to accurately and fairly reflect the provision of things of value to foreign officials."[15]

The Hillary Clinton campaign definitely stands compromised by accepting contributions from people who own and have derived substantial wealth from these corporations that have violated the FCPA and have been caught paying large and multiple bribes in many foreign countries to further their businesses and thereby make profits! How can the campaign accept huge contributions from people connected to corporations (like Stryker Corporation) that have violated the FCPA?

---

15   https://www.sec.gov/litigation/admin/2016/34-77261.pdf

What can she possibly be speaking at corporations (like Qualcomm and GE) that have violated the FCPA for several years? How will she explain to the American public the rationale behind her making frequent paid[16] speeches to large corporations that regularly break the law, offer bribes, and engage in corporate crime? I really have no answers!

---

16   Almost all the 84 entities including corporations paid hefty fees to Hillary Clinton for her speeches!

Chapter 8

Wall Street Regulation, Revolving Door, Conflicts of Interest, and the Hillary Clinton Campaign

While on the topic of corporate crime and regulation, it needs to be emphasized that there is growing concern over the lack of appropriate regulation and supervision of Wall Street — especially, the vulnerability of small investors is a critical issue here. In fact, this is one of the key issues of the 2016 U.S. presidential election.

First, one of the primary reasons for the existing weak regulatory system is the near seamless shift of key people from Wall Street to regulatory and supervisory bodies through the "reverse revolving door" phenomenon. Top executives of Wall Street firms (and representatives of special interest groups including lobbyists) have been known to take up positions in the government or the regulatory set up. Henry Paulson, the Treasury Secretary of the United States during the years 2006–2009, came to the Treasury after nearly 32 years at Goldman Sachs. (See Table 8.1 below for other examples.) There are others who have built up extremely close working relationships with the regulators and supervisors, in particular those who oversee or regulate Wall Street.

Table 8.1: Henry Paulson[1]			
Name	**Designation**	**Period**	**Remarks**
Henry Paulson	United States Secretary of the Treasury	July 10, 2006– January 20, 2009	Chairman and Chief Executive Officer, Goldman Sachs 1974 - 2006. His compensation package reportedly was $37 million in 2005. His net worth has been estimated at over $700 million.

Robert Rubin is yet another of those who made the switch from Wall Street to government. It must be recalled here that much of the foundations for the de-regulation that took place during former President Bill Clinton's second term, was laid during Rubin's tenure. It is of course common knowledge what this de-regulation ultimately did in terms of repealing the Glass-Steagall Act, thereby resulting in the 2008 financial crisis.[2]

Table 8.2: Robert Rubin[3]			
Name	**Designation**	**Period**	**Remarks**
Robert Rubin	United States Secretary of the Treasury	January 11, 1995– July 2, 1999	Before his government service, Rubin spent 26 years at Goldman Sachs, eventually serving as a member of the board and co-chairman from 1990 to 1992.

---

1   Wikipedia — https://en.wikipedia.org/wiki/Henry_Paulson
2   This is an opinion expressed in the final report of the Financial Crisis Inquiry Commission (FCIC) — http://fcic-static.law.stanford.edu/cdn_media/fcic-reports/fcic_final_report_full.pdf
3   Wikipedia — https://en.wikipedia.org/wiki/Robert_Rubin

Table 8.2: Robert Rubin[3]			
Name	Designation	Period	Remarks
			As Treasury Secretary during 1995–99, Rubin oversaw the loosening of financial industry underwriting guidelines, which had been intact since the 1930s. From November to December 2007, he served temporarily as chairman of Citigroup and resigned from the company on January 9, 2009. He received more than $126 million in cash and stock during his tenure at Citigroup, up through and including Citigroup's bailout by the U.S. Treasury. Rubin received over $17 million in compensation from Citigroup and a further $33 million in stock options as of 2008.

Often called the reverse revolving door phenomenon, these people have established a very strong pro-financial sector/Wall Street bias in policy formulation and regulatory enforcement by regulators and supervisors that oversee their (former) industry, former employers and/or related institutions. This oftentimes results in de-regulation to the detriment of the end user.

Second, is the shift of key people from government institutions to Wall Street through the normal revolving door phenomenon. There are the cases where important functionaries from regulatory and supervisory bodies and governments have moved (either through a permanent or temporary relationship) to lucrative private-sector positions at Wall Street firms. Two examples are relevant here:

1. Paid speeches delivered by former government position holders — all the Wall Street speeches by Hillary and Bill Clinton would come under this category; and

2. The other example is where people like Lawrence Summers, Timothy Geithner, or Robert Rubin for that matter, who, after having served as Treasury Secretary, went on to work with Wall Street firms like D. E. Shaw, Warburg Pincus,[4] and Citigroup respectively.

Table 8.3: Lawrence Summers and Timothy Geithner[5]			
Name	**Designation**	**Period**	**Remarks**
Lawrence Summers	United States Secretary of the Treasury	July 2, 1999– January 20, 2001	Post Government, Summers has worked as an advisor to hedge fund D. E. Shaw & Co, Citigroup and the NASDAQ OMX Group while resuming his role as a tenured, Harvard professor. In June 2011, Summers joined the board of directors of Square, a company developing an electronic payment service, and became a special adviser at venture capital firm Andreessen Horowitz.
Timothy Geithner	United States Secretary of the Treasury	January 26, 2009– January 25, 2013	American economic policy maker and central banker. He was previously the president of the Federal Reserve Bank of New York from 2003 to 2009. He now serves as president of Warburg Pincus, a Wall Street private equity firm.

Typically, such people use their regulatory and government experience and long-standing connections to benefit their new employer or industry directly as well as indirectly (e.g. through lobbying for a supportive regulatory policy environment,[6] in public procurement and so on). This

---

4   A Wall Street private equity firm.
5   Wikipedia — https://en.wikipedia.org/wiki/Lawrence_Summers and https://en.wikipedia.org/wiki/Timothy_Geithner
6   The case of the Dodd Frank legislation is one example here and the lobbying

has not only led to a lax regulatory environment and poor supervision by their former colleagues (with regard to Wall Street) but has also resulted in the drafting and framing of policies hugely supportive to Wall Street, and a de-regulated environment, especially at the expense of end user client protection and well being. Again, as noted before, we all know that the 2008 financial crisis resulted from a massive de-regulation due to lobbying, campaign contribution (both individual as well as to PACs), and other similar efforts.[7]

Third, there have also been situations where former decision makers (including policy makers and executive decision makers) have become paid advocates and use their knowledge of and connections with governmental agencies, regulators, and supervisors to advance the interests of Wall Street companies. This again would be part of Wall Street lobbying which has been discussed above.

Given the above context of the reverse and normal revolving door phenomenon, it is important to discuss the very "special" case study of BlackRock, particularly in the context of the Hillary Clinton campaign. BlackRock, an asset management company, is headed by Larry Fink, the man who has often been touted as a potential candidate for treasury secretary[8] in a Hillary Clinton administration — if and when it takes shape — for three key reasons:

(a) Fink's staff members have been at the forefront raising money for the Clinton campaign in a big way. For example, BlackRock's senior Managing Director Matthew Mallow is a "Hillblazer" who has helped raise $100,000 or more in donations. Clinton

---

database is replete with examples of lobbying by various Wall Street firms with former government staff!

7   This is an opinion expressed in the final report of the Financial Crisis Inquiry Commission (FCIC) — http://fcic-static.law.stanford.edu/cdn_media/fcic-reports/fcic_final_report_full.pdf

8   'Larry Fink and His BlackRock Team Poised to Take Over Hillary Clinton's Treasury Department' — https://theintercept.com/2016/03/02/larry-fink-and-his-blackrock-team-poised-to-take-over-hillary-clintons-treasury-department/

even reportedly held a fundraiser[9] at Mallow's New York City home.

(b) Individual staff members of BlackRock have contributed as much as $57,257 to the Hillary Clinton campaign.

(c) Hillary Clinton echoes ideas very similar[10] to that of Larry Fink as far as prescriptions go for Wall Street and the larger United States economy. She is said to rely on Fink's ideas, at least with regard to Wall Street and its regulation.

There are serious issues including conflicts of interest in the reality of Larry Fink as Treasury Secretary. The consequences of such a reverse revolving door appointment could well be disastrous for the United States of America and the world economy. One of major reasons for the 2008 financial crisis is the fact that Wall Street lobbied[11] so hard to have the industry de-regulated (including the shattering of the Glass-Steagall Act). In light of this, the idea of having Wall Street industry

9   'Hillary Clinton Doing Finance Industry Fundraiser Just Before Iowa' — https://theintercept.com/2016/01/26/hillary-clinton-doing-back-to-back-finance-industry-fundraisers-just-before-iowa/

10   'BlackRock's Larry Fink May Be Stepping Up his Play for Treasury Secretary' — http://fortune.com/2016/02/04/blackrock-larry-fink-treasury-secretary/ (In a recent letter to CEOs, the BlackRock CEO took a page out of Hillary Clinton's playbook.); 'Wall Street CEO sounds a lot like Hillary Clinton' —http://money.cnn.com/2016/02/03/investing/hillary-clinton-larry-fink-blackrock/

11   "Changes in the regulatory system occurred in many instances as financial markets evolved. However, as the report will show, the financial industry itself played a key role in weakening regulatory constraints on institutions, markets, and products. It did not surprise the Commission that an industry of such wealth and power would exert pressure on policy makers and regulators. From 1999 to 2008, the financial sector expended $2.7 billion in reported federal lobbying expenses; individuals and political action committees in the sector made more than $1 billion in campaign contributions. What troubled us was the extent to which the nation was deprived of the necessary strength and independence of the oversight necessary to safeguard financial stability." — 'Final Report Of The National Commission On The Causes Of The Financial And Economic Crisis In The United States', Submitted by The Financial Crisis Inquiry Commission, Pursuant to Public Law 111-21, January 2011, Page number 18

insiders[12] make policy does not appear to be a sound one.

The potential Treasury Secretary appointment aside, there are several other issues related to Larry Fink and BlackRock that make it extremely inappropriate for Hillary Clinton to even accept contributions from BlackRock/Larry Fink and/or use BlackRock staff as bundlers for collecting campaign contributions.

First, BlackRock has a huge global presence — while it reportedly manages $3.3 trillion worth of assets directly, it is said to indirectly advise in the management of $9 trillion worth assets[13]. Thus, BlackRock is also a firm that has become too big to fail — an issue central to the U.S. 2016 presidential elections with regard to Wall Street firms[14]. Enlisting the support of firms like BlackRock in any manner is therefore most inappropriate, as BlackRock itself is too large an institution and one that poses significant systemic risk, not just for the United States economy but the inter-connected global economy as well.

Second, given the trillions that flow through BlackRock, the question that needs asking is whether it is indeed appropriate to have the "global market influenced by one firm and the perspective of one

---

12   We know what happened when Paulson of Goldman Sachs fame was in charge of the Treasury during 2006–2009 — the crisis burgeoned and exploded as there were huge conflicts of interest.

13   'Larry Fink's $12 Trillion Shadow' — http://www.vanityfair.com/news/2010/04/fink-201004. Other estimates put the total of managed + advised assets at 15 trillion. See 'BlackRock executive Charles Hallac, dies at 50', — http://www.reuters.com/article/us-blackrock-copresident-idUSKCN0R92J320150909#4TSA SgekEB6rCw3G.97

14   The too-big-to-fail issue concerns the size of the already large financial institutions. In this context, it should be noted that many of the financial institutions of 2016 are much larger than their counterparts of 2008 when the financial crisis occurred. In addition, several of them hold much riskier assets than in 2008. Therefore, the argument is that the large financial institutions of today represent a huge systemic risk to the economy and therefore have to be broken into institutions that are less risky and can be better managed. This is the essence of the too-big-to-fail argument which is dominating the discussion in the United States Presidential elections of 2016.

man — Larry Fink."[15] This is especially relevant when one consider(s) the fact that Fink and BlackRock committed several blunders in the past:[16]

(a) Fink and BlackRock were strong backers of the 'Lehman Brothers' management, even as the bank was crashing. It has been reported that BlackRock purchased a huge amount of Lehman stock (at $28/share), three months before Lehman went bust;

(b) BlackRock, is also said to have had close to $8 billion of collateralized-debt-obligation deals that defaulted in 2007 and 2008, thereby contributing to the 2008 financial crisis in the United States; and

(c) BlackRock's purchase of the well known Manhattan housing complex, Stuyvesant Town and Peter Cooper Village — a $5.4 billion transaction that went into default and resulted in investors who bought equity losing large amounts of money. Take the case of the $200 billion California Pension and Retirement System (Calpers), reportedly the largest pension fund in the United States, which lost close to $500 million.[17]

Third, most interestingly, Clinton's long-term aide Cheryl Mills, who is also embroiled in the private email/unsecure server controversy that is reportedly being investigated by the Federal Bureau of Investigation (FBI), is a member of the board of BlackRock as well as the Clinton Foundation. Again, it raises serious conflict of interest issues, given what happened in the 2008 financial crisis and BlackRock's own past.

Fourth, BlackRock is a very strange entity that manages a huge amount of global assets. To the best of my knowledge, BlackRock is

15   'Larry Fink's $12 Trillion Shadow' — http://www.vanityfair.com/news/2010/04/ fink-201004

16   'Larry Fink's $12 Trillion Shadow' — http://www.vanityfair.com/news/2010/04/ fink-201004

17   'Larry Fink's $12 Trillion Shadow' — http://www.vanityfair.com/news/2010/04/ fink-201004

neither a bank nor is it an insurance company. It is most certainly not a central bank. In addition, it cannot be categorized as a unit of the finance ministry. Last but not the least, while it is not a sovereign wealth fund, it reportedly advises as well as owns such institutions. The larger point to make here is that BlackRock is an asset management company that virtually has a free run, as it is unregulated and is most often a backroom boy. However, the key issue of relevance here is that there are very few companies, countries, and regions on this Earth that this huge asset manager does not handle or advise. Put differently, BlackRock, in just a short span of 27 years, has got around to managing several trillion dollars in assets, making it the single largest investor on the face of this planet.

In terms of wealth, it is said to manage more wealth than what Japan or Germany have in GDP. Indeed, only the United States, China, and India perhaps have a larger GDP than BlackRock has assets under management. Moreover, when one includes the assets that BlackRock advises along with those it manages, BlackRock has control of close to $15 trillion in assets[18] — only the United States and China have a higher GDP than this.[19]

In fact, BlackRock[20] is omnipresent as can be seen from the following table:

---

18   'BlackRock executive Charles Hallac, dies at 50' — http://www.reuters.com/article/us-blackrock-copresident-idUSKCN0R92J320150909#4TSASgekEB6rCw3G.97

19   The above two paragraph's are paraphrased from 'Exposing BlackRock: Who's Afraid of Lawrence Fink?' — http://www.counterpunch.org/2015/12/11/exposing-blackrock-whos-afraid-of-lawrence-fink/

20   In many ways, BlackRock is the largest financial institution in the world. It is reported to be a prominent shareholder in around 40% of all U.S. companies that are traded publicly. — See 'Exposing BlackRock: Who's Afraid of Lawrence Fink?' — http://www.counterpunch.org/2015/12/11/exposing-blackrock-whos-afraid-of-lawrence-fink/

Table 8.4: BlackRock's Shareholding in Banks and Corporations[21]	
Major U.S. Banks	JPMorgan Chase, Citigroup, Bank of America, Goldman Sachs, Morgan Stanley, and Wells Fargo.
American Corporations and Companies	Walmart, General Electric, General Motors, Ford, AT&T, Verizon, Google, Apple, Exxon Mobil, Chevron, Microsoft, Johnson & Johnson, Facebook, Berkshire Hathaway, Gilead Sciences, Pfizer, Procter & Gamble, Merck, Intel, Coca-Cola, Walt Disney Company, Home Depot, Philip Morris, VISA, McDonald's, Cisco Systems, PepsiCo, IBM, Oracle, Comcast, Lockheed Martin, MasterCard, Starbucks, Boeing and ConocoPhillips, along with several thousand smaller brands.

What is even more interesting is that, despite its humungous size and widespread influence, BlackRock is said to be unregulated. This is because, unlike banks, asset management firms neither invest nor manage their own money. Rather, they do this function for and on behalf of their diversified clientele who are often banks, corporations, insurance companies, pension funds, sovereign wealth funds, central banks, and foundations. That is why BlackRock is best referred to as a "hidden giant" that very few of us have knowledge about[22] — a Goliath that is so powerful that it could even wreck the United States and the global economy in a jiffy, when things actually go wrong.

It is indeed scary then that a firm with such huge conflicts of interest caused by its presence in virtually all major industries is contributing to

---

21 Compiled from, 'Exposing BlackRock: Who's Afraid of Lawrence Fink?' — http://www.counterpunch.org/2015/12/11/exposing-blackrock-whos-afraid-of-lawrence-fink/

22 'Exposing BlackRock: Who's Afraid of Lawrence Fink?' —http://www.counterpunch.org/2015/12/11/exposing-blackrock-whos-afraid-of-lawrence-fink/

and raising money for the Hillary Clinton campaign and its founder is being talked of as the likely Treasury Secretary in a future Hillary Clinton administration.

Larry Fink is surely not doing all of this for nothing as there are no free lunches . . . ever! This is surely something that needs to be remembered in this context!

Fifth, there is much of this revolving door phenomenon going on at BlackRock itself with key personnel[23] moving to and from government/public policy positions and so on. A further case of huge conflicts of interest. Take for example the following:

Table 8.5: From Government to BlackRock — People and Positions[24]		
Name	**Former Position**	**Position at BlackRock**
Christopher Meade	Former general counsel at the Treasury Department. She spent 2010–2015 at Treasury, with three years as general counsel.	Serves in a similar capacity at BlackRock.
Katheryn Rosen	Senior policy adviser to Barney Frank (reportedly an adviser to the Clinton campaign) on the House Financial Services Committee, helping to write Dodd-Frank. She became deputy assistant secretary at Treasury in February 2011 working to build the Financial Stability Oversight Council, the Treasury-led super-regulator monitoring systemic risk.	Is managing director at BlackRock. Prior to government work, Rosen spent 14 years as a managing director with JPMorgan Chase.

---

23   http://www.blackrock.com/corporate/en-in/investor-relations/company-overview-and-governance/board-of-directors

24   Compiled from, 'Larry Fink and His BlackRock Team Poised to Take Over Hillary Clinton's Treasury Department' — https://theintercept.com/2016/03/02/larry-fink-and-his-blackrock-team-poised-to-take-over-hillary-clintons-treasury-department/

Table 8.5: From Government to BlackRock — People and Positions[24]		
Name	Former Position	Position at BlackRock
Kendrick Wilson	Advised Treasury while it managed the financial crisis and its fallout in 2008 and 2009. Advised the merger of Bank of America and failed subprime lender countrywide while at Treasury.	Is a vice chairman at BlackRock since 2010.
Michael Pyle	Was a senior adviser to Lael Brainard when she served as undersecretary to the Treasury for international affairs. Worked at the White House for the National Economic Council and the Office of Management and Budget. Said to be an economic policy adviser to the Clinton campaign.	He worked as a director at BlackRock until at least October 2015.
Cheryl Mills	Clinton's chief of staff at the State Department. Previously, Mills was deputy White House counsel in the Bill Clinton administration.	Cheryl Mills is presently on the board of directors of the Clinton Foundation[25] as well as BlackRock. She is Clinton's closest and most trusted (former) aide.

Sixth, an added reason is BlackRock's nature of business and its role in shaping regulation, post 2008 crisis. The kind of work that BlackRock does, as an asset manager, poses a systemic risk to the financial system. Yet, BlackRock and Larry Fink do not accept the view that

---

25   https://www.clintonfoundation.org/about/board-directors and http://www.blackrock.
      com/corporate/en-in/investor-relations/company-overview-and-governance/board-
      of-directors

asset managers are systemically important financial institutions as this could lead to capital requirements being made larger. Further, BlackRock, Fink, and Hillary Clinton are united in their stand against the reinstatement of the Glass-Steagall Act. Incidentally, the man who was responsible for the shattering of The Glass-Steagall Act, Sanford Weill[26] himself wants it brought back . . . today! Further, Fink and Hillary Clinton have very, very similar views on Wall Street and that is surely not a coincidence.

One final point — as stated in the very beginning of this chapter, Clinton's financial reform strategy is reportedly silent with regard to regulating (asset management) firms like BlackRock as a systemically important financial institution.[27] If that is not a conflict of interest, I wonder what is.

Finally, see what the SEC says in its order[28] about BlackRock and its ability to manage conflict of interest — an issue of great concern in the 2016 U.S. presidential election.

"This matter concerns investment adviser BlackRock's[29] failure to disclose a conflict of interest involving the outside business activity of one of its portfolio managers. Daniel J. Rice, III was a well-known, long-standing top-performing energy sector portfolio manager.

---

26   'Weill Puts Glass-Steagall Back on Washington's Agenda' — http://www. americanbanker.com/issues/177_143/sandy-weill-puts-glass-steagall-back-onwashingtons-agenda-1051271-1.html; 'Former Citigroup CEO: Big banks don't work' —http://money.cnn.com/2015/11/12/investing/citigroup-john-reed-glass-steagall/

27   'Larry Fink and His BlackRock Team Poised to Take Over Hillary Clinton's Treasury Department' — https://theintercept.com/2016/03/02/larry-fink-and-his-blackrock-team-poised-to-take-over-hillary-clintons-treasury-department/

28   https://www.sec.gov/litigation/admin/2015/ia-4065.pdf

29   BlackRock Advisors, LLC, a Delaware limited liability company headquartered in Wilmington, Delaware, is an investment adviser registered with the Commission. According to its Form ADV filed in June 2014, BlackRock has assets under management of approximately $452 billion. BlackRock is a subsidiary of BlackRock, Inc., an investment management firm with assets under management of approximately $4.3 trillion as of December 31, 2013.

Rice joined BlackRock in 2005 and managed BlackRock energy-focused registered funds, private funds, and separate accounts. In 2007, Rice founded Rice Energy, L.P. — a Rice family-owned-and-operated oil and natural gas production company. Rice was the general partner of Rice Energy and personally invested approximately $50 million in the company. Rice's three sons were the CEO, CFO, and VP of Geology of Rice Energy.

In February 2010, Rice Energy formed a joint venture with Alpha Natural Resources, Inc. (ANR), a publicly-traded coal company held in the BlackRock funds and accounts managed by Rice. By June 30, 2011, ANR stock was the largest holding (9.4%) in the Rice-managed $1.7 billion BlackRock Energy & Resources Portfolio, primarily as a result of ANR acquiring two other public companies held in that portfolio. BlackRock knew of Rice's involvement with and investment in Rice Energy as well as the joint venture with ANR, but failed to disclose Rice's conflict of interest to the BlackRock funds' boards of directors or to BlackRock advisory clients.

BlackRock also failed to adopt and implement written compliance policies and procedures reasonably designed to prevent violations of the Advisers Act and the rules thereunder, as required by Section 206(4) of the Advisers Act and Rule 206(4)-7 thereunder, concerning the outside activities of its employees, including how they should be assessed and monitored for conflict purposes, and when an employee's outside activity should be disclosed to the BlackRock funds' board of directors or to BlackRock advisory clients. BlackRock's chief compliance officer (CCO), Bartholomew A. Battista, caused BlackRock's compliance-related violations.

BlackRock and Battista also caused the registered funds' failure to have the funds' chief compliance officer report to the funds' boards of directors — in violation of Rule 38a-1(a)(4)(iii)(B) under the Investment Company Act of 1940 — Rice's violations of BlackRock's private investment policy. BlackRock and Battista knew about Rice's violations, and knew or should have known that they were not reported to the funds' boards.

As a result of the conduct described above, BlackRock willfully[30] violated Section 206(2) of the Advisers Act, which prohibits an investment adviser from engaging in any transaction, practice, or course of business that operates as a fraud or deceit upon a client or prospective client.[31] BlackRock breached its fiduciary duty by failing to disclose a conflict of interest — namely Rice's involvement with and investment in Rice Energy — to the BlackRock funds' boards of directors or to advisory clients.

As a result of the conduct described above, BlackRock willfully violated Section 206(4) of the Advisers Act and Rule 206(4)-7 thereunder by failing to adopt and implement written policies and procedures reasonably designed to prevent violations of the Advisers Act and its rules. BlackRock failed to adopt and implement written policies and procedures to assess and monitor the outside activities of its employees and to disclose conflicts of interest to the funds' boards and to advisory clients. Battista caused BlackRock's compliance-related violations.

As a result of the conduct described above, BlackRock and Battista caused certain BlackRock funds' violations of Rule 38a-1(a) under the Investment Company Act. Rule 38a-1(a)(4)(iii)(B) requires registered investment companies, through their chief compliance officer, to provide a written report at least annually to the fund's board of directors that

---

30   SEC order Original Footnote 1: A willful violation of the securities laws means merely "that the person charged with the duty knows what he is doing." *Wonsover v. SEC*, 205 F.3d 408, 414 (D.C. Cir. 2000) (quoting *Hughes v. SEC*, 174 F.2d 969, 977 (D.C. Cir. 1949)). There is no requirement that the actor "also be aware that he is violating one of the Rules or Acts." Id. (quoting *Gearhart & Otis, Inc. v. SEC*, 348 F.2d 798, 803 (D.C. Cir. 1965)).

31   SEC order Original Footnote 2: A violation of Section 206(2) of the Advisors Act does not require scienter, but, rather, may rest on a finding of simple negligence. *SEC v. Steadman*, 967 F.2d 636, 643 n.5 (D.C. Cir. 1992) (citing *SEC v. Capital Gains Research Bureau*, Inc., 375 U.S. 180, 195 (1963)).

addresses each material compliance matter that occurred since the date of the last report. Rule 38a-1, in pertinent part, defines a "material compliance matter" as any compliance matter about which the fund's board of directors would reasonably need to know to oversee fund compliance, and that involves, without limitation, a violation of the policies and procedures of its investment adviser. BlackRock and Battista caused the failures by certain BlackRock funds to report all material compliance matters — namely Rice's violations of BlackRock's private investment policy — to their boards of directors.

Accordingly, pursuant to Sections 203(e) and 203(k) of the Advisers Act and Sections 9(b) and 9(f) of the Investment Company Act with respect to BlackRock, and pursuant to Section 203(k) of the Advisers Act and Section 9(f) of the Investment Company Act with respect to Battista, it is hereby ORDERED that:

D. Respondent BlackRock shall, within thirty (30) calendar days of the entry of this Order, pay a civil money penalty in the amount of $12 million to the Securities and Exchange Commission. ... If timely payment is not made, additional interest shall accrue pursuant to 31 U.S.C. 3717."

In an election where the key issue is 'big money in politics', 'corrupt campaign finance system' and 'conflicts of interest and campaign funding', any association with an entity like BlackRock is a definite no-no, let alone getting them to mobilize campaign funds. If true, the proposal to make Larry Fink Treasury Secretary is fraught with danger and should be completely avoided for reasons outlined earlier! It remains to be seen whether such instances of blatant conflicts of interest will cost Hillary Clinton the U.S. presidential election to be held in November 2016.

Chapter 9

The Clinton Foundation, Its Donors/Trustees and the 2016 Hillary Clinton Campaign

No book on the 2016 Hillary Clinton campaign can be complete without a discussion of the Clinton Foundation, an important institution in Hillary Clinton's scheme to become President.

Many who have donated to the Clinton Foundation have also contributed to her 2008 and 2016 presidential bid. Likewise, there have been newcomers who have supported her through her campaign and who have now hopped on the Clinton Foundation bandwagon as donors.

This chapter takes a look at five specific case studies in an attempt to understand the links between the Clinton Foundation and its donors, some of whom are also supporters of Hillary Clinton for the 2016 presidential run. I also take a closer look at the antecedents of some of the foundation's donors and trustees who have contributed to Hillary Clinton's campaign in 2016.

The Case of The Blackstone Group

The first case study pertains to The Blackstone Group L.P., which was founded in 1985 as a mergers and acquisitions specialist. Today, Blackstone has grown into one of the world's largest private equity firms. Headquartered at 345 Park Avenue in Manhattan, New York City, Blackstone has eight other offices in the United States. Globally, it has offices in London, Paris, Düsseldorf, Sydney, Tokyo, Hong Kong, Singapore, Beijing, Shanghai, Madrid, Mumbai, and Dubai.

Among its noteworthy achievements is a $4 billion initial public offering (IPO) completed in 2007, making it one of the first major private equity firms to list shares on a public exchange.

Another aspect about Blackstone worthy of mention here is that it has been one of the largest investors in leveraged buyout transactions over the last ten years.[1]

Blackstone has been a major supporter of the Clintons and has specifically made donations to the Clinton Foundation in the range of $250,001 to $500,000. In addition, several key staff members of the Blackstone Group have contributed a sum total of $101,700 to pro-Clinton super PACs as listed in Table 9.1 below:

Table 9.1: The Blackstone Group Contribution to pro-Clinton PACs						
Contributor Name	Employer	Occupation	City	State	Zip	Amount (in $)
Hillary Victory Fund						
Wien, Byron	The Blackstone Group	Vice Chairman	New York	NY	10065	33,400
Zelin, Steve	The Blackstone Group	Banker	Larchmont	NY	10538	33,400
Agarwal, A.J.	The Blackstone Group	Senior Managing Director	New York	NY	10012	16,700
James, Hamilton	The Blackstone Group	President	New York	NY	10065	16,700
Kaden, David	The Blackstone Group	The Blackstone Group	New York	NY	10024	1,000

---

1   https://en.wikipedia.org/wiki/The_Blackstone_Group

Table 9.1: The Blackstone Group Contribution to pro-Clinton PACs						
Contributor Name	Employer	Occupation	City	State	Zip	Amount (in $)
Pieper, Jeanette	The Blackstone Group	Marketing	Brooklyn	NY	11201	500
Total						**101,700**
Source: Data from Federal Election Commission, http://www.fec.gov/						

Furthermore, several Blackstone staff have also contributed individually to the Hillary Clinton 2016 presidential run. The total contribution from individual staff members is around $54,000.[2]

If there is one point that Hillary Clinton has been making time and again in this 2016 campaign, it is the call for tougher action on financial crime. Call it the Sanders effect or whatever, the fact is that Hillary Clinton's call to enforce criminal prosecution of Wall Street executives who engage in financial crime is indeed symptomatic of the winds of change that seem to be blowing across America.

What is really ironical though is the fact that, while Hillary Clinton traverses the United States, talking tough and promising action against "corporate wrongdoers and shadow banks" as well as cracking down on "investment firms that offer banking services outside the purview of traditional financial regulations," her own campaign is partially funded by money from personnel of a large Wall Street firm that is considered one of the United States' biggest shadow banks. Interestingly, this same shadow bank was recently fined by the SEC for supposedly "ripping off its clients."[3]

In an article titled "Hillary Clinton Denounces Corporate Crime While Accepting Cash from Blackstone, Firm Sanctioned by SEC,"[4]

---

2   www.fec.gov

3   All quotes in this paragraph are from 'Hillary Clinton Denounces Corporate Crime While Accepting Cash From Blackstone, Firm Sanctioned By SEC' — http://www.ibtimes.com/political-capital/hillary-clinton-denounces-corporate-crime-while-accepting-cash-blackstone-firm

4   'Hillary Clinton Denounces Corporate Crime While Accepting Cash From Blackstone, Firm Sanctioned By SEC' — http://www.ibtimes.com/political-capital/hillary-clinton-denounces-corporate-crime-while-accepting-cash-blackstone-firm

the *International Business Times* noted that Blackstone's President held a fundraiser for Clinton and the money is said to have been donated to Hillary Clinton's 2016 campaign.

That is not all. There is even more interesting news. According to the aforementioned *International Business Times* report, this fundraiser was just about two months after Blackstone settled with the Securities and Exchange Commission on charges that it had used monitoring fees to enrich itself at the expense of investors.

Recall that this practice of Wall Street firms enriching themselves at the expense of investors was also reported in the case of the $7 billion Employee Retirement System of the State of Rhode Island where D.E. Shaw, Davidson Kempner, OZ Domestic Partners, and other Wall Street firms are managing[5] the said pension fund.

Looks like it's the same old story again and perhaps this is how Wall Street builds its own wealth? Also recall what happened in the case of Calpers,[6] the $200 billion California Pension and Retirement System, where again $500 million was lost due to the carelessness of a Wall Street asset manager, namely BlackRock.[7]

As in the Rhode Island case, the investors[8] in the Blackstone funds who were apparently harmed were the major public pension systems in the states of California, Florida, and New Jersey, all of which hold the retirement savings of educators, police officials, firefighters, and other government workers. According to the International Business Times article, municipal and state pension systems that had invested close to $9.7 billion were supposedly affected in the three Blackstone funds case.

---

5   Refer case study of D. E. Shaw given in Chapter 2.

6   'Larry Fink's $12 Trillion Shadow' — http://www.vanityfair.com/news/2010/04/fink-201004

7   Refer case study of BlackRock given in Chapter 8.

8   According to the research firm Preqin cited in the *International Business Times* article the investors were the major public pension systems in the states of California, Florida and New Jersey — http://www.ibtimes.com/political-capital/hillary-clinton-denounces-corporate-crime-while-accepting-cash-blackstone-firm

In fact, reportedly Blackstone executives have stated that state pension funds are too generous. One such comment was supposedly made on January 5, 2010 (at a webcast for Blackstone's clients) by Byron R. Wien, vice chairman, Blackstone Advisory Partners LP, Blackstone's global advisory business.

Wien is reported to have said,

> "The retirement benefits for state workers, really not only in New York, California and New Jersey, but throughout the country, are very generous. Too generous. ... We literally can't afford the benefits we have given our retirees in state and local governments. And we have to change that."[9]

What is interesting in all of the above and the 2016 election is that Hillary Clinton has received the endorsement of a large group of major unions that have public employees as their constituents. She needs to remember that these public employees rely almost exclusively on the various public pension systems for their life after retirement. I wonder what she will tell them when they find out that she (Hillary Clinton) is backed by major Wall Street firms, many of whom have eroded their pension fund savings and returns. That would be a difficult question to answer under any circumstances.

That said, let us get back to the Securities and Exchange Commission (SEC) order against Blackstone. Specifically, it can be seen that the SEC — under the Investment Advisers Act Of 1940 (Release No. 4219 / October 7, 2015) and Administrative Proceeding (File No. 3-16887), in the Matter of Blackstone Management Partners L.L.C., Blackstone Management Partners III L.L.C., and Blackstone Management Partners IV L.L.C., Respondents — has given an order instituting cease-and-desist proceedings pursuant to section 203(k) of the investment advisers act of 1940.[10]

---

9   http://www.pionline.com/article/20100628/PRINT/306289980/blackstone-in-repair-mode-after-wien-flap

10   https://www.sec.gov/litigation/admin/2015/ia-4219.pdf   and   http://www.businessinsider.com/byron-wien-state-government-retirement-benefits-too-high-2011-1?IR=T

The SEC order notes that:

"These proceedings arise from inadequate disclosures that involved two distinct breaches of fiduciary duty by private equity fund advisers Blackstone Management Partners L.L.C., Blackstone Management Partners III L.L.C., and Blackstone Management Partners IV L.L.C. (collectively, 'Blackstone').

First, from at least 2010 through March 2015, upon either the private sale of a portfolio company or an initial public offering (IPO), Blackstone terminated certain portfolio company monitoring agreements and accelerated the payment of future monitoring fees as set forth in the agreements. Although Blackstone disclosed that it may receive monitoring fees from portfolio companies held by the funds it advised, and disclosed the amount of monitoring fees that had been accelerated following the acceleration, Blackstone failed to disclose to its funds, and to the funds' limited partners prior to their commitment of capital, that it may accelerate future monitoring fees upon termination of the monitoring agreements.

Second, in late 2007, Blackstone negotiated a single legal services arrangement with its primary outside law firm (the 'Law Firm') on behalf of itself and the funds. For the majority of legal services performed by the Law Firm beginning in 2008 and continuing through early 2011, Blackstone received a discount that was substantially greater than the discount received by the funds. The disparate legal fee discounts were not disclosed to the funds or the funds' limited partners until August 2012. Because of its conflict of interest as the recipient of the accelerated monitoring fees and the beneficiary of the disparate legal fee discounts, Blackstone could not effectively consent to either of these practices on behalf of the funds it advised. As a result, Blackstone breached its fiduciary duty to the funds in violation of Section 206(2) of the Advisers Act and also violated Section 206(4) of the Advisers Act and Rule 206(4)-8 there under.

Blackstone separately violated Section 206(4) of the Advisers Act and Rule 206(4)-7 there under by failing to adopt and implement written policies and procedures reasonably designed to prevent violations of the Advisers Act arising from the undisclosed receipt of fees and conflicts of interest.

Section 206(2) of the Advisers Act prohibits investment advisers from directly or indirectly engaging "in any transaction, practice, or course of business which operates as a fraud or deceit upon any client or prospective client." A violation of Section 206(2) of the Advisers Act may rest on a finding of simple negligence. *SEC v. Steadman*, 967 F.2d 636, 643 n.5 (D.C. Cir. 1992) (citing *SEC v. Capital Gains Research Bureau, Inc.*, 375 U.S. 180, 195 (1963)). Proof of scienter is not required to establish a violation of Section 206(2) of the Advisers Act. *Id.* As a result of the conduct described above, BMP, BMP III, and BMP IV violated Section 206(2) of the Advisers Act.

Section 206(4) of the Advisers Act and Rule 206(4)-8 thereunder make it unlawful for any investment adviser to a pooled investment vehicle to "make any untrue statement of a material fact or omit to state a material fact necessary to make the statements made, in the light of the circumstances under which they were made, not misleading, to any investor or prospective investor in the pooled investment vehicle" or "engage in any act, practice, or course of business that is fraudulent, deceptive, or manipulative with respect to any investor or prospective investor in the pooled investment vehicle." As a result of the conduct described above, BMP, BMP III, and BMP IV violated Section 206(4) of the Advisers Act and Rule 206(4)-8 thereunder.

Section 206(4) of the Advisers Act and Rule 206(4)-7 thereunder require registered investment advisers to adopt and implement written policies and procedures reasonably designed to prevent violations of the Advisers Act and its rules. As a result of the conduct described above, BMP, BMP III, and BMP IV violated Section 206(4) of the Advisers Act and Rule 206(4)-7 thereunder.

Accordingly, pursuant to Section 203(k) of the Advisers Act, it is hereby ORDERED that:

A.   Respondents BMP, BMP III, and BMP IV cease and desist from committing or causing any violations and any future violations of Sections 206(2) and 206(4) of the Advisers Act and Rules 206(4)-7 and 206(4)-8 thereunder.

B.   Respondents BMP, BMP III, and BMP IV shall pay, jointly and severally, disgorgement and prejudgment interest as follows:

i.   Respondents shall pay a total of $28,911,756 consisting of disgorgement of $26,225,203 and prejudgment interest of $2,686,553 (collectively, the "Disgorgement Fund") to compensate the Funds and limited partners therein that invested in private equity transactions from 2010 to March 2015 that resulted in payment of undisclosed accelerated monitoring fees;

ii.   Within ten (10) days of the entry of this Order, Respondents shall deposit the full amount of the Disgorgement Fund into an escrow account acceptable to the Commission staff and shall provide the Commission staff with evidence of such deposit in a form acceptable to the Commission staff. If timely deposit of the Disgorgement Fund is not made, additional interest shall accrue pursuant to SEC Rule of Practice 600;

iii. Respondents agree to be responsible for all tax compliance responsibilities associated with distribution of the Disgorgement Fund and may retain any professional services necessary. The costs and expenses of any such professional services shall be borne by Respondents and shall not be paid out of the Disgorgement Fund; and ...

C.   Respondents BMP, BMP III, and BMP IV shall pay, jointly and severally, within ten (10) days of the entry of this Order, a civil monetary penalty in the amount of $10,000,000 to the Securities and Exchange Commission for transfer to the general fund of the United States Treasury, subject to Section 21F(g)(3) of the Securities Exchange Act of 1934. If timely payment is not made, additional interest shall accrue pursuant to 31 U.S.C. § 3717."

The above excerpt clearly indicates that The Blackstone Group has been charged with serious violations by the SEC and the question that begs to be asked all over again is: "How and why did the Hillary Clinton campaign and the Clinton Foundation take contributions from such an institution? This is an especially critical question given what Hillary Clinton has been saying all through her campaign in terms of reigning in Wall Street professionals engaging in financial crime. On the face of it, this is once again proof that high-sounding rhetoric and the actual action on the ground don't match at all.

The Case of Vinod Gupta

Next in line is the case of Vinod Gupta, the former chief executive officer (CEO) and chairman of infoUSA (now infoGroup) and also a former trustee of the William J. Clinton Foundation.[11] He has donated a sum ranging between $1,000,000 and $5,000,000 to the Clinton Foundation and has also been a key contributor to the Hillary Clinton campaign. A perusal of Vinod Gupta's LinkedIn profile suggests that he has been extremely close to the Clintons. Among the things stated by Vinod Gupta in his profile[12] are the following:

- His appointment by President Clinton to serve as a trustee of the John F. Kennedy Center for the Performing Arts in Washington, D.C.

---

11   This is also stated in by his LinkedIn profile.

12   See https://www.linkedin.com/in/vinodgupta1 and other sources including, 'The Clinton Foundation Reeks of Crooks, Thieves, and Hoods' — http://www.nationalreview.com/article/419791/clinton-foundation-reeks-crooks-thieves-and-hoods-deroy-murdock and 'Revealed: Four Clinton Foundation Trustees Charged or Convicted of Financial Crimes' — http://www.breitbart.com/big-government/2015/05/07/revealed-four-clinton-foundation-trustees-charged-or-convicted-of-financial-crimes/

- His nomination and confirmation to be the United States Consul General to Bermuda

- His nomination to be the United States Ambassador to Fiji

That certainly is a wonderful profile! Like any other successful businessman, Vinod Gupta also has a well-developed political network but has been considered particularly close to the Clintons for a long time. Not only has he contributed to Hillary Clinton's presidential campaign in 2016, he had as well earlier supported Hillary in the Democratic presidential primaries of 2008.[13]

While Vinod Gupta's profile, including his having served as a trustee of the William Jefferson Clinton Foundation, makes for interesting reading and glowing praise, what it does not reveal, for obvious reasons, is that he was earlier charged by the SEC, which noted as follows:

"From 2003 through 2007, Vinod Gupta, the former CEO and Chairman of infoUSA Inc. (now InfoGroup Inc.) ('Info'), engaged in fraud by receiving from Info approximately $9.5 million of unauthorized and undisclosed perquisites, including for the personal use of jets; costs associated with a yacht, homes, automobiles, and life insurance policies; personal credit card expenses; and club memberships and related costs.

For the same period, Info entered into related party transactions totaling approximately $9.3 million with two entities that Gupta controlled, and one entity with which he was affiliated, without disclosing the transactions in Info's public filings with the Commission.

Separately, in March and April 2005, Gupta purchased 55,000 shares of Opinion Research Corporation ('ORC') after he had taken steps on behalf of Info to acquire ORC. Info later acquired ORC. In breach of his fiduciary duty to Info, Gupta failed to inform Info's other board members of the material fact that he had purchased ORC shares for his own benefit. Gupta obtained realized and unrealized ill-gotten gains

---

13   See www.fec.gov

from his ORC trading totaling approximately $240,700, which he has turned over to Info."[14]

A specific look at the SEC's complaints reveal shocking details. The complaints stated[15] that:

- During the period 2003 to 2007, Gupta improperly used corporate funds of $3 million towards personal jet travel expenses for himself, family, and friends to travel to South Africa, Italy, and Cancun.

- Investor money of $2.8 million was used by Gupta to pay for expenses related to his yacht. Likewise, $1.3 million of investor funds were directed to pay for Gupta's expenses related to his personal credit cards and other costs associated with 28 club memberships, 20 automobiles, homes around the country, and three personal life insurance policies.

- Gupta failed to inform Info's other board members of the material fact that he had purchased shares of an Info acquisition target for his own ill-gotten financial benefit.

Furthermore, along with Vinod Gupta, the former chairman of Info's audit committee, Vasant H. Raval, and two of the company's former chief financial officers, Rajnish K. Das and Stormy L. Dean, were also charged by the SEC for enabling Gupta to carry out the scheme in which he "funneled illegal compensation to himself in the form of perks worth millions of dollars."[16]

As Robert Khuzami, Director of the SEC's Division of Enforcement put, "Gupta stole millions of dollars from Info shareholders by treating the company like it was his personal ATM" and "other corporate officers

---

14   In The United States District Court For The District Of Nebraska, *Securities And Exchange Commission, (Plaintiff) Vs. Vinod Gupta,* Defendant — https://www.sec.gov/litigation/complaints/2010/comp21451-gupta.pdf

15   'SEC Charges Former Executives in Illegal Scheme to Enrich CEO With Perks', Press Release, Washington, D.C., March 15, 2010 — https://www.sec.gov/news/press/2010/2010-39.htm

16   SEC press release dated March 15, 2010 given above

also abused their positions of trust by looking the other way instead of standing up for investors and bringing the scheme to a halt."[17]

Donald M. Hoerl, Director of the SEC's Denver Regional Office, added, "Officers and directors must ensure that shareholders receive accurate and complete disclosure of all compensation paid to executives. Raval, as chairman of the audit committee, neglected these duties and allowed the money to flow to Gupta unbeknownst to investors."[18]

In fact, if we go back to the 2008 global financial crisis, compensation was one factor among many that contributed to the financial crisis of 2008 in the United States and elsewhere. It looks like Vinod Gupta was taking a leaf out of the playbook of the Wall Street firms.

Again, Gupta's proximity to the Clinton support system and campaign clearly show the interface between corruption, big money, and politics!

Interestingly, Gupta, Raval, and Info agreed to settle the SEC's charges. Gupta agreed to pay disgorgement of $4,045,000, prejudgment interest of $1,145,400, and a penalty of $2,240,700. He also consented to an order barring him from serving as an officer or director of a public company, and placing restrictions on the voting of his Info common stock.[19]

Clearly, the Hillary Clinton campaign does not seem too concerned about accepting contributions and support from the likes of Vinod Gupta, a man clearly seen by the SEC as having committed fraud and having been charged as such by it. What is even more shocking is the fact that Vinod Gupta was a trustee of the Clinton Foundation, an indication of the degree of proximity he shares with the Clintons.

The Case of Sant Singh Chatwal

The case of Sant Singh Chatwal exposes the nexus between politics and corruption even better. Let us rewind in time to 2010 to an interview

---

17   Ibid.
18   Ibid.
19   'SEC Charges Former Executives in Illegal Scheme to Enrich CEO With Perks', Press Release, Washington, D.C., March 15, 2010 — https://www.sec.gov/news/press/2010/2010-39.htm

given in *Leaders magazine* (Volume 33, Number 3) by Sant Singh Chatwal who noted in the interview[20] and I quote,

> "My father said, if you give 10 percent of your profit to people who need the money, whether they're poor or needy, that 10 percent will multiply 1,000 times. ... That is one reason I am a Trustee of the Clinton Foundation. President Clinton was my friend before he became President, and he offered me a position in the White House — I said, no because I'm a businessman."

There are other sources[21] that suggest the Sant Singh Chatwal was a trustee of the Clinton Foundation. While there appears no dispute on this count, i.e., Sant Singh Chatwal was indeed a trustee of the Clinton Foundation, unfortunately, we are not able to access a clear list of past trustees from the Clinton Foundation either from their filings to the IRS or their annual reports. This point deserves emphasis here since it reflects on the transparency (specifically the lack of it) and governance that the Clintons publicly claim to espouse. Apart from being a trustee of the Clinton Foundation in the past, Sant Singh Chatwal also donated to the Clinton 2008 presidential run as an individual as did his son, Vikram Chatwal. His company, Hampshire Hotels & Resorts, LLC has donated between $250,001 and $500,000 to the Clinton Foundation as per data given in the Foundation website.[22]

While all of the eloquent talk of sharing and gifting to the needy sounds great, I came across an interesting piece of information about a court case in the United States District Court, Eastern District of New York, Criminal Division. The case was The United States of America vs. Sant Singh Chatwal, Defendant. The case talks of "The Conspiracy to Violate the Election Act." Specifically, it mentions a conspiracy to violate the Election Act by the defendant Sant Singh Chatwal[23] (and others).

---

20   http://www.leadersmag.com/issues/2010.3_jul/pdfs/chatwal.pdf
21   https://en.wikipedia.org/wiki/Sant_Singh_Chatwal; http://www.bornrich.com/sant-singh-chatwal.html
22   https://www.clintonfoundation.org/contributors
23   http://images.politico.com/global/2014/04/17/chatwalinformationlel_signed_1.pdf

"In or about and between March 2007 and August 2011, both dates being approximate and inclusive, within the Eastern District of New York and elsewhere, the defendant SANT SINGH CHATWAL, together with others, did knowingly and willfully conspire to make, and cause to be made, contributions of money, aggregating $25,000 and more in a calendar year, in the names of others, to the Candidates, all of whom were candidates for federal office, contrary to Title 2, United States Code, Sections 441f and 437g(d) (1) (A) (i).

In furtherance of this conspiracy and to effect its objectives, within the Eastern District of New York and elsewhere, the defendant SANT SINGH CHATWAL, together with his co-conspirators, did commit, and did cause to commit, among others, the following:

OVERT ACTS

In or about September 2008, in New York, New York, CHATWAL, together with others, reimbursed the CI[24] for campaign contributions from the Group A1 Straw Donors and the Group A3 Straw Donors that the CI had previously obtained by reducing by $50,000 the amount of interest that the CI owed on a $2.5 million loan CHATWAL previously made to the CI.

On or about October 2, 2010, in New York, New York, CHATWAL and the CI delivered to Candidate B campaign contributions from straw Donors totaling approximately $19,200.

In or about July 2011, from his office in Queens, New York, John Doe #1[25] submitted the July Invoice to Northquay, a company controlled

---

24   A "Cooperating Informant", an individual, whose IDENTITY is known to the United States Attorney (The "CI"), was a business associate of CHATWAL — page 4 of the document accessed at http://images.politico.com/global/2014/04/17/chatwalinformationlel_signed_1.pdf

25   John Doe # 1, an individual whose identity is known to the United States Attorney, was a contractor whose construction company contracted with entities operated by Chatwal to perform millions of dollars in construction work at Chatwal's business

by CHATWAL, in the amount of $129,745, which invoice included approximately $69,000 in reimbursement for campaign contributions that John Doe #1 had raised for Candidate C by reimbursing the Group C Straw Donors.

In or about and between June 2012 and July 2012, both dates being approximate and inclusive, within the Eastern District of New York and elsewhere, the defendant SANT SINGH CHATWAL, together with others, did knowingly and corruptly persuade another person, to wit: John Doe #1, with intent to hinder, delay or prevent the communication to one or more law enforcement officers of the United States: to wit, the Law Enforcement Officers, of information relating to the commission, or possible commission, of one or more federal offenses, to wit: the Federal Offenses."[26]

Thus, Chatwal, was convicted of one count[27] of Conspiracy to Violate the Federal Election Campaign Act and one count of Witness Tampering and subjected to a fine of $500,000 plus other charges.

Table 9.2: Sant Singh Chatwal Convicted of Two Counts	
Title & Section	**Nature of Offense**
18 USC §371 and 3551 et seq;	Conspiracy to violate the Federal Election Campaign Act
18 USC, 1512(b)(3) and 3551 et seq;	Witness tampering

All of this activity does not provide a very flattering picture of the kind of company both the Clintons and the Clinton Foundation have kept in the past.

---

properties and at one of Chatwal's personal residences in Old Brookville, New York ("Old Brookville") — page 4 of the document accessed at http://images.politico.com/global/2014/04/17/chatwalinformationlel_signed_1.pdf

26   http://images.politico.com/global/2014/04/17/chatwalinformationlel_signed_1.pdf

27   http://www.nyindia.us/images/Sant-Chatwal-Judgment.pdf

Considering that they could once again become the first couple of the United States, it is critical to consider how effective Hillary Clinton will be in keeping the corrupt and criminal from tarnishing the precincts of the pristine White House.

The Case of Victor Phillip Michael Dahdaleh

Moving on, let us look at the case of Victor Phillip Michael Dahdaleh, who is the owner and chairman of the Dadco group of companies, which is involved in investment, manufacturing, and trading. Established in 1915, the founding company is said to have had operations in Europe, North America, the Middle East, Africa, and Australia.

As per his website, the 72-year-old Jordanian born Victor Dahdaleh claims that he has held several honorary positions that include serving on the board of the William J. Clinton Foundation[28] as a trustee. Together, Victor P. Dahdaleh & The Victor Phillip Dahdaleh Charitable Foundation have donated between $1,000,001 to $5,000,000 to the Clinton Foundation. That's a huge sum indeed.

Interestingly, Victor Dahdaleh is also one of the names that has cropped up in the recent Panama Papers expose. He has been confirmed as the mysterious "Consultant A" named in U.S. court documents. Consultant A is supposed to have given out millions and millions of dollars as inducement to personnel of a Persian Gulf smelting company in return for supplier contracts to one of the world's largest aluminum companies. Incidentally, Dahdaleh's client, which is a subsidiary of Alcoa, admitted to being on the wrong side of the law as it confessed to a U.S. bribery charge in 2014 in relation to the above scandal. Alcoa and its unit are reported to have together paid one of the largest anti-corruption fines — about $384 million — in the history of the United States.[29]

---

28   http://victordahdaleh.com/

29   See the CBC article and its quote — 'Panama Papers confirm Canadian billionaire and university benefactor as mystery man in global bribery case'— http://www.cbc. ca/news/business/panama-papers-victor-dahdaleh-alcoa-bribery-case-1.3598527 — "The huge leak of offshore financial records reveals Dahdaleh, a 72-year-old Jordanian-born metals magnate, is indeed, as long suspected, the mysterious

In fact, a look at the relevant SEC order[30] should throw more light on this matter:

"1. These proceedings arise from violations of the Foreign Corrupt Practices Act of 1977 (the 'FCPA') [15 U.S.C. § 78dd] by Respondent Alcoa Inc. ('Alcoa') concerning alumina sales to Aluminum Bahrain B.S.C. ('Alba'), an aluminum manufacturer owned primarily by the Kingdom of Bahrain.

2. Between 1989 and 2009, Alcoa of Australia ('AofA') and Alcoa World Alumina LLC ('AWA') (collectively, the 'AWAC Subsidiaries') retained a consultant to act as their middleman in connection with sales of alumina to Alba and knew or consciously disregarded the fact that the relationship with the consultant was designed to generate funds that facilitated corrupt payments to Bahraini officials. The consultant was paid a commission on sales where he acted as an agent and received a markup on sales where he acted as a purported distributor. On sales where the consultant acted as a purported distributor, no legitimate services were provided to justify the role of the consultant as a distributor. The consultant used these funds to enrich himself and pay bribes to senior government officials of Bahrain.

3. The commission payments to the consultant and the alumina sales to the consultant made pursuant to the distribution agreements were improperly recorded in Alcoa's books and records as legitimate commissions or sales to a distributor and did not accurately reflect the transactions. The false entries were initially recorded by the AWAC Subsidiaries which were then consolidated into Alcoa's books and records. During the relevant period, Alcoa also lacked sufficient internal controls to prevent and detect the improper payments."

---

middleman known in U.S. court documents as "Consultant A"

30   https://www.sec.gov/litigation/admin/2014/34-71261.pdf

Further, as per the SEC order, the main entity is:

> "6. Alcoa World Alumina and Chemicals ('AWAC') is an unincorporated global bauxite mining and alumina refining enterprise formed in 1995 between Alcoa and Alumina Limited ('Alumina'), the majority and minority owners of AWAC, respectively. AWAC operates through a number of affiliated enterprise companies, including AofA and AWA, with each enterprise company being owned by Alcoa and Alumina in proportion to their respective ownership interests in the AWAC enterprise. In matters of strategy and policy, the AWAC enterprise companies receive direction and counsel from a 'Strategic Council' that is chaired by Alcoa. Alcoa controls the Strategic Council and as such the operations and personnel of AWAC report to Alcoa personnel in New York."

The consultant is referred to in the SEC order as Consultant A and as per the same SEC order, Consultant A is described as

> "an international middleman who resides in London and is a citizen of Canada, Jordan, and the United Kingdom. Consultant A had close contacts with certain members of Bahrain's Royal Family, some of whom were senior officials in the Government of Bahrain. Consultant A met with Alcoa executives to discuss matters relating to the relationship with Alba. Consultant A operates through many shell companies, including Alumet Ltd ('Alumet') and AA Alumina and Chemicals Ltd ('AAAC')."

Note that the SEC order states that "Consultant A operates through many shell companies, including Alumet Ltd. ('Alumet') and AA Alumina and Chemicals Ltd. ('AAAC')."

The SEC order further notes:

> "13. From at least 1989 to 2009, AofA supplied alumina to Alba through a series of multi-year contracts. During this period, Alba

was one of Alcoa's largest alumina customers purchasing a total of nearly 19 million metric tons beginning with an annual volume of 300,000 metric tons increasing to 1.6 million metric tons.

14. Beginning in approximately 1989, AofA retained Consultant A to assist in longterm contract negotiations with Alba and Bahraini government officials, including the negotiation and execution of a new long-term alumina supply agreement in 1990 (the '1990 Supply Agreement.')

15. By 1996, Consultant A was playing a significant role in the relationship between the AWAC Subsidiaries and Alba. Around this time, Alba complained to the AWAC Subsidiaries that it was paying an above-market price for alumina. AofA learned that Alba was seeking to increase its alumina supply requirements from 600,000 metric tons a year up to 970,000 metric tons a year, and that other major global suppliers of alumina were seeking to capture these additional requirements. The AWAC Subsidiaries' sales team decided that, to 'comply with business norms in the Middle East[,]' the AWAC Subsidiaries would propose supplying some of Alba's alumina through Alumet, which was one of Consultant A's shell companies, which would pay the 'required commission.' An AofA manager proposed using Consultant A as the intermediary because Consultant A was 'well versed in the normal ways of Middle East business' and 'will keep the various stakeholders in the Alba smelter happy....'"

It must be emphasized that the SEC order again refers to Consultant A as operating a shell company called "Alumet." This point needs emphasis here. Remember this as it becomes even more significant later.

The SEC order, which notes that,

"38. The recipients of the corrupt payments included a senior Bahraini official, members of the board of directors of Alba, and senior management of Alba. Examples of the corrupt payments include:

- In August 2003, Consultant A's shell companies made 2 payments totaling $7 million to accounts for the benefit of a Bahraini government official who Consultant A had been retained to lobby. Two weeks later, Alcoa and Alba signed an agreement in principle to have Alcoa participate in Alba's plant expansion.

- In October 2004, Consultant A's shell company paid $1 million to an account for the benefit of that same government official. Shortly thereafter, Alba agreed in principle to Alcoa's offer for the 2005 Alba Supply Agreement.

- In or around the time of the execution of the final 2005 Alba Supply Agreement, Consultant A-controlled companies paid another Bahraini government official and/or his beneficiaries $41 million in three payments."

The point to be noted is that nearly $49 million were paid out by Consultant A controlled shell companies.

The SEC order further notes the following violations:

"D. Under Section 30A(a) of the Exchange Act it is unlawful for any issuer, officer, director, employee, or agent of such issuer or any stockholder thereof acting on behalf of the issuer, to make use of the mails or any means or instrumentality of interstate commerce corruptly in furtherance of an offer, payment, promise to pay, or authorization of the payment of any money, or offer, gift, promise to give, or authorization of the giving of anything of value to any foreign official or any person, while knowing that all or a portion of such money or thing of value will be offered, given, or promised, directly or indirectly, to any foreign official for the purposes of (i) influencing any act or decision of such foreign official in his official capacity, (ii) inducing such foreign official to do or omit to do any act in violation of the lawful duty of such official, or (iii) securing any improper advantage in order to assist such issuer in obtaining or retaining business for or with, or directing business to, any person. [15 U.S.C. § 78dd-1].

E.   Additionally, under Section 30A(g) of the Exchange Act it is unlawful for any issuer organized under the laws of the United States, or a State, territory, possession, or commonwealth of the United States or for any United States person that is an officer, director, employee, or agent of such issuer or a stockholder thereof acting on behalf of such issuer, to corruptly do any act outside the United States in furtherance of an offer, payment, promise to pay, or authorization of the payment of any money, or offer, gift, promise to give, or authorization of the giving of anything of value to any of the persons or entities set forth in paragraphs (i), (ii), and (iii) of subsection (a) of this section for the purposes set forth therein, irrespective of whether such issuer or such officer, director, employee, agent, or stockholder makes use of the mails or any means or instrumentality of interstate commerce in furtherance of such offer, gift, payment, promise, or authorization.

F.   This Order contains no findings that an officer, director or employee of Alcoa knowingly engaged in the bribe scheme. As described above, Alcoa violated Section 30A of the Exchange Act by reason of its agents, including subsidiaries AWA and AofA, indirectly paying bribes to foreign officials in Bahrain in order to obtain or retain business. AWA, AofA, and their employees all acted as "agents" of Alcoa during the relevant time, and were acting within the scope of their authority when participating in the bribe scheme. As described above, Alcoa exercised control over the Alumina Segment, including the AWAC Subsidiaries. Alcoa appointed the majority of seats on the AWAC Strategic Council, and the head of the Global Primary Products group served as its chair. Alcoa and AofA transferred personnel between them, including alumina sales staff; Alcoa set the business and financial goals for AWAC and coordinated the legal, audit, and compliance functions of AWAC; and the AWAC Subsidiaries' employees managing the Alba alumina business reported functionally to the global head of the Alumina Segment. Alba was a significant alumina customer for Alcoa's Alumina Segment and during the relevant period, members of Alcoa senior management met both with Alba officials and Consultant A to discuss matters related to the Alba relationship, including a proposed joint venture between Alcoa and Alba. During this time, Alcoa was aware that Consultant A was an agent and distributor with respect to AofA's sales of alumina to Alba and that terms of related contracts were reviewed and approved by senior managers of Alcoa's Alumina Segment in the United States.

G. Under Section 13(b)(2)(A) of the Exchange Act issuers are required to make and keep books, records, and accounts, which, in reasonable detail, accurately and fairly reflect the transactions and disposition of the assets of the issuer. [15 U.S.C. § 78m(b)(2)(A)].

H. Under Section 13(b)(2)(B) of the Exchange Act issuers are required to devise and maintain a system of internal accounting controls sufficient to provide reasonable assurances that (i) transactions are executed in accordance with management's general or specific authorization; (ii) transactions are recorded as necessary (I) to permit preparation of financial statements in conformity with generally accepted accounting principles or any other criteria applicable to such statements, and (II) to maintain accountability for assets; (iii) access to assets is permitted only in accordance with management's general or specific authorization; and (iv) the recorded accountability for assets is compared with the existing assets at reasonable intervals and appropriate action is taken with respect to any differences. [15 U.S.C. § 78m(b)(2)(B)].

I. **As described above, Alcoa violated Section 13(b)(2)(A) of the Exchange Act by improperly recording the payments, to Consultant A, as agent commissions when the true purpose of these payments was to make corrupt payments to Bahraini officials. Alcoa violated Section 13(b)(2)(A) when Alcoa recorded the sales to Consultant A as a distributor.** The false entries were initially recorded by the AWAC Subsidiaries which were then consolidated and reported by Alcoa in its consolidated financial statements. Alcoa also violated Section 13(b)(2)(B) by failing to devise and maintain sufficient accounting controls to detect and prevent the making of improper payments to foreign officials."

Further, as the SEC order notes:

"Respondent's subsidiary AWA has agreed, with the United States Department of Justice, Criminal Division, Fraud Section, to plead guilty for criminal conduct relating to certain of the findings in the Order."

This is very significant because ALCOA INC's subsidiary AWA has agreed to plead guilty of criminal conduct.

The SEC therefore ordered that:

"A.　Pursuant to Section 21C of the Exchange Act, Respondent Alcoa cease and desist from committing or causing any violations and any future violations of Sections 30A, 13(b)(2)(A) and 13(b)(2)(B) of the Exchange Act;

B.　Respondent shall pay disgorgement of $175,000,000. ... If timely payment of disgorgement is not made within 14 days of when due, additional interest shall accrue pursuant to SEC Rule of Practice 600."

Two issues deserve mention in the above SEC order. First, is the fact that ALCOA INC's subsidiary AWA has agreed to plead guilty of criminal conduct. Second, is that the SEC confirms the use of Alumet Ltd. (Shell Company of Consultant A) in this criminal activity.

Logically, the next question that arises is, "Who is Consultant A who owns the shell companies Alumet Ltd ('Alumet') and AA Alumina and Chemicals Ltd ('AAAC')"?

A search of the ICIJ database[31] proves that Victor Philip Dahdaleh is the beneficiary of 'Alumet Ltd.', incorporated in the British Virgin Islands, which also has him listed as the shareholder of Alumet Ltd.

31　https://offshoreleaks.icij.org/

— it says Victor Phillip Michael Dahdaleh is the shareholder of Alumet Ltd. Alumet Ltd. has its address listed as Hani Saliba Rizeq Qushiar Chemin, de La Jaque 41, Lausanne, Geneva. Victor Phillip Dahdaleh's address is given as 28 Eaton Place, Belgravia, London SWIX 8AF.

Additionally, the Panama Papers March 2007 email,[32] which is given below, is cited in the CBC article[33] and it shows beyond doubt that "Consultant A" who owns the shell company "Alumet Ltd." is Victor Philip Dahdaleh.

"From: Victor Phillip Dahdaleh [mailto:zzzz@dadcogroup.com]
Sent: Friday, March 30, 2007 4:47 PM

To: *Mossack Fonseca & Co. BVI Ltd
Subject: Alumet Limited 22812

Attention: Xxxxxxxxx Xxxx

Mosseck Fonseca

Greetings! Further to my telecom with one of your colleagues today, and as requested, this email confirms that in my capacity as the owner and director of Alumet, I hereby appoint the following to be additional directors to the above company:

Xxxx Xxxxxxx, Hamilton House, St. Julian's Avenue, St. Petersport, Guernsey, GY1 1 WA tel: +44 1481 xxx xxx; fax: +44 1481 xxx xxx

Xxxx Xxxxxxx, Hamilton House, St. Julian's Avenue, St.Petersport, Guernsey, GY1 1 WA tel:+44 1481 xxx xxx;fax: +44 1481 xxx xxx

---

32   https://assets.documentcloud.org/documents/2842261/2007-03-30-Victor-Dahdaleh-Email-to-Mossack.pdf

33   'Panama Papers confirm Canadian billionaire and university benefactor as mystery man in global bribery case' — http://www.cbc.ca/news/business/panama-papers-victor-dahdaleh-alcoa-bribery-case-1.3598527

This should be effective Friday 30 March 2007. Please record this in the registration. Please confirm.

On another subject, I am considering the incorporation of one or two BVI companies. Would you kindly send to me details on how to proceed with this?

Thank you for your assistance in these matters.

Best regards

Victor Phillip Dahdaleh,

Tel: +44 7711 xxx xxx, e-mail: xxxx@dadcogroup.com"

It is thus apparent that it is Victor Philip Dahdaleh who is 'Consultant A' mentioned in the SEC's order pertaining to ALCOA INC. (the respondent), where the SEC has charged the various stakeholders with serious 'criminal' offences and also levied a huge fine of $175 million.

Please recall that this SEC order pertains to Foreign Corrupt Practices Act violations including payment of bribes.

Given the above, it is indeed truly baffling as to how the Clinton Foundation has accepted huge sums of money from Victor P. Dahdaleh & The Victor Phillip Dahdaleh Charitable Foundation as well as how the Clinton Foundation had made him a trustee. I am truly shocked by these activities and by the close association of the Clintons with people like Victor P. Dahdaleh. Again, I sincerely hope that a Hillary Clinton Presidency, if and when it happens, would keep out such people from the White House!

The Case of Bank of America/Merrill Lynch

The fifth and last case in this chapter is that of Bank of America/Merrill Lynch (BoA/ML), which is yet another favorite of the Clintons. While Hillary gave one speech to BoA/ML, Bill delivered four speeches. While four of these speeches were made during period 2011–2015, one speech was in the pre-financial crisis era (2001–2007). A total of $1,300,000 was received as speaking fees by the Clintons.

In addition, several staff (including senior management) of Bank of America/Merrill Lynch have contributed (individually) to the Hillary Clinton 2016 presidential run for a total of $123,362.[34]

In addition, to top it all off, Bank of America Corporation gave $100,001 to $250,000 to the Clinton Foundation while Bank of America Foundation gave $500,001 to $1,000,000. Huge sums indeed!

While Bank of America/Merrill Lynch is one of the largest banks in the United States, it must, however, be remembered that Bank of America reached a settlement of $16.7 billion with the federal and state joint working group formed to investigate wrong doing in the pre-financial crisis mortgage-backed securities market.

In totality, Bank of America has since 2008 reportedly, "entered into or been subject to 51 major legal settlements, judgments, and regulatory fines. Taken together, they add up to $91.2 billion in monetary and nonmonetary damages."[35]

A list of key settlements by Bank of America reached in 2014 alone are provided in table 9.3 below, which certainly does not paint a picture of a well-functioning, rule-abiding Wall Street bank by any measure.

Table 9.3: Bank of America Settlements in Year 2014			
S. No	**Date**	**Issue**	**Settlement and/ or Judgment Amount**
1.	Still pending	Sale of toxic mortgage backed securities sold by bank and its legacy companies.	Ambac is reportedly asking is $2.5 billion in damages.
2.	September 2014	Over reporting of regulatory capital.	SEC fine is $7.65 million.

---

34   Federal Election Commission (FEC) data — see www.fec.gov — data as of May 1, 2016.

35   The Complete List: 'Bank of America's Legal Fines and Settlements Since 2008' — http://www.fool.com/investing/general/2014/10/01/the-complete-list-bank-of-americas-legal-fines-and.aspx

Table 9.3: Bank of America Settlements in Year 2014			
S. No	Date	Issue	Settlement and/ or Judgment Amount
3.	August 2014	Sale of shoddy residential mortgage-backed securities (principally by Countrywide Financial) in the years leading up to the crisis.	$16.65 billion settlement with Federal/State agencies.
4.	July 2014	Sale of toxic mortgage backed securities sold by bank and its legacy companies.	Settlement of $650 million with American International Group (AIG).
5.	April 2014	Forcing customers to sign up for extra credit card products.	Consumer Financial Protection Bureau fine is $727 million.
6.	April 2014	Securities fraud claims.	Settles with Allstate. Amount not known. Value of securities as per lawsuit is $167 million.
7.	April 2014	Securities fraud claims mainly related to Residential Mortgage Backed Securities (RMBS) sold by Countrywide Financial.	Settles with Allstate. Amount not known. Allstate reportedly asking $700 million.
8.	March 2014	Toxic second-lien RMBS.	$950 million settlement with Financial Guaranty Insurance Co.

Table 9.3: Bank of America Settlements in Year 2014			
S. No	Date	Issue	Settlement and/ or Judgment Amount
9.	March 2014	Defrauding Fannie Mae and Freddie Mac by Bank of America and mainly Countrywide Financial.	$9.5 billion settlement with Federal Housing Finance Agency.
10.	March 2014	Security fraud charges associated with Bank of America acquiring Merrill Lynch.	Bank of America and former CEO Ken Lewis settle $25 million.
11.	February 2014	Kickback scheme inflating the cost of insurance that homeowners were forced to buy.	Settles $228 million (Insurance dispute).
Compiled from several sources including The Fool.com[36], Bank of America, U.S. Department of Justice, New York Attorney General's Office, Securities and Exchange Commission, Federal Trade Commission, Reuters, Bloomberg, *The New York Times*, and *The Wall Street Journal and other web sources including court documents*. Citations as per original sources.			

Additionally, Merrill Lynch, which has merged with Bank of America, has been charged with following:

(a) "The Securities and Exchange Commission ... charged Merrill Lynch with making faulty disclosures about collateral selection for two collateralized debt obligations (CDO) that it structured and marketed to investors, and maintaining inaccurate books and records for a third CDO. Merrill Lynch agreed to pay $131.8 million to settle the SEC's charges."[37]

(b) "The Securities and Exchange Commission ... charged two Merrill Lynch entities with using inaccurate data in the course of executing

---

36   http://www.fool.com/investing/general/2014/10/01/the-complete-list-bank-of-americas-legal-fines-and.aspx

37   'SEC Charges Merrill Lynch With Misleading Investors in CDOs' — https://www.sec.gov/News/PressRelease/Detail/PressRelease/1370540492377

short sale orders. Merrill Lynch agreed to admit wrongdoing, pay nearly $11 million, and retain an independent compliance consultant in order to settle the charges."[38]

(c)   "The Financial Industry Regulatory Authority (FINRA) announced ... that it has censured and fined Merrill Lynch Professional Clearing Corp. (Merrill Lynch PRO) $3.5 million for violating Regulation SHO, an SEC rule that established a regulatory framework to govern short sales and prevent abusive naked short selling. FINRA also censured and fined its affiliated broker-dealer, Merrill Lynch, Pierce, Fenner & Smith Incorporated (Merrill Lynch), $2.5 million for failing to establish, maintain and enforce supervisory systems and procedures related to Regulation SHO and other areas."[39]

The above clearly shows the kind of wrong doing that Bank of America, Merrill Lynch and its associates engaged in at various times. What is really perplexing is the fact that Hillary Clinton/Bill Clinton were delivering paid speeches at Bank of America/Merrill Lynch despite the fraudulent environment prevalent at these institutions. More shockingly, huge donations ranging from $100,001 to $250,000 to the Clinton Foundation (by Bank of America Corporation) and $500,001 to $1,000,000 to the Clinton Foundation (by Bank of America Foundation) have been received.

This is yet another example of how "corrupt" money plays a role in the political process. Given the proximity that Bank of America and Merrill Lynch have with the Clintons, and given the kind of issues and problems that these institutions face in their regular operations, what good is any promise or guarantee that Bank of America and Merrill Lynch will not "curry" favors from Hillary Clinton, if and when she becomes President?

---

38   'Merrill Lynch Admits Using Inaccurate Data for Short Sale Orders, Agrees to $11 Million Settlement'— https://www.sec.gov/news/pressrelease/2015-105.html
39   'FINRA Fines Merrill Lynch a Total of $6 Million for Reg SHO Violations and Supervisory Failures' — https://www.finra.org/newsroom/2014/finra-fines-merrill-lynch-total-6-million-reg-sho-violations-and-supervisory-failures

Overall, the basic question from the five case studies presented in this chapter is simple and straight:

Given Hillary Clinton's supposed promises made through her election tirade against corporate crime and her emphasis on the need to crackdown on such activities, isn't her ability to match her actions with her rhetoric severely compromised by:

(a) the Clinton Foundation's association with and acceptance of huge sums of money in each of the aforementioned cases;

(b) her campaign's acceptance of money from Blackstone, Vinod Gupta, and Bank of America detailed above;

(c) the Clinton Foundation's reported use of Vinod Gupta, Victor Dahdaleh, and Sant Singh Chatwal as its trustees; and

(d) Hillary and Bill's acceptance of invitations to deliver several paid speeches to Bank of America and Merrill Lynch.

Friends, what more can I say? I rest my case.

Chapter 10

Hillary Clinton, the Trans-Pacific Partnership And Free Trade-Agreements (1993–2016)

As the West Virginia primary drew closer, Hillary Clinton's opposition to the Trans-Pacific Partnership (TPP) became more strident and stronger in substantive terms as she categorically stated, "I oppose the TPP agreement."[1]

This was quite in contrast with her statements on several occasions in the past when she had spoken glowingly about the TPP.

First, let's rewind back to when Hillary Clinton was Secretary of State and see what her stand on TPP was, as revealed in her speeches and remarks.[2]

Instance # 1

Hillary Clinton's Speech delivered as Secretary of State on "Regional Architecture in Asia: Principles and Priorities" at the Imin Center-Jefferson Hall, Honolulu, Hawaii, USA on January 12, 2010.

Hillary Clinton's Remarks: "To advance economic opportunity, we

---

1   'Clinton Commits: No TPP, Fundamentally Rethink Trade Policies' — http://www.huffingtonpost.com/entry/clinton-commits-no-tpp-fu_b_9887124.html?section=india

2   There are some over 40 instances where she mentioned TPP in a very positive manner! Not all of these are included here and just a sampling of 10 instances across countries is provided.

must focus on lowering trade and investment barriers, improving market transparency, and promoting more balanced, inclusive, and sustainable patterns of economic growth. ... In addition, the United States is engaging in the Trans-Pacific Partnership trade negotiations as a mechanism for improving linkages among many of the major Asia-Pacific economies."[3]

Hillary came out in support of lowering trade and investment barriers and also mentioned the Trans-Pacific Partnership (TPP) in a positive light, in the context of improving inter-linkages among the major Asia-Pacific economies. This is quite in contrast with the stand she has taken on TPP during the 2016 presidential primary season.

Instance # 2

Remarks made by Hillary Clinton, as Secretary of State, in the presence of Vietnam Deputy Prime Minister and Foreign Minister Pham Gia Khiem at the Government Guest House, Hanoi, Vietnam, on July 22, 2010.

> **Hillary Clinton's Remarks:** "And we are particularly seeking to promote economic progress in Vietnam through broad-based growth built on Vietnam's integration into the regional and global economy. We discussed our shared interest in expanding trade to create jobs in both countries. And I am very much supportive of Vietnam's participation as a full member in the Trans-Pacific partnership."[4]

Here, she is actively seen canvassing for Vietnam's participation in the TPP.

Instance # 3

Remarks made by Hillary Clinton, as Secretary of State, on United States Foreign Policy delivered at Council on Foreign Relations, Washington, D.C., USA on September 8, 2010.

---

3   'Remarks on Regional Architecture in Asia: Principles and Priorities' — http://www.state.gov/secretary/20092013clinton/rm/2010/01/135090.htm

4   'Remarks With Vietnam Deputy Prime Minister And Foreign Minister Pham Gia Khiem' — http://www.state.gov/secretary/20092013clinton/rm/2010/07/145034.htm

Hillary Clinton's Remarks: "We want to realize the benefits from greater economic integration. In order to do that, we have to be willing to play. To this end, we are working to ratify a free trade agreement with South Korea, we're pursuing a regional agreement with the nations of the Trans-Pacific Partnership, and we know that that will help create new jobs and opportunities here at home."[5]

She can be seen canvassing for the TPP, which she believes will have a positive impact through greater economic integration. The key point here is that after having said all of this, she opposes TPP during the primary election season. Wonder why?

Instance # 4

Remarks made by Hillary Clinton as Secretary of State on America's Engagement in the Asia-Pacific at Kahala Hotel, Honolulu, HI, USA on October 28, 2010.

Hillary Clinton's Remarks: "Because the progress we see today is the result not only of the hard work of leaders and citizens across the region, but the … the American business leaders and entrepreneurs who invested in new markets and formed trans-Pacific partnerships …

Few countries punch as far above their weight as Singapore, and we're working together to promote economic growth and integration, leveraging Singapore's leadership in ASEAN and the role it has played in negotiating the Trans-Pacific Partnership. …

We are also pressing ahead with negotiations for the Trans-Pacific Partnership, an innovative, ambitious multilateral free trade agreement that would bring together nine Pacific Rim countries, including four new free trade partners for the United States, and potentially others in the future. 2011 will be a pivotal year for this agenda. Starting with the Korea Free Trade Agreement, continuing with the negotiation of the

---

5   'Remarks on United States Foreign Policy' — http://www.state.gov/
        secretary/20092013clinton/rm/2010/09/146917.htm

Trans-Pacific Partnership, working together for financial rebalancing at the G-20, and culminating at the APEC Leaders Summit in Hawaii, we have a historic chance to create broad, sustained, and balanced growth across the Asia Pacific and we intend to seize that."[6]

The above quotation clearly illustrates the optimism that Hillary Clinton shared for the TPP when she was Secretary of State. Given this, her present anti TPP stance, during the 2016 election season, seems inexplicable since, to the best of my knowledge, there have been no credible statements from her giving reasons for this crucial change in her position with regard to TPP.

Instance # 5

Remarks made by Hillary Clinton as Secretary of State after signing ceremonies at Hanoi in the presence of Vietnamese Foreign Minister Pham Gia Khiem on October 30, 2010.

Hillary Clinton's Remarks: "And the foreign minister and the prime minister and I talked about how to expand this trade relationship, including through the Trans-Pacific Partnership. The United States, Vietnam, and seven other countries finished a third round of negotiations on the TPP this month and we hope that Vietnam can conclude it in internal process and announce its status as a full member of the partnership soon."[7]

Yet another instance of Hillary Clinton actively pushing the TPP, this time in Vietnam.

Instance # 6

Remarks made by Hillary Clinton as Secretary of State at the Town Interview Hosted by Media Prima at the International Islamic University of Malaysia, Kuala Lumpur Malaysia on November 2, 2010.

---

6   'America's Engagement in the Asia-Pacific' — http://www.state.gov/
     secretary/20092013clinton/rm/2010/10/150141.htm
7   'Remarks With Vietnamese Foreign Minister Pham Gia Khiem' — http://
     www.state.gov/secretary/20092013clinton/rm/2010/10/150189.htm

Hillary Clinton's Remarks: "So in our meetings with your government officials and even in my conversation with the prime minister earlier today, we of course talked about our bilateral relationship but we also talked about the role that Malaysia is playing in the Trans Pacific Partnership, a new free trade agreement that will enhance market access, but also working to support Afghanistan and the people there with training and medical services."[8]

Hillary Clinton is seen talking about the benefits of the TPP in terms of enhancing market access. If that is the case and if Hillary Clinton is a firm believer in free trade, why oppose it now during the 2016 election season?

Instance # 7
Secretary Clinton's Remarks at a Meeting with Kuala Lumpur Embassy Staff and Their Families, Kuala Lumpur, Malaysia on November 2, 2010.

Hillary Clinton's Remarks: "We have some very exciting work on the Trans-Pacific Partnership, enhancing trade and investment (inaudible) that will promote closer cooperation."[9]

In this speech, Hillary Clinton talks very positively about TPP and its benefits including enhancing trade and investment. Again, if an agreement is so positive in its impact, why does Hillary Clinton oppose it now (during the 2016 election season), especially after having canvassed for it so heavily when she was Secretary of State, just a few years ago. To date, to the best of my knowledge, I have not seen a credible explanation for the change in Hillary Clinton's position on TPP.

Instance # 8
Hillary Clinton's Remarks as Secretary of State with Malaysian Foreign

---

8   'Townterview Hosted by Media Prima in Malaysia' — http://www.state.gov/
     secretary/20092013clinton/rm/2010/11/150325.htm
9   'Secretary Clinton's Meeting with Kuala Lumpur Embassy Staff and
     Their Families' — http://www.state.gov/secretary/20092013clinton/
     rm/2010/11/150319.htm

Minister Anifah Aman, Ministry of Foreign Affairs, Kuala Lumpur, Malaysia on November 2, 2010.

> **Hillary Clinton's Remarks:** "Finally, we are pleased that Malaysia joined last month's negotiations for the Trans-Pacific Partnership. That is a pact that would expand markets and create a level playing field for people in every country that does participate."[10]

Hillary Clinton's speech clearly underlined her happiness over Malaysia joining the negotiations for the TPP, which she believed would expand markets (not just access) and create a level playing field (which is a basic dictum of free trade).

Instance # 9

Hillary Clinton's Remarks as Secretary of State at the Pratt & Whitney Trade Event, Subang Airport, Kuala Lumpur, Malaysia on November 3, 2010.

> **Hillary Clinton's Remarks:** "That is why the United States is very pleased by Malaysia's decision to join the negotiations for the Trans Pacific Strategic Economic Partnership. This regional trade agreement will promote shared success by expanding markets and building a level playing field for workers in every country that participates.
>
> No one can do this alone. The days of going it alone in the global economy are behind us. Building shared prosperity is a goal that we can only achieve together"[11]

In the course of above speech, Hillary Clinton touched upon a very important concept, that of building shared prosperity, implying that the TPP would play a crucial role in the same. So, why this reversal of views against TPP during the 2016 election season?

10　'Remarks with Malaysian Foreign Minister Anifah Aman' — http://www.state.gov/secretary/20092013clinton/rm/2010/11/150321.htm

11　'Remarks at the Pratt & Whitney Trade Event' — http://www.state.gov/secretary/20092013clinton/rm/2010/11/150330.htm

Instance # 10

Hillary Clinton's Remarks as Secretary of State With New Zealand Prime Minister John Phillip Key and New Zealand Foreign Minister Murray Stuart McCully at the Parliament Theatrette, Wellington, New Zealand on November 4, 2010.

> **Hillary Clinton's Remarks:** "Well, let me say that we discussed at some length, both the foreign minister and I and then the prime minister and I, the way forward on trade. We are very committed to the Trans Pacific Partnership, and New Zealand, again, is playing a leading role. And we want to expedite the negotiations as much as possible. So we are exploring ways that we can try to drive this agenda. I am absolutely convinced that opening up markets in Asia amongst all of us and doing so in a way that creates win-win situations so that people feel that trade is in their interests. ...
>
> So we are very committed to TPP. ...But our priority is to really focus on the TTP and see how fast we can move that towards completion, and I think that's very much in both New Zealand's and the United States' interests."[12]

Yet another instance of Hillary Clinton unequivocally underlining her commitment to the TPP, a free trade agreement that she suddenly finds unacceptable today during the 2016 election season.

Summary of Position on TPP

From all of the above direct quotes from Hillary's speeches in various locations[13], it is very clear that she was an ardent supporter of free trade and TPP . . . at least as long as she was Secretary of State.

To phrase it differently, she supported it so long as she was not

---

12   'Remarks With New Zealand Prime Minister John Phillip Key and New Zealand Foreign Minister Murray Stuart McCully' — http://www.state.gov/secretary/20092013clinton/rm/2010/11/150390.htm

13   There are over 40 speeches where she has spoken positively about the TPP, when she was Secretary of State.

running for the post of the President of the United States. Perhaps, the general mood of the American Public and the stand of Bernie Sanders seem to have pushed Hillary Clinton to the far left and forced her to oppose the TPP. That is the only explanation that I can come up with to explain her volte-face.

Hillary's Free Trade and Trade Agreement Flip Flop

In fact, if you look at Hillary Clinton's record on free trade and trade agreements in general, you will notice that she has numerous "flip flops" The following instances from the year 1996 onwards will shed even greater light on it.

Position on Free Trade # 1

Way back in 1996, when she was First Lady, Hillary Clinton's comments on NAFTA were quite revealing of her stance then. This is what she says:

> "Oh I think everybody is in favor of free and fair trade and I think that NAFTA is proving its worth!" [14]

This was a very positive comment indeed with regard to free trade. It clearly reflects Hillary Clinton's thinking with regard to international trade back in the mid-1990s.

Position on Free Trade # 2

In her brilliant speech on Values and Priorities of the 21st Century, (Recorded 2/2/1998), at the World Economic Forum (WEF) Davos, she argues that:

> "There was a very effective business effort in the United States on behalf of NAFTA."[15]

---

14   https://www.youtube.com/watch?v=jW4XPRA2jIk
15   http://www.c-span.org/video/?100018-1/21st-century-priorities; 'Hillary Rodham Clinton at the Annual Meeting of the World Economic Forum' — http://clinton3.nara.gov/WH/EOP/First_Lady/html/generalspeeches/1998/19980202.html

In fact, a viewing of the entire video will reveal that she also spoke completely in favor of free markets and said that the debate was settled on the matter. In fact, she cites the organization of the economy around free markets as a major accomplishment of the past century and goes on to state that the ability of the free market — to create jobs, enhance income and wealth and foster investment — cannot be disputed.

Again, as the First Lady, her comments were very positive and her speech truly eloquent and impressive.

Position on Free Trade # 3

Let us move ahead to the year 2000 and to a speech before the Working Families Party March 26, 2000 as part of her campaign for the New York Senate Seat, in the 2000 Election Cycle. Hillary Clinton said the following:

"I think the NAFTA agreement was flawed."[16]

The key point to note is that Hillary Clinton was seeking election for the New York Senate seat in year 2000. This is was her first election cycle for the U.S. Senate! Whether this comment was a genuine change of heart reflecting changing times and situations or a mere statement made before an election is any body's guess.

Position on Free Trade # 4

Let us move to the time when she was a Senator and after she had written and released her first memoir, *Living History* (2003). In her memoir, she passes an opinion on NAFTA:

"Creating a free trade zone in North America... would expand U.S. exports, create jobs, and ensure that our economy was reaping the

---

16   'Hillary's Record: Pretending to Oppose Trade Agreements' — http://www.huffingtonpost.com/ian-fletcher/hillary-promised-to-reneg_b_8267424.html?section=india; 'Fact Check: Obama Continues To Mislead on Hillary and NAFTA' — http://web.archive.org/web/20081212012728/http://www.hillaryclinton.com/news/release/view/?id=6175 and numerous other sources.

benefits, not the burdens, of globalization."[17]

Note the emphasis on free trade and NAFTA bringing in the benefits of globalization to the United States — this again was a very positive view of Hillary Clinton with regard to trade.

Position on Free Trade # 5

Moving on, let us look at July 31, 2003 when the Senate Bill was passed through a vote for the HR 2739 — U.S.-Singapore Free Trade Agreement Implementation Act — Key Vote. This is how Hillary Clinton voted:

Table 10.1: Hillary Clinton's Vote for Singapore Free Trade Agreement	
State	NY
District	Jr
Name	**Sen. Hillary Rodham Clinton**
Party	Democratic
Vote	**Yea**[18]

The details of the vote are given below:

- U.S.-Singapore Free Trade Agreement Implementation Act
- Passed by Senate
- Date: July 31, 2003
- Issues: Trade
- Bill: U.S.-Singapore Free Trade Agreement Implementation Act
- Yea: 66
- Nay: 32
- Bill Passed (Senate)

---

17   Hillary Clinton 2003, Living History, (New York: Scribner, 2003), p 182.

18   HR 2739 — U.S.-Singapore Free Trade Agreement Implementation Act — Voting Record — https://votesmart.org/bill/votes/12021#.Vx4MGHpj560

Hillary Clinton's support for the U.S. Singapore Free Trade Agreement was indeed reflected in the manner she voted.[19]

Position on Free Trade # 6

On the same day, i.e., July 31, 2003, the Senate Bill passed through a vote for the HR 2738 — U.S.-Chile Free Trade Agreement Implementation Act — Voting Record. This is how Hillary Clinton voted:

Table 10.2: Hillary Clinton's Vote for Chile Free Trade Agreement	
State	NY
District	Jr
Name	**Sen. Hillary Rodham Clinton**
Party	Democratic
Vote	**Yea**

The details of these are given below:

- Passed by Senate
- Date: July 31, 2003
- Issues: Trade
- Bill: U.S.-Chile Free Trade Agreement Implementation Act
- Yea: 65
- Nay: 32
- Bill Passed (Senate)

Hillary Clinton support for the U.S. Chile Free Trade Agreement was again clearly reflected in the manner she voted.[20]

19　HR 2739 — U.S.-Singapore Free Trade Agreement Implementation Act — Voting Record — https://votesmart.org/bill/votes/12021#.Vx4MGHpj560

20　HR 2738 — U.S.-Chile Free Trade Agreement Implementation Act — Voting Record — https://votesmart.org/bill/votes/7878#.Vx4P23pj560

Position on Free Trade # 7

On July 15, 2004, the Senate Bill passed through a vote for the HR 4759 — United States-Australia Free Trade Agreement Implementation Act — Bill Passed. This is how Hillary Clinton voted:

Table 10.3: Hillary Clinton's Vote for Australia Free Trade Agreement	
State	NY
District	Jr
Name	**Sen. Hillary Rodham Clinton**
Party	Democratic
Vote	**Yea**

The details of the vote are given below:

- Passed by Senate
- Date: July 15, 2004
- Issues: Trade
- Bill: United States-Australia Free Trade Agreement Implementation Act
- Yea: 80
- Nay: 16
- Bill Passed (Senate)

Hillary Clinton's positive stance on the U.S. Australia Free Trade Agreement was again reflected in the manner she voted.[21]

Position on Free Trade # 8

On July 21, 2004, the Senate Bill passed through a vote for the

---

21   U.S. Senate Roll Call Votes 108th Congress — 2nd Session — http://www.senate.gov/legislative/LIS/roll_call_lists/roll_call_vote_cfm.cfm?congress=108&session=2&vote=00156

S 2677 — United States-Morocco Free Trade Agreement Implementation Act — Bill Passed. This is how Hillary Clinton voted:

Table 10.4: Hillary Clinton's Vote for Morocco Free Trade Agreement	
State	NY
District	Jr
Name	**Sen. Hillary Rodham Clinton**
Party	Democratic
Vote	**Yea**

The details of the vote are given below:

- Passed by Senate
- Date: July 21, 2004
- Issues: Trade
- Bill: United States-Morocco Free Trade Agreement Implementation Act
- Yea: 85
- Nay: 13
- Bill Passed (Senate)

Hillary Clinton's support for the U.S. Morocco Free Trade Agreement was very positive as reflected in the manner she voted.[22]

Position on Free Trade # 9

On June 30, 2005, the Senate Bill passed through a vote for the S. 1307 (Dominican Republic-Central America-United States Free Trade Agreement Implementation Act) — Bill Passed. This is how Hillary Clinton voted:

---

22   U.S. Senate Roll Call Votes 108th Congress — 2nd Session — http://www.senate.gov/legislative/LIS/roll_call_lists/roll_call_vote_cfm.cfm?&congress=108&session=2&vote=00159

Table 10.5: Hillary Clinton's Vote for CAFTA Free Trade Agreement	
State	NY
District	Jr
Name	**Sen. Hillary Rodham Clinton**
Party	Democratic
Vote	**Nay**

The details of the vote are given below:

- Passed by Senate
- Date: June 30, 2005
- Issues: Trade
- Bill: (Dominican Republic-Central America-United States Free Trade Agreement Implementation Act)
- Yea: 54
- Nay: 45
- Bill Passed (Senate)

Hillary Clinton voted against the Dominican Republic-Central America-United States Free Trade Agreement Implementation Act.[23]

One might wonder whether her change in position was specific to that particular agreement or if it was influenced by the fact that she was seeking re-election to the Senate at that point in time — this aspect has to be considered and researched deeply.

Although, in a subsequent *Time magazine* interview (February 1, 2007), Hillary Clinton does provide the rationale for voting against CAFTA. She is reported to have said that she voted against CAFTA because there were no labor or environmental standards in the agreement

---

23   U.S. Senate Roll Call Votes 109th Congress — 1st Session — http://www.senate.gov/legislative/LIS/roll_call_lists/roll_call_vote_cfm.cfm?congress=109&session=1&vote=00170

and also that free trade cannot be a free ride (without rules).[24]

Position on Free Trade # 10

On July 29, 2006, the Senate Bill passed through a vote for the S. 3569
— United States-Oman Free Trade Agreement Implementation Act —
Bill Passed. This is how Hillary Clinton voted:

Table 10.6: Hillary Clinton's Vote for Oman Free Trade Agreement	
State	NY
District	Jr
Name	**Sen. Hillary Rodham Clinton**
Party	Democratic
Vote	Yea

The details of the vote are given below:

- Passed by Senate
- Date: July 29, 2006
- Issues: Trade
- Bill: United States-Oman Free Trade Agreement Implementation Act
- Yea: 60
- Nay: 34
- Bill Passed (Senate)

Hillary Clinton's support for the United States-Oman Free Trade
Agreement Implementation Act was evident as reflected in the manner
she voted.[25]

---

24   'Hillary: "I Have to Earn Every Vote"' — http://content.time.com/time/nation/
      article/0,8599,1584649,00.html

25   U.S. Senate Roll Call Votes 109th Congress — 2nd Session — http://
      www.senate.gov/legislative/LIS/roll_call_lists/roll_call_vote_cfm.
      cfm?congress=109&session=2&vote=00190

Position on Free Trade # 11

In a *Time magazine* interview published in 2007, Hillary Clinton is reported to have made several statements with regard to trade agreements.[26] Looking at the interview, it appears that while Hillary Clinton continued to support the basic premise of NAFTA and free trade, she was asking for tougher negotiations and better enforcement. Likewise, from what Hillary said with regard to CAFTA, it is obvious that she is looking for minimum standards on certain aspects with regard to trade agreements, which is a good thing because we need trade that is child labor free, has fair and equal wages (including by gender), and the like. At least, that is what she claims as her reason for voting against CAFTA and that seems a fair argument.

Position on Free Trade # 12

In 2007, on the campaign trail seeking the Democratic Party nomination for the 2008 presidential election, Hillary Clinton said that she would oppose "the ratification of a free trade pact with South Korea" as she believed that it would negatively impact the U.S. auto industry and its performance. She is also reported to have commented that the U.S.-South Korea free trade agreement would result in a loss of jobs for the middle class, enhance the U.S. trade deficit, and most importantly, make America less competitive.[27]

This is a very significant point and it would be good to keep this in mind as the actual passage of the Korean free trade agreement did eventually come about, but much later, when Hillary Clinton was Secretary of State and I am sure you are curious to know what she said then.

Position on Free Trade # 13

Talking about the pending trade agreements with regard to Peru, South Korea, Panama, and Colombia on her Presidential campaign trail in 2008, Clinton is reported to have said that, while she supported the

---

26   'Hillary: "I Have to Earn Every Vote"' —http://content.time.com/time/nation/article/0,8599,1584649,00.html

27   'Hillary Clinton slams proposed U.S.-Korea trade pact' — http://www.reuters.com/article/us-clinton-korea-idUSN0939324020070609

Peru free trade agreement, she would oppose the pending free trade agreements with South Korea, Colombia, and Panama. Among other things, she also talked of appointing a "trade enforcer" if and when she became President of the United States to monitor and enforce trade agreements.[28]

It is, however, important to note that she was not part of the voting in the U.S. Senate with regard to the Peru free trade bill, which was passed as shown below.

On December 4, 2007, the Senate Bill passed through a vote for the H.R. 3688 — United States-Peru Free Trade Agreement Implementation Act — Bill Passed. This is how Hillary Clinton voted:

Table 10.7: Hillary Clinton's Vote for Peru Free Trade Agreement	
State	NY
District	Jr
Name	Sen. Hillary Rodham Clinton
Party	Democratic
Vote	Absent

The details of this vote are given below:

- Passed by Senate
- Date: December 4, 2007
- Issues: Trade
- Bill: United States-Peru Free Trade Agreement Implementation Act
- Yea: 77
- Nay: 18

---

28   Hillary Clinton Statement on Pending Trade Agreements — http://web. archive.org/web/20081127135532/http:/www.hillaryclinton.com/news/release/ view/?id=4113

- Not Voting: 5

- Bill Passed (Senate)

Hillary Clinton's support for the United States-Peru Free Trade Agreement Implementation Act was not positive, as she did not vote on this.[29] Here, it needs to be mentioned that there was a Democratic primary debate scheduled on December 13, 2007 — see Democratic Candidates Debate in Johnston, Iowa.[30] Only Hillary can clarify if that was the reason for absenting herself.

Position on Free Trade # 14
In 2008, she again voiced her opinion strongly against the Colombia free trade agreement. She even promised to get the Congress to reject the Colombia Free Trade Agreement.[31]

Position on Free Trade # 15
Thereafter, from 2009 to 2013, when she was Secretary of State, she constantly supported free trade and free trade agreements as is evident from the 10 instances of speeches[32] given earlier. In fact, her released statement on the State Department website at the time of passage of the Panama free trade agreement says it all:

"The Free Trade Agreements passed by Congress tonight will make it easier for American companies to sell their products to South Korea, Colombia and Panama, which will create jobs here at home. The Obama Administration is constantly working to deepen our economic engagement throughout the world and these agreements are an example of that commitment.

---

29   U.S. Senate Roll Call Votes 110th Congress — 1st Session — http://www.senate.gov/legislative/LIS/roll_call_lists/roll_call_vote_cfm.cfm?&congress=110&session=1&vote=00413

30   Presidential Debates — 1960–2016 — http://www.presidency.ucsb.edu/ws/index.php?pid=76123

31   'Clinton reiterates opposition to Colombia trade pact' — http://articles.latimes.com/2008/apr/09/nation/na-penn9

32   In fact, there are over 40 instances where she spoke in favor of the TPP.

The stakes are not just economic. South Korea, Colombia and Panama are three important partners in strategically vital regions. With the passage of these agreements, America has delivered for our friends and allies. I want to thank Presidents Lee, Santos and Martinelli for their patience and willingness to partner with the Obama Administration as these agreements moved through Congress.

But our work is not yet done. We will not be content until these agreements are fully implemented so that American exporters can reap the benefits as soon as possible."[33]

Now, during the Democratic primary season in 2015–2016, she has opposed the very same TPP that she spoke so strongly for when she was Secretary of State. While her opposition to TPP was muted during the electioneering in 2015, by the time of the West Virginia primary in May 2016, she had come full circle and was opposing it very strongly.

Summary of Hillary's Position on Trade
In summary, one can make the following basic inferences from the above discussion. Hillary Clinton's position on trade has not been consistent over time. Her support for free trade appears to be somewhat related to whether or not, she holds a position (official or unofficial) at the time. As First Lady, she was strongly in support of free trade and NAFTA. When she sought election for the New York Senate seat in 2000, she voiced her opposition to NAFTA and also free trade. When she wrote her first memoir, *Living History* (2003), she spoke glowingly of the Clinton era and was positive in her references to NAFTA and free trade. Then she supported a spate of free trade agreements (through 2003–06) with Singapore, Chile, Australia, Morocco, and Oman while opposing CAFTA in 2005. The reasons for opposing CAFTA have already been elaborated. In 2007–2008, she again voiced her opposition to NAFTA and also the trade agreements with South Korea, Colombia, and Panama

---

33   'Passage of Colombia, Panama, and South Korea Trade Agreements' — https://blogs.state.gov/stories/2011/10/13/passage-colombia-panama-and-south-korea-trade-agreements#sthash.ZloicUCP.dpuf

while speaking in favor of the Peruvian free trade agreement. However, she did not vote for the Peruvian free trade agreement. Whether or not this was because of the Democratic primary debate (December 13, 2007) — hardly ten days away from when the actual Senate voting took place with regard to the Peruvian free trade agreement (December 4, 2007) — is something that only she can clarify.

From 2009 onwards until she remained Secretary of State in 2013, she espoused very strong support for all free trade agreements including South Korea, Panama, and Colombia — trade deals that she had previously opposed during her first presidential primary run. In several of her speeches and remarks as demonstrated earlier, she actively promoted the TPP, time and again, which she is now opposing in 2015–16, during her second presidential run. All of this leaves one baffled over what she will actually do with regard to trade deals, if and when she becomes the President of the United States. It's a very big and important question, but Hillary's track record does not permit a clear answer!

Chapter 11

The Hillary Clinton Email Saga

I came across this very intriguing piece of information on the official website of the U.S. House of Representatives, The Select Committee on Benghazi, (majority website) and it pertains to the Hillary Clinton email saga. I reproduce a statement from this press release and quote it below:

> "It is the FBI, not the Benghazi Committee that is investigating the mishandling of classified information in connection with Secretary Clinton's use of an unsecure, private server to conduct official U.S. government foreign policy."[1]

From the above, it can be inferred that the U.S. House of Representatives, The Select Committee on Benghazi (majority website), has clarified that the then Secretary of State, Hillary Clinton had indeed used an unsecured private server to conduct official U.S. government foreign policy.

The same has now been confirmed in the Inspector General's report of May 2016.[2]

A second issue is relevant here — Hillary Clinton has frequently

---

1   'Statement on Latest Release of Clinton Emails' — https://benghazi.house.gov/news/press-releases/statement-on-latest-release-of-clinton-emails

2   'Office of the Secretary: Evaluation of Email Records Management and Cyber security Requirements' — https://assets.documentcloud.org/documents/2842723/State-IG-Report-Clinton-Server.pdf

called the FBI investigation (with regard to her email issue) as a "security review". However, if you look at what the FBI specializes in — it is criminal investigation. Therefore, it may well be inferred that, given that the FBI is investigating Hillary Clinton's email saga as per the U.S. House of Representatives statement given above, Hillary Clinton is under criminal investigation by the FBI. This fact needs to be noted.

That said, conducting foreign policy through a private unsecure email is indeed a serious issue if you consider the duties of the Secretary of State and I quote from the official website that lists the duties of the Secretary of State:[3]

"Under the Constitution, the President of the United States determines U.S. foreign policy. The Secretary of State, appointed by the President with the advice and consent of the Senate, is the President's chief foreign affairs adviser. The Secretary carries out the President's foreign policies through the State Department and the foreign service of the United States.

Created in 1789 by the Congress as the successor to the Department of Foreign Affairs, the Department of State is the senior executive Department of the U.S. Government. The Secretary of State's duties relating to foreign affairs have not changed significantly since then, but they have become far more complex as international commitments multiplied. These duties — the activities and responsibilities of the State Department — include the following:[4]

(1) Serves as the President's principal adviser on U.S. foreign policy;

(2) **Conducts negotiations relating to U.S. foreign affairs[5];**

(3) Grants and issues passports to American citizens and exequaturs to foreign consuls in the United States;

---

3   Duties of the Secretary of State — http://www.state.gov/secretary/115194.htm
4   All activities and responsibilities highlighted in bold have direct implications for national defense and national security!
5   This activity and responsibility has direct implications for national defense and national security!

(4)   **Advises the President on the appointment of U.S. ambassadors, ministers, consuls, and other diplomatic representatives;**

(5)   **Advises the President regarding the acceptance, recall, and dismissal of the representatives of foreign governments;**

(6)   **Personally participates in or directs U.S. representatives to international conferences, organizations, and agencies;**

(7)   **Negotiates, interprets, and terminates treaties and agreements;**

(8)   **Ensures the protection of the U.S. Government to American citizens, property, and interests in foreign countries;**

(9)   **Supervises the administration of U.S. immigration laws abroad;**

(10) Provides information to American citizens regarding the political, economic, social, cultural, and humanitarian conditions in foreign countries;

(11) **Informs the Congress and American citizens on the conduct of U.S. foreign relations;**

(12) Promotes beneficial economic intercourse between the United States and other countries;

(13) Administers the Department of State;

(14) **Supervises the Foreign Service of the United States.**

In addition, the Secretary of State retains domestic responsibilities that Congress entrusted to the State Department in 1789. These include the custody of the Great Seal of the United States, the preparation of certain presidential proclamations, the publication of treaties and international acts as well as the official record of the foreign relations of the United States, and the custody of certain original treaties and international agreements. **The Secretary also serves as the channel of communication between the Federal Government and the States on the extradition of fugitives to or from foreign countries."** [6]

In the above, it must be noted that activities and responsibilities 2, 4, 5, 6, 7, 8, 9, 11, and 14 (given above) have direct implications for national

---

6   Duties of the Secretary of State — http://www.state.gov/secretary/115194.htm

defense and national security. In addition to these, the activities and responsibilities shown in bold in the paragraph immediately above also have serious implications for national defense and national security as "The Secretary also serves as the channel of communication between the Federal Government and the states on the extradition of fugitives[7] to or from foreign countries."

All of these again clearly underline the fact that the duties of the Secretary of State are hugely concerned with national defense and national security, especially, in the changing world of the last three decades where fugitives like Osama Bin Laden have waged war on the United States property, both in the homeland and elsewhere across the globe while hiding in other countries.

It goes without saying that foreign policy has serious defense implications. Foreign policy cannot be conducted in isolation as nations everywhere (The United States included) attempt to build alliances against the global threat of transnational terrorism, which was in fact brought to the United States mainland via the despicable terrorist attacks of 9/11/2001. Therefore, there is always a national security aspect and thereby a national defense component of foreign policy, which needs to be recognized explicitly. Every foreign policy advisor, including the United States Secretary of State, would most certainly be aware of that.

Dealing with transnational terrorism is therefore a very integral part of foreign policy and be it 9/11/2001 in the United States, 7/7/2005 (in London), 26/11/2008 (in India), or the more recent Paris and Brussels attacks, it is foreign policy that will have to take a lead in ensuring national security. The national defense implications of this fact cannot be overemphasized. In fact, national security and national defense strategies are now an integral part of foreign policy because the foreign policy advisor (such as the United States Secretary of State) has the responsibility to ensure the safety and security of a nation's assets, properties, and citizens worldwide. I don't think there should be any doubts with regard to this.

---

7   The word fugitive should be interpreted to normally include terrorists like Osama Bin Laden, who have waged war on the United States of America.

Having said that, let's get back to the statement as given in the press release dated January 8, 2016 on the (majority) website of The Select Committee on Benghazi, House of Representatives. The statement also talks of classified information and we will get to that later. For now though, what is of immediate concern, and what should concern every American is the fact that the U.S. House of Representatives, The Select Committee on Benghazi, majority website[8] has put forth the statement that "Secretary Clinton used an unsecure, private server to conduct official U.S. government foreign policy." This fact has been reiterated by the Inspector General's (IG's) report of May 2016.[9]

It has to be said at this stage that Hillary Clinton's actions in using her private unsecure server to conduct official U.S. government foreign policy, was not quite in the best interests of the United States. This is a severe lack of judgment and compromise of security by one of the highest-ranking officials in the United States whose responsibilities (by default) also *include* security.

That said, let's fast forward and see what happened in Afghanistan just after Secretary of State John Kerry visited Afghanistan on Sunday, April 10, 2016. The horrific explosions that occurred after Secretary Kerry's visit make it very clear that in today's violent world, foreign policy is always closely intertwined with national defense and security.

Read the following news article — "Blasts rattle Kabul after US secretary of state John Kerry's visit to push for new Taliban peace talks,"[10] and you will automatically come to the same judgment.

Having set the context, let us now look at a set of emails[11] from

---

8   'Statement on Latest Release of Clinton Emails' — https://benghazi.house.gov/news/press-releases/statement-on-latest-release-of-clinton-emails

9   'Office of the Secretary: Evaluation of Email Records Management and Cyber security Requirements' — https://assets.documentcloud.org/documents/2842723/State-IG-Report-Clinton-Server.pdf

10   'Blasts rattle Kabul after US secretary of state John Kerry's visit to push for new Taliban peace talks' — http://www.abc.net.au/news/2016-04-10/blasts-rock-afganistan-after-us-secretary-of-state-visit/7313860

11   https://wikileaks.org/clinton-emails/emailid/2358

Hillary Clinton dated July 1, 2010 where the subject matter is a bomb blast in Pakistan.

"BOMB AT SUFI SHRINE

UNCLASSIFIED U.S. Department of State Case

No. F-2014-20439 Doc No. C05769248

Date: 08/31/2015

RELEASE IN FULL

From: Sullivan, Jacob J <Sullivarth@state.gov>

Sent: Thursday, July 1, 2010 6:27 PM

To: H

Subject Re: Bomb at Sufi shrine

Yep

Original Message

From: H <HDR22@clintonemail.com>

To: Sullivan, Jacobi

Sent: Thu Jul 01 18:25:22 2010

Subject: Re: Bomb at Sufi shrine

Can you get me more info about the shrine?

Original Message —

From: Sullivan, Jacob i <Sullivanh@state.gov>

To: H

Sent: Thu Jul 01 18:24:02 2010

Subject: Fw: Bomb at Sufi shrine

Fyi

Original Message —

From: Holbrooke, Richard

To: Sullivan, Jacobi

Sent: Thu Jul 01 18:07:11 2010

Subject: Fw: Bomb at Sufi shrine

Jake please pass to hillary. I will call. She may want to, especially given forthcoming trip. R PS--tell her I had a good (I think)u talk with Misha S today. Hope it helps trip.

Original Message —

From: Nasr, S Vali R

To: HolbrookeR@state.govs <HolbrookeR@state.gov >

Sent: Thu Jul 01 17:32:48 2010

Subject: Bomb at Sufi shrine

Richard 3 bombs devastated the shrine of Data Ganjbakhsh (the most sacred Muslim place in all of South Asia, and the shrine S was supposed to go to). Aside from loss of life, this is a major blow to Pakistan. I recommend that you call Qureshi, Nawaz and Pasha (who will be here tomorrow). This will either break Pakistanis or will get them into the fight. This shrine is deeply tied to the foundation of Islam in Pakistan.

Vali Nasr"[12]

The stakeholders in the above email trail (with the positions held by them then) are:

- Hillary Clinton, Secretary of State, The United States Government,
- Jacob Sullivan, Deputy Chief of Staff to the Secretary of State, Hillary Clinton
- Richard Holbrooke, Special Adviser on Pakistan and Afghanistan,

---

12   https://wikileaks.org/clinton-emails/Clinton_Email_August_Release/ C05769248.pdf

working under President Barack Obama and Secretary of State
Hillary Clinton

- Vali Nasr, Senior Advisor to the U.S. Special Representative
  for Afghanistan and Pakistan, Ambassador Richard Holbrooke,
  between 2009 and 2011

Was it right for such a high profile team to communicate on very
sensitive matters through the private unsecure email of Hillary Clinton,
then Secretary of State? Irrespective of whether or not laws were violated,
it was clearly irresponsible on the part of such a high profile team to
communicate on such a sensitive topic via a private unsecure server,
especially, on the eve of the well-publicized Secretary of State's visit to
Pakistan and Afghanistan, both of which are very sensitive regions and
have been linked to transnational terrorism.

It must be mentioned that Hillary Clinton's private unsecure email
server was indeed shown to be unsecure[13] after it was reportedly hacked
by Marcel Lazăr Lehel (aka Guccifer). Please recall that *Russia Today*[14]
has already previously published emails – about the Benghazi Embassy
attacks – supposedly hacked from the then Secretary of State Hillary
Clinton and Sydney Blumenthal, her advisor.

Anyway, getting back to the bomb blast of 2010 at a Sufi Shrine in
Pakistan as mentioned in Hillary Clinton's email shown earlier, I quote
from the BBC writing about these blasts in an article titled, "High alert
after Pakistan shrine suicide blasts."[15] The key issue to note here is that
when Pakistan was in a state of high alert after a bomb blast and the

---

13   'Jailed hacker Guccifer boasts, "I used to read [Clinton's] memos... and then do
      the gardening"' — https://pando.com/2015/03/20/exclusive-interview-jailed-
      hacker-guccifer-boasts-i-used-to-read-hillarys-memos-for-six-seven-hours-and-
      then-do-the-gardening/; 'No "coincidence" Romanian hacker, Guccifer, extradited
      amid Clinton probe' —http://www.foxnews.com/politics/2016/04/08/source-no-
      coincidence-romanian-hacker-guccifer-extradited-amid-clinton-probe.html

14   Hillary Clinton's "hacked" Benghazi emails: FULL RELEASE — https://www.
      rt.com/usa/complete-emails-guccifer-clinton-554/

15   Analysis, By Aleem Maqbool, BBC News, Islamabad, "No group has yet said that
      it carried out the attack, but the finger of blame is being pointed at the Taliban." —
      http://www.bbc.com/news/10486925

United States Secretary of State (i.e., Hillary Clinton) was visiting the country shortly thereafter, was she not aware of the national security and strategic implications in that context?

Furthermore, did this matter not concern national defense for the United States, especially after 9/11, and also given the fact that the Taliban regime in Afghanistan and Pakistani Taliban are known to have continuously helped Al Qaeda and Osama Bin Laden? In 2010, Osama Bin Laden was apparently still living in Abbottabad, Pakistan. In addition, let's not forget the fact that the United States has been fighting a drone war against the Pakistani terrorists in the Waziristan areas as well.

In the light of all that was going on, how correct and appropriate was it for emails to be sent — to the Secretary of State and by the Secretary of State — through an unsecured private server especially considering the fact that the content of the message was about a bombing incident in a foreign country that was supposedly under terrorist attack. Remember, Pakistan was the next stop for the Secretary of State who was planning to visit and did in fact visit shortly thereafter on July 18, 2010. If these unsecured emails of July 1, 2010 are not of concern to national security and defense, especially given the fact that Osama Bin Laden was still alive then and perhaps already living in Abbottabad, one wonders what will be.

As noted above, Hillary Clinton was scheduled to travel[16] to Pakistan and Afghanistan on July 18, 2010. An interview[17] she gave to *Fox News* at the time clearly proves her trip was concerned as much with foreign policy as with national defense and security, especially given the context of what was happening in Pakistan and the region.

In the interview,[18] Hillary talks of the terrorist threats to the United

---

16   'Secretary Clinton: Travel to Pakistan, Afghanistan, Republic of Korea, and Vietnam' — http://www.state.gov/secretary/20092013clinton/trvl/2010/144613.htm

17   Interview With Greta Van Susteren of *Fox News* — http://www.state.gov/secretary/20092013clinton/rm/2010/07/144969.htm

18   Interview With Greta Van Susteren of *Fox News* — http://www.state.gov/secretary/20092013clinton/rm/2010/07/144969.htm

States, the requirement for a much more cooperative relationship with Pakistan to counter such terrorist threats, and the dire need to prevent Afghanistan from becoming a failed state and so on.

This reiterates the point that Hillary Clinton was using her private and unsecured email server to communicate about United States foreign policy, a subject closely intertwined with national security and defense. Furthermore, this communication happened within the context of a global environment prevalent with transnational terrorism and transnational terrorist organizations like Al Qaeda and other networks (like ISIS) operational in foreign countries like Pakistan and elsewhere from where they have plotted and attacked the United States and other countries.

It is thus established that Hillary Clinton, as Secretary of State, was entrusted with and had lawful possession and control of information, relating to foreign policy, national security, and national defense (as shown in the examples and emails above and there are numerous other examples and emails that can be provided). It is also very clear that when Hillary Clinton was Secretary of State, she, permitted the above information (as demonstrated in the July 1, 2010 email trail above) related to foreign policy, national security and national defense to be removed from their proper place of custody, the secure United States government server(s), where they belonged and had them stored on an unsecured private email server. I am not sure that was wise under any circumstances and we will find out whether her actions violated the relevant laws of the land in the United States.

There are many more emails that went through Hillary Clinton's private unsecured server. I have analyzed them and their content clearly concerned issues of national defense, national security, foreign government information, and foreign policy. That being the case, it appears that Hillary Clinton by sending such emails via a private unsecured server when she was Secretary of State may have violated the following section of the law:

Take for example, U.S. Code › Title 18 › Part I › Chapter 37 › § 793[19].

---

19   https://www.law.cornell.edu/uscode/text/18/793

This section of the law does not talk of classified information and it just mentions information pertaining to national defense as shown below:

"U.S. Code › Title 18 › Part I › Chapter 37 › § 793[20]

"18 U.S. Code § 793 — Gathering, transmitting or losing defense information

f) Whoever, being entrusted with or having lawful possession or control of any document, writing, code book, signal book, sketch, photograph, photographic negative, blueprint, plan, map, model, instrument, appliance, note, or information, relating to the national defense, (1) through gross negligence permits the same to be removed from its proper place of custody or delivered to anyone in violation of his trust, or to be lost, stolen, abstracted, or destroyed, or (2) having knowledge that the same has been illegally removed from its proper place of custody or delivered to anyone in violation of its trust, or lost, or stolen, abstracted, or destroyed, and fails to make prompt report of such loss, theft, abstraction, or destruction to his superior officer — Shall be fined under this title or imprisoned not more than ten years, or both."[21]

Note that the word "classified" does not appear in this section of the law. It must be understood that this section does not require the information to be classified in any manner. All it requires is for the information to pertain to national defense and national security and as the email trail given earlier proves, the subject matter of the emails did pertain to national defense and national security indeed. Thus, it appears from the above that Hillary Clinton's sending out national defense and national security information through a private email and unsecure server may have constituted a violation of the above section of the law.

Therefore, Hillary Clinton's statements that she did not send out "classified" information via her private email on an unsecure server,

---

20   https://www.law.cornell.edu/uscode/text/18/793
21   https://www.law.cornell.edu/uscode/text/18/793

does not hold water. Her statements are irrelevant as far as this section goes because the focus here is on the transmittal of "information" (not classified) pertaining to national defense and national security which by default are highly interconnected. **Thus, Hillary Clinton appears to have violated 18 U.S. Code § 793 — "Gathering, transmitting or losing defense information."**

It has already been proven that Hillary Clinton in fact used her private email located on an unsecure server to conduct United States foreign policy. The example email trail given therein also proves the subject matter concerned foreign policy, national defense, and national security, in addition to pertaining to foreign governments. That being the case, it also appears that Hillary Clinton also violated the following section of the law:

"18 U.S. Code § 1924 — Unauthorized removal and retention of classified documents or material

Current through Pub. L. 114-38. (See Public Laws for the current Congress.)

- US Code

- Notes

(a) Whoever, being an officer, employee, contractor, or consultant of the United States, and, by virtue of his office, employment, position, or contract, becomes possessed of documents or materials containing classified information of the United States, knowingly removes such documents or materials without authority and with the intent to retain such documents or materials at an unauthorized location shall be fined under this title or imprisoned for not more than one year, or both.

(b) For purposes of this section, the provision of documents and materials to the Congress shall not constitute an offense under subsection (a).

(c)   In this section, the term 'classified information of the United States' means information originated, owned, or possessed by the United States Government concerning the national defense or foreign relations of the United States that has been determined pursuant to law or Executive order to require protection against unauthorized disclosure in the interests of national security.

(Added Pub. L. 103–359, title VIII, § 808(a), Oct. 14, 1994, 108 Stat. 3453; amended Pub. L. 107–273, div. B, title IV, § 4002(d)(1)(C)(i), Nov. 2, 2002, 116 Stat. 1809.)"[22]

The supposed legal violation is due to the nature of the information transmitted in Hillary Clinton's email, which meets the definition of 'classified information' given in section (c) above, i.e., information pertaining to foreign policy, national defense, national security, and foreign governments. In fact, section 1.4 (d) of the presidential executive order 13526 (dated 2009) on classified national security information also confirms the above. As per the Executive Order 13526, classified information would include:

"Information, whose unauthorized disclosure could reasonably be expected to cause identifiable or describable damage to the national security... and it pertains to one or more of the following:

(a)   military plans, weapons systems, or operations;

(b)   foreign government information;

(c)   intelligence activities (including covert action), intelligence sources or methods, or cryptology;

(d)   foreign relations or foreign activities of the United States, including confidential sources;

(e)   scientific, technological, or economic matters relating to the national security;

---

22   https://www.law.cornell.edu/uscode/text/18/1924

(f)   United States Government programs for safeguarding nuclear materials or facilities;

(g)   vulnerabilities or capabilities of systems, installations, infrastructures, projects, plans, or protection services relating to the national security; or

(h)   the development, production, or use of weapons of mass destruction."[23]

At the minimum, items (b), (c), (d) and (e) have been part of Hillary Clinton's email exchanges and therefore, there is no doubt that Hillary Clinton was transmitting classified information by definition, irrespective of whether they had been categorized as classified or not.

Thus, while Hillary Clinton has consistently denied the presence of classified information in her emails, the fact that she conducted foreign policy through her private email on an unsecure server means that she *was* dealing with classified information. In addition, as the example email transcript given earlier shows, there was foreign government information, foreign policy information, national defense information, and national security information in the emails. Such information is by definition classified as per section (c) 18 U.S. Code § 1924 and as per the presidential Executive Order 13526. There can be no ambiguity here.

A related issue deserves mention. As per the presidential Executive Order 13526 the responsibility for classification of material (documents, information, emails etc.) also happens to fall on the agency head amongst others. While there can be authorized persons for classifying material within an agency, the ultimate responsibility for timely classification of sensitive material undoubtedly falls on the head of the agency, which, in this case means Hillary Clinton. As head of the State Department by virtue of her being the Secretary of State, *she* was responsible[24] for the timely classification of her emails. While why she did not do it as the

---

23   Executive Order 13526 — Classified National Security Information — https://www.whitehouse.gov/the-press-office/executive-order-classified-national-security-information

24   See Executive Order 13526.

agency head is an important question, the fact that she was responsible for getting her emails classified, and did not do so, is a point that cannot be overlooked.

Furthermore, having failed in her responsibility, it must be mentioned that she also did not hand over custody of her emails in her private unsecured server to the State Department, which, in my opinion, perhaps prevented other authorized persons from classifying them. Therefore, when the emails themselves were not available for classification, Hillary Clinton's argument that she did not transmit any "classified information" through her private email via an unsecure server is simply smoke and mirrors because it was *she* who failed in her responsibility to classify them (or get them classified) when in fact they were most definitely in need of classification.

Thus, irrespective of whether the emails were classified or not, the fact that they contained information relating to foreign governments, foreign policy, national defense and national security, make these emails as classified (by default and by definition).

To put it differently, Hillary Clinton conducted foreign policy and communicated with foreign government personnel and dignitaries via her private email (using an unsecure server) and by definition, that information is classified. Likewise, she communicated on matters concerning national defense and national security with her private email using an unsecure server and by definition, that information is also classified. Therefore, without a doubt, it appears that all of her correspondence given above would most definitely be *classified information* in some form or the other. **This being the case, it appears that Hillary Clinton could have violated 18 U.S. Code § 1924 — "Unauthorized removal and retention of classified documents or material."**

One additional point needs to be made here. It has been reported that over 30,000 emails were supposedly deleted[25] from her private unsecure server and there seems to be no way of knowing what was

---

25   'Final Clinton emails coming today' — http://thehill.com/policy/national-security/270984-final-clinton-emails-coming-today

in those messages, unless the FBI has retrieved the emails. One key question here is whether the deletion of those emails is in itself wrong. Specifically, I wonder whether this deletion of over 30,000 emails is a violation of the United Stated Federal Records Act (1950).

The law (44 U.S. Code § 3301 — Definition of records) defines a record as:

"(a) Records Defined. —

   (1)   In general. — As used in this chapter, the term "records" —

       (A)   includes all recorded information, regardless of form or characteristics, made or received by a Federal agency under Federal law or in connection with the transaction of public business and preserved or appropriate for preservation by that agency or its legitimate successor as evidence of the organization, functions, policies, decisions, procedures, operations, or other activities of the United States Government or because of the informational value of data in them; and

       (B)   does not include —

           (i)   library and museum material made or acquired and preserved solely for reference or exhibition purposes; or

           (ii)   duplicate copies of records preserved only for convenience.

   (2)   Recorded information defined. —

       (a)   For purposes of paragraph (1), the term "recorded information" includes all traditional forms of records, regardless of physical form or characteristics, including information created, manipulated, communicated, or stored in digital or electronic form.

   (b)   Determination of Definition. —

           The   Archivist's   determination   whether   recorded

information, regardless of whether it exists in physical, digital, or electronic form, is a record as defined in subsection (a) shall be binding on all Federal agencies.

(Pub. L. 90–620, Oct. 22, 1968, 82 Stat. 1299; Pub. L. 94–575, § 4(c) (2), Oct. 21, 1976, 90 Stat. 2727; Pub. L. 113–187, § 5(a), Nov. 26, 2014, 128 Stat. 2009.)"[26]

The law also notes with regard to destruction and /or removal of Federal governmental records the following:

"Records Management by Federal Agencies, 44 U.S.C. Chapter 31 — § 3106. Unlawful removal, destruction of records

(a) FEDERAL AGENCY NOTIFICATION. — The head of each Federal agency shall notify the Archivist of any actual, impending, or threatened unlawful removal, defacing, alteration, corruption, deletion, erasure, or other destruction of records in the custody of the agency, and with the assistance of the Archivist shall initiate action through the Attorney General for the recovery of records the head of the Federal agency knows or has reason to believe have been unlawfully removed from that agency, or from another Federal agency whose records have been transferred to the legal custody of that Federal agency.

(b) ARCHIVIST NOTIFICATION. — In any case in which the head of the Federal agency does not initiate an action for such recovery or other redress within a reasonable period of time after being notified of any such unlawful action described in subsection (a), or is participating in, or believed to be participating in any such unlawful action, the Archivist shall request the Attorney General to initiate such an action, and shall notify the Congress when such a request has been made."[27]

---

26   https://www.law.cornell.edu/uscode/text/44/3301
27   Records Management by Federal Agencies — http://www.archives.gov/about/laws/fed-agencies.html

Three issues need mentioning here:

(1) First, is the fact that over 30,000 emails were deleted. In spite of the report from Hillary that they were personal emails pertaining to 'Yoga' etc., who can verify whether official federal records were not contained in the destroyed emails? The FBI could have done that, but given that the emails are not available, there is no way to honestly tell if federal records were not destroyed.

(2) Second, the other issue is with emails that were turned over to the State Department by Hillary Clinton after the email controversy erupted. I am sure that by storing these official emails on a private unsecure server Hillary Clinton undoubtedly prevented them from being kept in the place that they had to be statutorily stored — the official secure government server. This surely meets the condition of unlawful removal of federal records from the place they belong and therefore appears to constitute a violation of the above section of the Federal Records Act.

(3) Third, is the issue regarding the role of the agency head — in this case Hillary Clinton was the head of the State Department — in preserving federal records. She herself was bound by duty to safeguard the federal records and notify the appropriate authorities[28] of any action that caused the federal records to be displaced from where they should have been originally stored. Indeed, this makes the matter doubly serious.

Thus, from the above, it can be said that Hillary Clinton could have violated the Federal Records Act, 44 U.S.C. Chapter 31 — § 3106 — "Unlawful removal, destruction of records."

One another interesting fact needs to be noted with regard to the email saga. Hillary Clinton signed a Non-Disclosure Agreement (NDA), on January 22, 2009. As per this, she agreed to protect highly classified

---

28   The Archivist in turn, is duty bound to initiate action through the Attorney General and also notify the Congress of the same.

information, and also acknowledged that her failure to do so could result in criminal prosecution.

This is what she said in the NDA:

> "I have been advised that any breach of this Agreement may result in my termination of my access to SCI and removal from a position of special confidence and trust requiring such access as well as the termination of my employment or other relationships with any Department or Agency that provides me with access to SCI. In addition, I have been advised that any authorized disclosure of SCI by me may constitute violations of United States criminal laws, including provisions of Sections 793, 794, 798 and 952, Title 18 United States Code; and of Section 783(b), Title 50, United States Code. Nothing in this Agreement constitutes a waiver by the United States of the right to prosecute me for any statutory violation."[29]

> "I have been advised that the unauthorized disclosure, unauthorized retention, or negligent handling of SCI by me could cause irreparable injury to the United States or be used to advantage by foreign nation. I hereby agree that I will never divulge anything marked as SCI or that I know to be SCI to anyone who is not authorized to receive it without prior written authorization from the United States Government department or agency (hereinafter Department or Agency) that authorized my access to SCI.[30]

That being the case, I wonder how and why Hillary Clinton used her private email and unsecure server, which clearly violated the terms set out in her Non-Disclosure Agreement. It is clear that the emails, irrespective of whether they had been classified or not, contained classified information as per Executive Order 13526 as the subject matter concerned foreign governments, foreign policy, national defense, and national security.

---

29   http://freebeacon.com/wp-content/uploads/2015/11/HRC-SCI-NDA1.pdf
30   http://freebeacon.com/wp-content/uploads/2015/11/HRC-SCI-NDA1.pdf

In fact, what is really ironical in this whole episode is the fact that not only did Hillary Clinton conduct foreign policy, correspond with foreign dignitaries and officials and discuss aspects related to national security and national defense through the means of a private email from an unsecure server, she went the distance to shroud these actions with all sorts of explanations and excuses, which have now been nullified by the IG's report. Furthermore, what is very startling is the fact that she was rather casual about the whole thing as several instances[31] clearly demonstrate. This in fact shows her total disregard for the NDA that she had committed to and signed by herself.

It is in the above context that the FBI's investigation of Hillary Clinton's use of a private email and an unsecured server is indeed very serious. Being under such an investigation is neither appropriate for someone who once occupied the very important position of the Secretary of State of the United States nor is it apt for someone who could become the President of the United States of the future. A mere apology won't suffice, as there is clear indication that several sections of the law have been violated by the above action of Hillary Clinton.

Furthermore, in using a private email and unsecured server to conduct United States foreign policy, communicate with and about foreign governments, and discuss national defense and security issues, Hillary Clinton showed total indifference and lack of respect towards the very rules and regulations that people like her in positions of trusted authority (either when she was part of the Senate and/or Secretary of State) have helped establish. Once again, this does not befit a person who is campaigning to be the next President of the United States.

In addition to the above, several procedural aspects are evident from the emails themselves. These are highlighted below:

---

31   See 'Hillary Clinton Email Probe Update: New Emails Show Clinton Deliberately Used Unsecured Home Server Despite Security Risk' — http://www.inquisitr. com/3091393/hillary-clinton-email-probe-update-new-emails-show-clinton-deliberately-used-unsecured-home-server-despite-security-risk/; 'Another 57 Clinton email threads contain foreign governments' information' — http://mobile. reuters.com/article/idUSKCN0R22C120150902

(a) Hillary Clinton is reported[32] to have asked her key staff to take away the classification schemata and re-transmit the same information to her on a private email associated with an unsecure server. This needs to be investigated further in a thorough manner, as the implications of such an improper order are indeed very serious.

(b) Hillary Clinton, as the head of the State Department, was ultimately responsible for the classified material (information pertaining to foreign governments, foreign policy, national defense and national security) that her department either generated or received. That being the case, by transmitting this information through private email and an unsecure server, she ensured that this "classified information" was not available within the government and its secure email/servers where they really belonged. This is a major reason for the emails not having been classified. Today, when the emails are being released, the government withholds some information from the emails. Why? Because these emails contain classified information as defined in the Executive Order 13526.

(c) Further, the whole Hillary Clinton email saga itself, including the release of records as per the Freedom of Information Act (FOIA), has exposed to the whole world the process used to gather intelligence and this is a huge compromise of national security strategies. The use of outsiders like Blumenthal is a case in point; and

(d) Lastly, by sending classified information (information pertaining to foreign governments, foreign policy, national defense and national security) through a private email and unsecured server, Hillary Clinton exposed such information to

32   Please see the statement on latest release of Clinton emails — https://benghazi. house.gov/news/press-releases/statement-on-latest-release-of-clinton-emails This statement alludes to the above discussion. In this context, it must be mentioned that Hillary Clinton met with the FBI in early July 2016 as part of their investigation. This of course, was preceded by the untimely and inappropriate meeting that Bill Clinton had with Attorney General Loretta E. Lynch at the Phoenix airport.

potential cyber-attacks and hacking. While it is not definitely known whether Hillary Clinton's emails were hacked, the use of a private email and unsecured server by her meant that she was careless about such sensitive information, which indeed had to be safeguarded in the first place and which she had committed to safeguard as per her NDA.

In summary, Hillary Clinton conducted U.S. foreign policy through her private email and unsecure server and there can be no two ways about that. Much of the information pertained to foreign governments, foreign policy, national defense and national security and so it was actually classified, (even if it had not been classified). Part of the reason for these emails not being classified was the fact that Hillary Clinton kept them on a private email and private server, away from the State Department and government. It was also Hillary Clinton's duty to get them classified, which she did not do. In addition, many of those emails have now been supposedly destroyed and we can never find out what was actually in them. That thousands of emails were personal in nature and were about "Yoga" is hard to believe. If so, why were they deleted?

In addition, as noted earlier, there were many reported procedural violations like getting the classification schemata removed and transmitting the same (classified information) on an unsecure system.

Further, as far as the email saga goes, it smacks of the scant respect Hillary Clinton has for rules and regulations. The IG's report clearly proves that Hillary Clinton, despite being warned by the State Department, disregarded the rules/regulations and conducted foreign policy through her private email/unsecure server.

All in all, Hillary Clinton appears to have disregarded the terms set out in her non-disclosure agreement (NDA) that she herself signed as Secretary of State (SoS) by being careless and negligent about classified information (information pertaining to foreign governments, foreign policy, national defense and national security) — unintentionally or otherwise — and this is a huge error on her part. In doing so, she may have violated the laws of the United States (as noted earlier).

Irrespective of whether Hillary Clinton gets indicted, the use of a private email/unsecure server to conduct official business and foreign policy is certainly not acceptable as per the laws of the United States. In view of the IG's report, it is now clearly established that having conducted foreign policy and official business through a private email/unsecure server, Hillary Clinton tried her best to shroud what had happened with explanations that have since fallen flat. That makes matters even worse for Hillary and for the American public.

As noted above, and not to sound like a broken record, law is law and has to be applied impartially without fear, favor, or prejudice. As all of you would agree, it must apply equally to Hillary Clinton as it would apply to any member of the general public. Her position or the power she wields as a result should not afford her any immunity. Likewise, her status should not result in a case of overly zealous misplaced justice by finding her guilty if she truly is not.

It does not matter even if, as has been reported, "President Barack Obama said during an interview airing Sunday on CBS's 60 Minutes, Hillary Rodham Clinton's use of a private email server to conduct government business when she served as secretary of state was a mistake but didn't endanger national security."[33] With all due respect, I can only say that President Obama is entitled to his opinion but as the President of the United States, it would have been (more) appropriate if he had not commented on this issue which is supposedly under investigation by the FBI, which is part of his administration and has the,

> mission ... to protect and defend the United States against terrorist and foreign intelligence threats, to uphold and enforce the criminal laws of the United States, and to provide leadership and criminal justice services to federal, state, municipal, and international agencies and partners. It performs these responsibilities in a way that is responsive to the needs of the public and faithful to the Constitution of the United States.[34]

Incidentally, "The FBI is led by a Director, who is appointed by the

---

33   'Barack Obama says Hillary Clinton did not endanger national security' — http://www.telegraph.co.uk/news/worldnews/northamerica/usa/11925769/Barack-Obama-says-Hillary-Clinton-did-not-endanger-national-security.html

34   Paraphrased from, Frequently Asked Questions — https://www.fbi.gov/about-us/faqs

U.S. President and confirmed by the Senate for a term not to exceed 10 years."[35]

Therefore, as Ron Hosko, a former senior F.B.I. official who retired in 2014 and is now the president of the Law Enforcement Legal Defense Fund, said:

> "It was inappropriate for the president to suggest what side of the investigation he is on when the F.B.I. is still investigating."[36]

As the ultimate custodian of the constitution in the United States, President Obama could have avoided making a statement that could well compromise/influence a federal investigation.

If Hillary Clinton has broken any law(s) in regards to the email issue, she is clearly liable for punishment as per the relevant sections of federal law. It is a matter of investigation at the moment and only the FBI and the concerned investigating officers can come to any sort of conclusion based on the material at hand.

To determine this, the FBI would have to diligently examine each and every piece of record including emails (personal and/or private) that were handed over by Hillary Clinton for investigation and also those that were supposedly deleted by her/her staff, correspondence from and to the White House and other stakeholders (across the world) by Hillary Clinton (including those from the White House supposedly asking her to use the government email and servers) and all other correspondence, documents and information (including any writing, code book, signal book, sketch, photograph, photographic negative, blueprint, plan, map, model, instrument, appliance, note etc.) related to her official duties as Secretary of State.

Only such a thorough and comprehensive examination of all the records can lead us to answer questions such as the above and thereby, bring us to understand whether Section 793 (f) and other relevant sections of the law were violated by Hillary Clinton both in terms of letter and spirit.

---

35 Frequently Asked Questions — https://www.fbi.gov/about-us/faqs

36 'Obama's Comments About Clinton's Emails Rankle Some in the F.B.I.'— http://www.nytimes.com/2015/10/17/us/politics/obamas-comments-on-clinton-emails-collide-with-fbi-inquiry.html?_r=0

Chapter 12

Hillary Clinton's Track Record In Foreign Policy

Foreign policy is a critical component of the governance of any country and it assumes greater importance in an increasingly interdependent and globalized economy. This is true especially for the world's only super-power — the United States — which is today involved in multiple roles across the global strategic context.

In the light of this, it is only fair and appropriate that we look at a presidential candidate's foreign affairs experience and judgment (including decision making) especially if that candidate had either served in a foreign policy position in an earlier administration and/or had, as a law maker, voted on the foreign policy decision made by a previous administration. Additionally, it also becomes important to analyze the presidential candidate's comments, opinions, and views with regard to foreign policy. As the presumptive nominee of the Democratic Party for the presidential election to be held in November 2016, Hillary Clinton's standpoints on foreign policy are critical and need close and careful consideration.

Foreign policy decision(s) can be made in 2 ways in the United States governance structure: 1) One way is, as a member of the Congress (i.e., the United States Senate and/or the United States House of Representatives), a person can vote in a foreign policy decision of the government; and 2) The other way is, as a key member of the presidential cabinet (especially, as Secretary of State), a person can advise the President in making a foreign policy decision.

Before moving forward, it is important to understand what constitutes a foreign policy decision in typical parlance. Here are a couple of relevant examples but they are by no means exhaustive:

(a) The decision to go to war with a foreign country;

(b) The decision to sign a trade agreement with a foreign country and so on.

In Hillary Clinton's case, given that she served as Senator for several years across multiple terms, we take a close look at her record of voting in the Senate with regard to foreign policy decisions to assess her foreign policy experience and judgment from an objective standpoint. Her views, opinions, and comments are also looked at to understand her stand on an issue and how her stated position influenced her in making a specific vote for or against a particular foreign policy decision made by the administration concerned.

Likewise, Hillary Clinton also served as a key member of the Obama Cabinet during the period (2009–2013) when she was Secretary of State. The Secretary of State is the chief foreign policy advisor to the President of the United States and so her input into decision making with regard to foreign policy is also examined and evaluated in this chapter.

Effectively, Hillary Clinton's foreign policy track record, judgment and decision-making are seen through the prism of two key roles played by her (i.e., Senator and Secretary of State) during a 13-year period from 2001–2013.

With regard to wars, conflicts, and regime changes, there is the war on terror (in Afghanistan), the Iraqi invasion of 2003, and the intervention in Libya from 2011 onwards. Of these, the war on terror is excluded from this analysis because the context of that war is rooted in the tragic 9/11 attacks on the World Trade Center (WTC) towers and the Pentagon. In many ways, this was a war that was forced on America by the tragic and horrific 9/11 attacks. Therefore, the analysis of wars/

conflicts/regime change is limited to the Iraqi invasion of 2003 and the support to Libyan rebels as they were the major conflict situations.[1] The Israeli-Palestinian conflict is also touched upon, especially with a focus on Iran's possible intervention against Israel.

However, before we get into the details, a general comment on Hillary Clinton's foreign policy record is in order. To put it candidly, her foreign policy record is a mixed bag. On the one hand, it must be acknowledged that she was one of the most energetic Secretaries of State, travelling far and wide during her tenure. It must also be recognized that she did play a major part in promoting free trade and bi-lateral agreements, especially in Asia and Africa. However, the real problem with Hillary Clinton's foreign policy is the mindset she carried to the Middle East whether it was Iraq, Libya, Iran, Palestine, or Syria.

First, her Senate vote for the President Bush-sponsored war on Iraq associated her with a disastrous war. No apology can reverse the huge injustices and alarming negative impact that the Iraq war had on the people of the region. That is not to mention the horrible effect of the U.S.-bound body bags that came back to America daily.

While George W. Bush and other neoconservatives were primarily responsible[2] for initiating the Iraq war, it must be noted that Hillary Clinton is the only one among the current crop of candidates contesting in the U.S. 2016 presidential elections who voted for the Iraq war. Her speech on the Senate floor in October 2002 is transcribed below and also the link provided to the video where she is seen speaking:

---

1   Honduras and Ukraine are other places of interest here, but they are kept out of the discussion due to lack of space and the fact that Iraq and Libya, as major foreign policy interventions, should provide sufficient insights into Hillary Clinton's foreign policy judgment and strategy.

2   A lot of the groundwork for this war, in my opinion, happened when (the Project for the New American Century — PNAC) wrote to President Clinton in 1998. Incidentally, it must be noted that Robert Kagan, co-founder of PNAC has endorsed Hillary Clinton in the presidential race. Another factor that needs to be noted is that there are several controversies surrounding a former Clinton administration appointee at Federal Aviation Administration (FAA), Jane Garvey. These and other issues are explored as part of another book — "9/11: The Unanswered Questions."

"Today, Mr. President, we are asked whether to give the President of the United States authority to use force in Iraq should diplomatic efforts fail to dismantle Saddam Hussein's chemical and biological weapons and his nuclear program.

I believe the facts that have brought us to this fateful vote are not in doubt. Saddam Hussein is a tyrant who has tortured and killed his own people, even his own family members, to maintain his iron grip on power. He used chemical weapons on Iraqi Kurds and on Iranians, killing over 20,000 people.

In 1998, the United States also changed its underlying policy toward Iraq from containment to regime change and began to examine options to effect such a change, including support for Iraqi opposition leaders within the country and abroad. In the 4 years since the inspectors, intelligence reports show that Saddam Hussein has worked to rebuild his chemical and biological weapons stock, his missile delivery capability, and his nuclear program. He has also given aid, comfort, and sanctuary to terrorists, including al-Qaida members, though there is apparently no evidence of his involvement in the terrible events of September 11, 2001.

It is clear, however, that if left unchecked, Saddam Hussein will continue to increase his capability to wage biological and chemical warfare and will keep trying to develop nuclear weapons. Should he succeed in that endeavor, he could alter the political and security landscape of the Middle East, which, as we know all too well, affects American security.

This is a difficult vote. This is probably the hardest decision I have ever had to make. Any vote that may lead to war should be hard, but I cast it with conviction."[3]

In the same speech, Hillary Clinton also talks of "regime change" and I quote,

---

3   http://www.c-span.org/video/?c4579045/sen-hillary-clinton-supporting-aumf-iraq — this is a speech delivered in the U.S. Senate by Senator Hillary Clinton and therefore, is in the public domain.

"Regime change will, of course, take longer but we must still work for
it, nurturing all reasonable forces of opposition."

Several questions come to my mind on America's Iraq war. Time and
again, Hillary supporters have defended her vote for the Iraq war by
saying it was done to ensure that Saddam Hussein complies with the
weapons inspection process. That is totally untrue because at the time of
the vote in the United States Senate (October 2002), four things[4] were
factually observable:

(1) First, the return of the weapons inspectors had already been
     agreed to by Saddam Hussein. This needs to be stated clearly
     and unequivocally!

(2) Second, Saddam Hussein's government showed that it was
     indeed committed to the weapons inspection process. It was
     in fact, negotiating with the United Nations Monitoring and
     Verification Commission on the details, which were formalized
     just a few weeks later.

(3) Third, as many people have argued, all of the above including
     point 2 could (perhaps) have been resolved much earlier if
     only the United States had not repeatedly postponed a UN
     Security Council resolution. It has been reported that the
     United States was keen to insert words in the resolution that
     would allow it to unilaterally construe and interpret the level
     of compliance.

(4) Four, if Hillary Clinton's desire was merely to push Saddam
     into complying with the weapons inspection process, then,
     why did she not vote[5] for the alternative Levin amendment

---

4   'The 5 Worst Excuses for Hillary Clinton's Vote To Invade Iraq' — http://
      inthesetimes.com/article/18813/the-five-lamest-excuses-for-hillary-clintons-
      vote-to-invade-iraq

5   U.S. Senate Roll Call Votes 107th Congress — 2nd Session — http://
      www.senate.gov/legislative/LIS/roll_call_lists/roll_call_vote_cfm.
      cfm?congress=107&session=2&vote=00235

(S.AMDT.4862 — Providing for Congressional Construction in the Consideration of the Joint Resolution (S.J.RES.45) that (would have) granted President Bush authority to use force, if and only if, Iraq defied subsequent UN demands regarding the inspections process.

Unfortunately, the net result is that Hillary Clinton did vote for a Republican-sponsored resolution that gave President Bush, the complete authority to invade Iraq at his will and pleasure. Without a doubt, that act has had disastrous consequences for the whole world.

Given that Hillary Clinton herself later admitted that there was no evidence linking Saddam Hussein to the horrific events of 9/11, what was the reason for her voting to go to war with Iraq? Ok, it may be argued that perhaps Saddam Hussein had in his possession weapons of mass destruction (WMD) that could have posed a global threat but where was the concrete evidence of this? What weapons of mass destruction (WMDs) did anyone finally find in Iraq? Sadly none. Last but not least, what have been the consequences of the Iraq war and the regime change? Without a doubt, answers to the above questions will reveal why the Iraq war is indeed America's biggest foreign policy blunder.

Saddam Hussein was a dictator and he did stifle democracy. Nevertheless, what was America's locus standi in intervening in the affairs of another country like Iraq? And why did America meddle in the Middle East at a time when it faced so many problems on the domestic front — including loss of American jobs overseas (outsourcing), decline of American manufacturing, income disparity and inequality across America, lack of affordable health care for all in America, rising student education debt in the United States and the like — note that all of the above continue to be serious issues even in election 2016.

One of the key questions that needs to be answered is: What have been the consequences of the removal of Saddam Hussein? Is not the birth and consolidation of the dreaded ISIS a major outfall of America's war in Iraq? These are questions that still remain unanswered and many Americans have been raising these issues time and again only for them to fall on deaf ears it seems.

Without a doubt, the consequences of the Iraq war are many:

(a) Several thousand people including innocent women and children have been slaughtered;

(b) Thousands of dead troops — both American as well as Iraqi;

(c) Death and destruction of Iraq including its monuments, cities etc;

(d) A broken Iraq in civil war and well on its way to becoming a failed state; and

(e) The birth and rapid growth of the dreaded Islamic State (ISIS).

Indeed, a direct consequence of the Iraq war is the burgeoning growth of the dreaded and horrific Islamic State and that is a stark reminder of the most deadly impact of the Iraq war. When I was writing this chapter, I saw a news flash on how the ISIS had murdered 14 people in a café in Iraq in absolute cold blood.[6] And when I was looking through the final edited version of the book, the news of the barbaric, cold-blooded and horrific mass killings at Orlando[7] left me dumbfounded with shock.

Therefore, Hillary Clinton's apologies for the Iraq war notwithstanding, her Senate vote for the Iraq war shows extremely poor foreign policy judgment. Agreed, Saddam Hussein was a dictator and a "bad guy" to his people, but his real threat to the world was an illusion created by the Project for the New American Century (PNAC). George Bush, and the other neo-conservatives, simply ignored intelligence inputs about lack of weapons of mass destruction (WMDs) with Saddam and started an unwanted war with Iraq. While it was initially thought that Saddam Hussein may have helped Al-Qaeda in the horrific 9/11 attack, that too

---

6   'ISIS in Iraq: Real Madrid fans killed as suicide gunmen attack cafe leaving 13 dead and 15 injured' — http://www.ibtimes.co.uk/isis-iraq-suicide-gunmen-attack-cafe-leaving-13-dead-15-injured-1559917

7   'Orlando shooting: 49 killed, shooter pledged ISIS allegiance' — http://edition.cnn.com/2016/06/12/us/orlando-nightclub-shooting/

was negated subsequently. Even President Bush is reported to have stated that Saddam Hussein did not participate in the gruesome 9/11 event.

That being the case, what was the justification to attack Iraq? Part of the reason was that the "neo cons" and President George W. Bush and his friends desired a "regime change." What kind of foreign policy is that? This gross-interference strategy in foreign policy is shocking and also the fact that Hillary Clinton too subscribed to such a view, possibly because she is more right of centre and also due to the fact that she may have had a war hawk like Henry Kissinger as her mentor.

Getting back to the issue of foreign policy judgment, it must be remembered that Saddam Hussein had steadied the religious boat in Iraq by virtue of his being a Sunni leader. The moment he was overthrown, instability crept in and today you see Sunni Muslims revolting through the dreaded ISIS. Agreed, Saddam Hussein was a bad guy, but how does that give America the authority to act against him, if he was neither a threat to America nor a threat globally? Thus, this interventionist "regime change" foreign policy strategy is what has caused this huge mess in Iraq and led to the birth of the despicable ISIS.

This is where good foreign policy judgment[8] could have helped prevent not only the war but more importantly the birth of the dastardly ISIS, which is a much, much worse threat than Saddam Hussein ever was.

I personally think that the decision to vote for the Iraq war by Hillary Clinton truly represents a huge black spot on her foreign policy record. It was bad foreign policy at its best and revealed a keen lack of foresight. I am compelled to point out the contrast to what Bernie Sanders said at the time in the context of the Iraq war:

---

8   Look at what Bernie Sanders said against the war on Iraq — https://www.youtube.com/watch?v=NdFw1btbkLM - this is a speech delivered in the U.S. Senate by Senator Hillary Clinton and therefore, is in the public domain.

"Thank you, Mr. Speaker. And I thank my friend from New Jersey for yielding. Mr. Speaker, I don't think any member of this body disagrees that Saddam Hussein is a tyrant, a murderer and a man who has started two wars. He is clearly someone who cannot be trusted — who cannot be trusted or believed. The question, Mr. Speaker, is not whether we like Saddam Hussein or not, the question is whether he represents an imminent threat to the American people and whether an attack would do more harm than good. Mr. Speaker, the Washington Post today reported that all U.S. Intelligence agencies now say despite what we've heard from the White House, that Saddam Hussein is unlikely to unleash a chemical or biological attack against the United States.

Even more importantly, our intelligence agencies say that should Saddam Hussein conclude that a U.S.-led attack could no longer be deterred, he might at that point launch a chemical or biological counterattack. In other words, there's more danger of an attack on the United States if we launch a precipitous invasion. Mr. Speaker, I don't know why the president feels, despite what our intelligence agencies are saying, that it is so important to pass an authorization of this magnitude, despite the support of our major allies including those fighting side by side with us in the war on terrorism.

...

Mr. Speaker, in the brief time I have, let me give you five reasons why I'm opposed to giving the President a blank check to launch a unilateral invasion and occupation of Iraq and why I will vote against this resolution.

One, I have not heard any estimates of how many young American men and women might die in such a war or how many tens of thousands of women and children in Iraq might also be killed. As a caring nation, we should do everything we can to prevent the horrible suffering that a war will cause. War must be the last recourse in international relations, not the first.

Second, I am deeply concerned about the precedent that a unilateral invasion of Iraq could establish in terms of international law and the role of the United Nations. If President Bush believes that the U.S. can go to war at anytime against any nation, what moral or legal obligation could our government raise if another country chose to do the same thing?

Third, the United States is now involved in a very difficult war against international terrorism, as we learned tragically on September 11. We are opposed by Osama Bin Laden and religious fanatics who are prepared to engage in a kind of warfare that we have never experienced before. I agree with Brent Scowcroft, Republican former national security advisor for President George Bush Sr., who stated, and I quote, "an attack on Iraq at this time would seriously jeopardize, if not destroy the global counterterrorist campaign we have undertaken."

Fourth, at a time when this country has a $6 trillion national debt and a growing deficit, we should declare that a war and a long-term American occupation of Iraq could be extremely expensive.

Fifth, I am concerned about the problems with so-called unintended consequences. Who will govern Iraq when Saddam Hussein is removed and what role will the U.S. play in an ensuing civil war that could develop in that country? Will moderate governments in the region dislodge Islamic populations? Will the conflict between Israel and the Palestinian authority be exacerbated? And these are a few questions that remain unanswered. If a unilateral invasion of Iraq is not the best approach, what should we do? In my view, the U.S. must work with the United Nations to make certain within clearly defined time lines that the U.N. Inspectors are allowed to do their jobs. These inspectors should undertake an unfettered search for Iraqi weapons of mass destruction and destroy them when found pursuant to past U.N. resolutions. If Iraq resists inspection and elimination of stockpiled weapons, we should stand ready to assist the U.N. in forcing compliance."[9]

---

9   https://www.youtube.com/watch?v=NdFw1btbkLM - this is a speech delivered in the U.S. Senate by Senator Bernie Sanders and therefore, is in the public domain.

If Hillary's vote for Iraq represented poor foreign policy judgment, then Libya was a complete fiasco. Indeed, Hillary Clinton's role in creating the mess in Libya needs no emphasis and is rather well known. Her statement, "We came, we saw, and he died!"[10] sums it all up.

Again, Libya was a classic example of policy gone wrong — the same interventionist "regime change" strategy back fired miserably. Gaddafi, like Saddam Hussein, was indeed a dictator and a bad man to his own people but he was not a supporter of Islamic fundamentalist forces. Thus, when the U.S. intervened and had Gaddafi overthrown and killed, they opened the veritable Pandora's Box and suddenly, Libya was in a state of complete chaos.

Additionally, the middlemen and Islamic terrorists started apportioning off Gaddafi's cache of arms and gold, which became the powerful ammunition that helped build the Islamic State. Let us not forget this truth. Therefore, without any doubt, and as President Obama himself has acknowledged, Libya is clearly a failed foreign policy effort and much of the blame will lie at the doorstep of Hillary Rodham Clinton, who was President Obama's chief foreign policy advisor.

Clinton's roles in Libya and Syria are best summed up in an article titled "Regime Change Madness: Hillary, Obama and Murderous Mayhem in the Muslim World". As the article argues:

"In the cases of both Libya and Syria, Mrs. Clinton ... contributed significantly to the horrific outcomes in her role as Obama's Secretary of State…and largely, the Hillary-led campaign created the basic context for a second revival of jihadism in Iraq and the rise and expansion of IS across vast swaths of both Syria and Iraq."[11]

One can go on with a list such of attempted "interventionist regime changes" in Syria, Honduras etc., all of which signify a flawed foreign policy effort, because this policy approach refused to even consider

---

10   https://www.youtube.com/watch?v=Fgcd1ghag5Y

11   'Regime Change Madness: Hillary, Obama and Murderous Mayhem in the Muslim World' — http://www.counterpunch.org/2016/01/08/regime-change-madness-hillary-obama-and-murderous-mayhem-in-the-muslim-world/

what would happen the day after the dictator or the bad guy was overthrown. Hillary Clinton, who was President Obama's chief foreign policy advisor in his first term, is much to blame for this disastrous foreign policy approach that has resulted in unprecedented global chaos and violence. In fact, that this flawed foreign policy is responsible for the growth and strengthening of the dastardly Islamic State needs no further emphasis.

It would be in order to consider one other point here. Even in the context of the Israel-Palestine-Iran conflict, Hillary Clinton's attitude is clearly that of a "war hawk" as people have largely described her. Recall the ABC interview clip where she says she will "obliterate Iran." Isn't it rather frightening to hear that from someone who's potentially a future President of the United States? This is what she said:

> "I want the Iranians to know that if I'm the president, we will attack Iran (if it attacks Israel)... In the next 10 years, during which they might foolishly consider launching an attack on Israel, we would be able to totally obliterate them," she said.[12]

The thought that the most powerful person on this planet has the courage to say that she would completely wipe out 77 million people in Iran is indeed horrific.

In summary, on the issue of war and foreign policy, Hillary Clinton's action in voting for the Iraq war was untenable to say the least. Having voted for the war that has caused so much devastation and destruction in Iraq, America, and elsewhere, I found it rather despicable that she could speak of Iraq as a great business opportunity for American Corporations.[13] Death and destruction apart, the Iraq war is the primary reason for the birth and growth of the dreaded ISIS and its horrific

---

12   https://www.youtube.com/watch?v=857guwaNbRc - Clinton in an interview on ABC's Good Morning America.

13   https://www.youtube.com/watch?v=sQq3hs_lXpY; 'Campaign 2016: Hillary Clinton Pitched Iraq As "A Business Opportunity" For US Corporations' — http://www.ibtimes.com/campaign-2016-hillary-clinton-pitched-iraq-business-opportunity-us-corporations-2121999

activities. Everyone, who voted for the Iraq war is in some way to blame for the horrific situation that we face today — the ISIS monster is without a doubt the result of the Iraq war and Hillary Clinton's vote for the war in Iraq can never be forgotten, whatever be her regrets today. This needs to be clearly and candidly stated.

Indeed President Obama acknowledges this and in a recent interview with Shane Smith, the founder of VICE News, President Barack Obama reportedly said: "ISIL is a direct outgrowth of Al Qaeda in Iraq that grew out of our invasion, which is an example of unintended consequences."[14]

Furthermore, Hillary Clinton's foreign policy approach of "regime change" has backfired so badly in Libya that it is a failed state today. In fact, Gaddafi's arms cache was looted soon after his death and distributed worldwide. It is often stated that much of the havoc/terror that the dreaded ISIS carries out today is done with the arms that were looted from Gaddafi's back yard. Therefore, the Libyan intervention has also been a total disaster.

If Iraq and Libya were examples of Hillary Clinton's bad judgment and poor ability to foresee the future, her statement on Iran is clearly the voice of a typical "war hawk". I see no difference between her and George W. Bush with regard to their views on Iraq and war in the Middle East. I am shocked that she talks of obliterating Iran and its 77 million people. Is that not both irresponsible and unacceptable given the humongous bloodshed we have had over the last decade? Should not war be the absolute last resort and should not peace and dialogue be the order of the day? Folks, I rest my case!

---

14   'ISIS: The "unintended consequences" of the US-led war on Iraq' — http://www.
        foreignpolicyjournal.com/2015/03/23/isis-the-unintended-consequences-of-the-
        us-led-war-on-iraq/

Chapter 13

Conclusion

In the preceding twelve chapters, we looked at various issues pertaining to Hillary Clinton's 2016 presidential run. While several niggling issues and different aspects related to her candidacy have been touched upon, it must be said that very rarely does one come across a candidate so well qualified. We must duly acknowledge her experience and qualifications for the position.

From being First Lady (during two terms of Bill Clinton's Presidency) to Senator (for several years across multiple terms) to Secretary of State (during the first term of the Obama Administration), Hillary Clinton has seen it all. If she becomes President of the United States, she would be the first woman to do so and if that happens, she and her husband Bill Clinton will be the first couple to have both been President of the United States — no small achievement by any standard.

While her achievements and experience have indeed raised expectations with regard to Hillary Clinton's candidacy, it must also be pointed out that, in truth, over the years Hillary has continually *flattered to deceive* in almost every "achievement."

Let's take a look at her lofty climb one step at a time to see how she arrived where she is today, on the cusp of becoming the first female President of The United States of America.

First, a significant number of names on her list of key supporters (large/ close campaign donors, corporate friends and others who have donated to the Clinton Foundation) are Wall Street veterans with the scars to prove it. Several of these veterans have reportedly either been charged or pronounced guilty of serious violations including financial fraud and the like. In fact, through their unscrupulous and nefarious actions, many of them have contributed in some degree to the 2008 financial crisis. There are numerous other supporters of questionable character as well, including corporate honchos, high net-worth individuals and others.

Some of her largest donors, both to her election campaign as well as to the Clinton Foundation, have been charged with serious violations including fraud by the Securities and Exchanges Commission (SEC). There are other "associates" who have been plucked from the bunch as examples by the Internal Revenue Service (IRS) and the Department of Justice (DoJ). Still others from this group have been charged with violations under the Foreign Corrupt Practices Act (FCPA), having bribed their way to profits and business overseas. Even in the homeland (on U.S. soil), there are similar "friends of Hillary" who have been convicted on various counts including political corruption and bribery — Paul Adler is a classic example of this. Many of Hillary's donors — in spite of her adamant posture on tax evasion by the rich — have evaded paying taxes by moving their operations and money to the very well established tax havens, especially outside the United States. Some of them have been named in Congressional reports with regard to tax abuse and tax evasion. Finally, there is the fact that some of the donors to the Clinton Foundation as well as to her election campaign have been named in the Panama Papers exposé that rocked the world and even led to the resignation of the Iceland Prime Minister.[1]

Therefore, I am not inclined to blindly believe that Hillary Clinton, as President, will be able to act decisively and strongly against corporate/political crime. She would have to take action against many of the very people who are mobilizing funds — by the hundreds of millions — directly and indirectly to put her, their favorite candidate, in the White House. What do these donors expect from her? What did she promise them?

---

1   'The Panama Papers: Here's What We Know' — http://www.nytimes.com/2016/04/05/world/panama-papers-explainer.html?_r=0

While Hillary Clinton may well deny the existence of any conflicts of interest from her lofty perch up there in her ivory tower, evidence down here at ground level indicates otherwise. I am inclined to question the likelihood that she will turn and act against corporate/political crime given that the guilty include several of her donors, benefactors, and friends of many years. Furthermore, it is hard to imagine that she is completely unaware of their questionable and even illegal actions and all the charges against them. That being the case, is it not unethical of her to have accepted their support knowing very well that she might have to act against them at a later time? There is no more proof required for this than what Elizabeth Warren, one of the most respected Senators in the United States today, stated with regard to the bankruptcy bill on video[2] (from time stamp: 2: 50). Specifically, Elizabeth Warren, as shown in the video, claims that Senator Hillary Clinton voted for the bankruptcy bill because of pressures from the consumer credit product companies. She also suggests that Senator Hillary Clinton was 'bought off' (see the video from time stamp 2:50 where she says that Hillary Clinton 'has taken money from the groups') by these consumer credit product companies. These are serious charges indeed and especially, coming from someone of the stature of Elizabeth Warren.

Of course Senator Warren has recently endorsed Hillary's candidature as the Democratic Party's Presidential nominee but surely the charges that she had leveled against Hillary Clinton continue to hold. Although Senator Warren may chosen to disregard her own observations for political or other considerations, an objective electorate would certainly need to factor in the points raised by her in the context of Hillary Clinton accepting campaign finance from Wall Street and corporate sources embroiled in many controversies and the pressure this would exert on any promised Presidential action (by Hillary) against corporate crime and regulation of Wall Street.

A second issue is campaign finance reform that has been discussed and debated extensively as part of the 2016 election campaign. Given

---

2   https://www.youtube.com/watch?v=N7ZnapWoG6E&feature=youtu.be

that much of Hillary Clinton's money (donations to her campaign as well as income from paid speeches) comes from large corporations and corporate donors, several of whom have been reportedly charged with corporate crime, it appears unlikely that Hillary Clinton, if she becomes President of the United States, will be able to eliminate big corrupt money from politics. Indeed as most Americans would argue, the corrupt campaign finance system is the bane of the American electoral polity, especially after Citizens United. Without a doubt, those corporate chieftains and large donors, who have contributed to Hillary Clinton's campaign, have paid the Clinton family large sums of money to deliver speeches and have donated huge amounts to the Clinton Foundation. Will they simply turn their backs on their investment and allow Hillary to reform the corrupt campaign finance system that they thrive on? Will they stand back and watch as she implements policies and protocols that go against their very substantial interests?

A third issue is the question of Hillary Clinton's position on free trade and trade agreements. The United States is one of the key international movers of free trade and much of what we have seen with regard to free trade in the last two decades has emanated from the United States. Therefore, any potential candidate for the post of the President of the United States must possess clarity with regard to trade-related issues. In my opinion, Hillary Clinton does not possess this clarity as is evident from her inconsistent track record of Senate voting and opinions on trade as given in Chapter 10. Therefore, it is my view that it would indeed be hard to predict what Hillary Clinton would do with regard to free trade and trade-related issues, if she becomes President.

Fourth is the issue of speeches that Hillary and Bill Clinton have delivered (in private) over the years to Wall Street firms (including the big banks) and other corporations. Clearly, these customized speeches and the payment for them, all done behind closed doors, raise serious questions about conflicts of interest. Two points need to be mentioned here. Several of the Wall Street firms and other corporations that Hillary and Bill made speeches to, had already been charged with serious violations by the SEC, IRS, DoJ and/or had committed serious violations under the FCPA *prior to their speaking engagements*. How could Hillary and Bill Clinton accept paid speaking assignments from them even while these corporations were under investigation by the various federal agencies? Was it mere coincidence that these suspect corporations invited Hillary and Bill at such an opportune time? What were Hillary and Bill Clinton telling UBS AG in their private meetings while the IRS was using every possible means under the law to get UBS AG to provide names of Americans (including tax evaders) holding bank accounts with it? Likewise, what did Hillary Clinton tell employees of Goldman Sachs — one of the firms that was largely (if not solely) responsible for the 2008 financial crisis — *in private*? Hillary Clinton, to date, has *refused* to release transcripts of these speeches. Similarly, what did Hillary Clinton tell the employees of Canadian Imperial Bank of Commerce (CIBC) against whose Caribbean operations the IRS had obtained a court order requiring CIBC to release names of Americans (including tax evaders) holding bank accounts with its Caribbean subsidiary?

By accepting invitations from them, taking huge sums of money as compensation for addressing them, and speaking at these institutions at that time, perhaps knowing full well that they were under the IRS scanner, Hillary Clinton exhibited extremely poor judgment.

Fifth, is the issue of war and foreign policy. Hillary Clinton's support for the Iraq war was outrageous, to say the least. Having voted for the war in Iraq that has caused so much devastation and destruction in Iraq, America, and elsewhere, I find it rather despicable that she cites Iraq as a great business opportunity for American corporations.[3] Death and destruction apart, the Iraq war is the primary reason for the birth and growth of the dreaded ISIS and its horrific activities. Everyone, who voted for the Iraq war is in some way to blame for the horrific situation that we face today. Many agree that the ISIS monster is without a doubt the result of the Iraq war and Hillary Clinton's vote

---

3   https://www.youtube.com/watch?v=sQq3hs_lXpY; 'Campaign 2016: Hillary Clinton Pitched Iraq As "A Business Opportunity" For US Corporations' — http://www.ibtimes.com/campaign-2016-hillary-clinton-pitched-iraq-business-opportunity-us-corporations-2121999

for the war in Iraq can never be forgotten, whatever her regrets might be today.

Furthermore, Hillary Clinton's foreign policy approach of "regime change" has backfired so badly in Libya that today it is a failed state. The vacuum left in the wake of Gaddafi has caused great havoc. In fact, Gaddafi's arms cache and gold were looted soon after his death and disbursed worldwide. It is often mentioned that much of the havoc/terror that the dreaded ISIS carries out today is with the arms that were looted from Gaddafi's back yard. The Libyan "intervention" has been a total disaster and it is undoubtedly, bad foreign policy at its very best.

Aside from that, the blame for the death of the American Ambassador and his staff at Benghazi again falls squarely on the people in the United States Federal Government — Hillary Clinton as Secretary of State was most certainly one of those at fault, having called for the "regime change" that turned to disaster in Libya with the untimely overthrow of Gaddafi. In fact, in an interview on *CBS News* in 2012, Hillary Clinton said the following about Gaddafi: "**We came, we saw, and he died.**"[4] This insensitivity was followed by a highly inappropriate giggle.

If Iraq and Libya are examples of Hillary Clinton's poor judgment and inability to foresee the future, her statement on Iran is typical of the worst "war hawk." I am shocked when she callously talks of "obliterating" Iran and its 77 million people. I see no difference between her and George W. Bush with regard to their views on Iraq and war in the Middle East. This ridiculous tactlessness is unsuitable at any time, let alone in the decade of tremendous bloodshed we have witnessed recently. Should not war be the absolute last resort and should not peace and dialogue be the order of the day? I'm not sure that Hillary Clinton's statement about obliterating Iran is something that Americans or anyone in the world wants to hear from a future President. This is not what the world expects of a responsible United States President. How could someone who may become the de facto leader of the world say such a thing?

---

4   https://www.youtube.com/watch?v=Fgcd1ghag5Y

The final issue, at least for now, is the email saga, which shows Hillary Clinton's scant respect for rules and regulations. The Inspector General's (IG's) report clearly proves that Hillary Clinton, despite being warned by the State Department, disregarded the rules and regulations and conducted foreign policy through her private email on an unsecure server.

Irrespective of whether or not Hillary Clinton gets indicted, the use of a private email and server to conduct official business and foreign policy is certainly not acceptable as per the laws of the United States. In the light of the IG's report, it is also clearly established that after having conducted foreign policy and official business through a private email and server, Hillary Clinton tried her best to shroud what had happened with a host of explanations that have fallen flat.

Indeed, Hillary Clinton has a lot of explaining to do on these important and relevant issues revealed here that go to the heart of people's trust in politics. If the members of Democratic Party decline their moral obligation to open their eyes and look for the obvious flaws in their candidate, how can they expect the American public to repose their faith in them and vote Hillary Clinton into office as the next President of the United States?

Before I close, I would like to make one final comment. Without a doubt, it needs to be reiterated that Hillary Clinton's experience and credentials are indeed unique. However, they stand severely compromised by her unholy alliances with Wall Street and corporate biggies, many of whom have been caught on the wrong side of the law once too often. By allowing such people to bankroll her campaign, Hillary has put herself in the truly unenviable position of having to bite the very hands that have fed her if she has to honor her electoral promise of going after the corrupt. The problem though is larger than Hillary herself in that, this is an issue that is germane to the electioneering process itself. That, in fact, is the primary reason why campaign finance has been dominating 2016 electoral debates as one of the most critical issues that need to be addressed if indeed America is to free itself from the clutches of Wall Street greed, self serving business interests and lobbyists who are out to take advantage of the system. Whether Hillary Clinton as the next President of the United States can and will usher in this much needed campaign finance reform is a question that perhaps only time can answer!

About the Author

Ramesh S Arunachalam wears many hats. In the last two decades, he has been a columnist (with the *Hindu Business Line* and *Moneylife*), an entrepreneur, a filmmaker and also a development practitioner working on issues pertaining to financial inclusion and livelihood security. His clients include both state and national governments, bi-lateral and multi-lateral agencies, and the private sector in countries across Asia, Africa, North America and Europe.

Title – Where Angels Prey
Author – Ramesh S Arunachalam
Size – 5.5 inches × 8.5 inches
No of Pages – 204
Binding – Paperback
ISBN – 978-9384439378

While the rest of the world reels under a severe financial crisis, India's microfinance sector enjoys an unprecedented boom. Why on earth are people investing such huge amounts of money in an obscure industry, especially at the time of global recession? And why is Wall Street suddenly so interested in India's poor?

That is exactly what Robert Bradlee, senior correspondent with *The New York Post*, sets off to investigate, along with his journalist friend, Chandresh. Little does he know that his search for a scoop would lead him through a complex multi-pronged web of deceit, fraud, manipulation and financial crime, remote controlled from distant lands by an entire chain of financial sector stakeholders.

Gripping, racy and meticulously researched, this financial thriller weaves in and out of the affluent world of high-powered boardrooms and the gruelling poverty of the remotest villages of India, to reveal the devastating truths that often lurk behind "good intentions".